eCommerce
Development:
Business to Consumer

Microsoft

Mastering

PUBLISHED BY
Microsoft Press
A Division of Microsoft Corporation
One Microsoft Way
Redmond, Washington 98052-6399

Library of Congress Cataloging-in-Publication Data pending.

Printed and bound in the United States of America.

3 4 5 6 7 8 9   WCWC   4 3 2 1 0 9

Distributed in Canada by Penguin Books Canada Limited.

A CIP catalogue record for this book is available from the British Library.

Microsoft Press books are available through booksellers and distributors worldwide. For further information about international editions, contact your local Microsoft Corporation office or contact Microsoft Press International directly at fax (425) 936-7329. Visit our Web site at mspress.microsoft.com.

Intel is a registered trademark of Intel Corporation. ActiveX, JScript, Microsoft, Microsoft Press, Visual Basic, Visual InterDev, Windows, and Windows NT are either registered trademarks or trademarks of Microsoft Corporation in the United States and/or other countries. Other product and company names mentioned herein may be the trademarks of their respective owners.

The example companies, organizations, products, people, and events depicted herein are fictitious. No association with any real company, organization, product, person, or event is intended or should be inferred.

Acquisitions Editor: Eric Stroo
Project Editor: Wendy Zucker

Acknowledgements

Authors:
Neetu Gangwani
Sangeeta Garg
Jayanthy K.R.
Developed with NIIT

Program Manager: Steve Merrill

Lead Instructional Designer: Steve Merrill

Instructional Designers:
Sangeeta Garg (NIIT)
Neetu Gangwani (NIIT)
Jayanthy K.R. (NIIT)

Production Manager: Miracle Davis

Production Coordinator: Gabriel Lamazares (S&T Onsite)

Media Production: Staci Dinehart (S&T Onsite)

Graphic Artist: Elizabeth Johanson (ArtSource)

Editors:
Reid Bannecker (S&T OnSite)
Ed Harper (MacTemps)

Build and Testing Manager: Julie Challenger

Testing: Test Goons

Book Production Coordinator: Katharine Ford (ArtSource)

Book Design: Mary Rasmussen (Online Training Solutions, Inc.)

Book Layout: Jennifer Murphy (S&T Onsite)

Companion CD-ROM Design and Development: Jeff Brown

Companion CD-ROM Production:
Jenny Boe
Eric Wagoner (Write Stuff)

About This Course

This course is intended for solution developers, companies that are starting to sell goods and services over the Internet, Certified Technical Edition Center (CTEC) trainers, commerce ISPs, and Web developers.

Prerequisite Skills

This book is designed for software developers who have a extensive experience in developing applications for the Internet. Before starting this book, you should be familiar with the following:

- Microsoft Visual InterDev as a development tool
- Microsoft Visual Basic Scripting Edition or some other scripting language
- ActiveX Data Objects (ADO) for accessing a local database
- SQL queries, recordsets, and cursors
- HTML
- Data Source Name (DSN)
- SQL and Microsoft Windows NT security

Course Content

The course content is organized into the following nine chapters:

Chapter 1: Understanding Electronic Commerce

Provides an introduction to electronic commerce (including the Commerce Server), an overview of the shopping process and a tour of a sample site.

Chapter 2: Building a Site

Shows students how to use the Site Foundation Wizard and the Site Builder Wizard to create a new site.

Chapter 3: Enhancing the Product Catalog

Shows students how to modify a wizard-generated site and use ADO to display product information.

Chapter 4: Managing a Shopping Cart

Shows students how to manage a shopping cart and implement upsell promotion.

Chapter 5: Processing Orders

Shows students how to create an order processing pipeline by using the plan template.

Chapter 6: Checking Out

Shows student how to capture shopper information, compute order value, and create a scriptor component for computing tax.

Chapter 7: Completing the Purchase Process

Shows students how to use the Purchase template of the Order Processing Pipeline and secure financial transactions.

Chapter 8: Tracking Shopper Information

Shows students how to track shoppers by using cookies and a registration database.

Chapter 9: Implementing Business-to-Business Commerce

Shows students how to track orders from business partners.

Labs

Most chapters in this course include a lab that gives the student hands-on experience with the skills learned in the chapter. A lab consists of one or more exercises that focus on how to use the information contained in the chapter. Lab hints, which provide code or other information to help you complete an exercise, are included in Appendix A.

To complete the exercises and view the accompanying solution code, you will need to install the lab files that are found on the accompanying CD-ROM.

Lab Setup

Software installation

To complete the exercises and view the accompanying solution code, you will need to install the following:

◆ Microsoft Windows NT Server version 4.0 and Windows NT Service Pack 5

◆ Microsoft Internet Explorer 5.0

◆ Microsoft Internet Information Server, version 4.0, along with Microsoft Transaction Server, Front Page Server Extensions, Microsoft Index Server, and Microsoft Data Access Components

◆ Microsoft SQL Server, version 7.0

◆ SiteServer 3.0 Commerce Edition

Detailed instructions for installing the required software are located in Appendix B in this book.

Hardware requirements:

To run the software for this course, you should have the following:

◆ Personal computer with a 300 MHz Pentium II processor

◆ 128 megabytes (MB) of RAM

◆ 4-gigabyte (GB) hard disk

◆ 12X CD-ROM drive

◆ Network adapter

◆ 4-MB video adapter

◆ Super VGA (SVGA) monitor (17-inch)

◆ Microsoft Mouse or compatible pointing device

◆ Sound card with amplified speakers

◆ Internet access

Lab Scenario

The labs in this course have you build a fictitious bookseller named Five Lakes Publishing. During the course, you will:

1. Create the foundation for the store.

2. Create the store itself and connect it to a product database.

3. Add and delete products in the database.

4. Create and enhance catalog pages.

5. Add product-search and cross-sell capabilities to the site.

6. Create and manage a shopping cart.

7. Add price promotions for individual items.

8. Add upsell capability.

9. Process orders by using the order-processing pipeline.

10. Capture shopper and order information.

11. Secure the business transaction.

12. Track shopper information.

Review Questions

This course includes several review questions at the end of each chapter. You can use these questions to test your understanding of the information that has been covered in the course. Answers are provided on the page following the review questions.

CD-ROM Contents

The *Building E-Commerce Solutions: Business to Consumer* CD-ROM that is included with this book contains multimedia, lab files, practice files, and sample code that you may wish to view or install on your computer's hard drive. To view the content on the CD-ROM you must use an HTML browser that supports frames. A copy of Internet Explorer has been included with this CD-ROM, in case you do not have a browser that supports frames installed on your computer. Please refer to the ReadMe file on the CD-ROM for further instructions on installing Internet Explorer.

To begin browsing the content included on the CD-ROM, open the file default.htm.

Lab Files

The starting point and solution for each lab is included in the CD-ROM. If you installed the labs from the CD, these files are in the folder *<install Folder>*\Labs\Lab*xx* on your hard disk. If you did not install the labs, you can find them in the folder \Labs\Lab*xx* on the CD-ROM. To install the lab files, go to the "Installing Course Files" page on the CD.

> **Note** 4.9 MB of hard disk space is required to install the labs.

Multimedia

This course provides an audio/video demonstration that illustrates security concepts discussed in Chapter 7. The following icon will appear in the margin, indicating that a multimedia title can be found on the accompanying CD-ROM.

Multimedia Icon

> **Note** You can toggle the display of the text of a demonstration or animation on and off by choosing **Closed Caption** from the **View** menu.

Sample Site

Included on the CD is the completed version of the sample site, Five Lakes Publishing. This is the final production version of the site on which you work throughout the book. It contains all of the files, and several user-interface enhancements, that would normally be found on a production site. Many of the user interface enhancements, however, were removed from the lab site to make it easier to work with.

Internet Links

The following icon appears in the margin next to an Internet link, indicating that this link is included on the accompanying CD-ROM.

Internet Link Icon

Conventions Used In This Course

The following table explains some of the typographic conventions used in this course.

Example of convention	Description
Sub, If, Case Else, Print, True, BackColor, Click, Debug, Long	In text, language-specific keywords appear in bold, with the initial letter capitalized.
File menu, **Add Project** dialog box	Most interface elements appear in bold, with the initial letter capitalized.
Setup	Words that you're instructed to type appear in bold.
Variable	In syntax and text, italic letters can indicate placeholders for information that you supply.
[expressionlist]	In syntax, items inside square brackets are optional.
{While | Until}	In syntax, braces and a vertical bar indicate a choice between two or more items. You must choose one of the items, unless all of the items are enclosed in square brackets.
```Sub HelloButton_Click()``` ```Readout.Text = _``` ```"Hello, world!"``` ```End Sub```	This font is used for code.
ENTER	Capital letters are used for the names of keys and key sequences, such as ENTER and CTRL+R.
ALT+F1	A plus sign (+) between key names indicates a combination of keys. For example, ALT+F1 means to hold down the ALT key while pressing the F1 key.
DOWN ARROW	Individual direction keys are referred to by the direction of the arrow on the key top (LEFT, RIGHT, UP, or DOWN). The phrase "arrow keys" is used when describing these keys collectively.

table continued on next page

Example of convention	Description
BACKSPACE, HOME	Other navigational keys are referred to by their specific names.
C:\Vb\Samples\Calldlls.vbp	Paths and file names are given in mixed case.

The following guidelines are used in writing code in this course:

◆ When used at the end of a line of code, the underscore (_) character indicates that the code continues on the next line. Do not type this character when creating your SQL statements or editing pages in Visual Interdev.

◆ Keywords appear with initial letters capitalized:

```
' Sub, If, ChDir, Print, and True are keywords.
Print "Title Page"
```

◆ Line labels are used to mark position in code (instead of line numbers):

```
ErrorHandler:
Power = conFailure
End Function
```

◆ An apostrophe (') introduces comments:

```
' This is a comment; these two lines
' are ignored when the program is running.
```

◆ Control-flow blocks and statements in **Sub, Function,** and **Property** procedures are indented from the enclosing code:

```
Private Sub cmdRemove_Click ()
    Dim Ind As Integer
    ' Get index
    Ind = lstClient.ListIndex
    ' Make sure list item is selected
    If Ind >= 0 Then
        ' Remove it from list box
        lstClient.RemoveItem Ind
        ' Display number
        lblDisplay.Caption = lstClient.ListCount
    Else
        ' If nothing selected, beep
        Beep
    End If
End Sub
```

♦ Intrinsic constant names appear in a mixed-case format, with a two-character prefix indicating the object library that defines the constant. Constants from the Visual Basic and Microsoft Visual Basic for Applications object libraries are prefaced with "vb"; constants from the ActiveX Data Objects (ADO) Library are prefaced with "ad"; constants from the Excel Object Library are prefaced with "xl". Examples are as follows:

```
vbTileHorizontal
adAddNew
xlDialogBorder
```

For more information about coding conventions, see "Programming Fundamentals" in the MSDN Visual Basic documentation.

Table of Contents

Chapter 1:
Understanding Electronic Commerce

Objectives

After completing this chapter, you will be able to:

- Explain what electronic commerce (e-commerce) is.
- Describe the need for e-commerce.
- Explain how business is transacted on an e-commerce site.
- List the features and requirements of a good e-commerce site.
- List a few e-commerce sites on the Internet.
- Explain what Commerce Server is.
- List the Commerce Server tools that enable the creation of customized e-commerce sites.

Overview of E-Commerce

This section introduces the key applications of, and the need for, e-commerce. You will also learn about the shopping process on an e-commerce site. This section includes the following topics:

- What Is E-Commerce?
- Why Use E-Commerce?
- How Does E-Commerce Work?

What Is E-Commerce?

E-commerce is a means of enabling and supporting the exchange of information, goods, and services between companies or between companies and their customers. It enables companies to be more efficient in their internal operations and more responsive to the needs and expectations of their customers. E-commerce technologies enable enterprises to exchange information instantaneously, eliminate paper-work, and advertise their products and services to a global market. E-commerce is divided into two categories: business-to-consumer and business-to-business commerce.

Business-to-Consumer Commerce

In business-to-consumer commerce, businesses create electronic storefronts that offer information, goods, and services to consumers. Internet "shopping malls" on the Web sell consumer goods ranging from cakes and wines to computers and cars.

An example of a business-to-consumer site is eToys.com (http://www.eToys.com).

Business-to-Business Commerce

Business-to-business commerce includes online wholesaling, in which businesses sell goods and services to other businesses on the Web. Business-to-business commerce is transacted by using Electronic Data Interchange (EDI) technologies. EDI defines the formats, data types, and routing instructions for the electronic exchange of business documents between companies' computer systems.

An example of a business-to-business site is openmarket.com (http://www.openmarket.com).

Why Use E-Commerce?

Because the Internet provides a flexible and dynamic marketplace to exchange goods, services, and information with consumers and business partners, it is becoming increasingly important for businesses to use the Internet to reach new markets. The greatest business advantage of being online is the ability to market products both locally and globally. The following list offers some reasons for companies to build commerce-enabled Web sites:

◆ **Low entry costs** A company can establish itself on the Internet, and open for business, with a relatively small investment. Thousands of companies operate simple, inexpensive sites that are successful in their markets.

◆ **Reduced transaction costs** Dealing with customers over the Web, whether to process orders or to attend to customer support, is cheaper than traditional marketing methods. For example, Dell Computer Corporation estimates that it saves eight dollars each time a customer checks the status of an order at the Dell Web site, instead of calling the company.

◆ **Access to the global market** With a traditional business, the target market may be the local community or, with a higher advertising budget, it may extend to neighboring communities. The Web extends the reach of even the smallest businesses by allowing them to market products globally.

◆ **Online distribution** The Web enables businesses to distribute data and software online.

◆ **Secure market share** Getting a business online protects its current offline market share from being eroded by an online entrepreneur. If a business enters the e-commerce market too late, competitors who have already established a Web presence may make a successful market entry more difficult.

How Does E-Commerce Work?

The following illustration shows how the e-commerce process works.

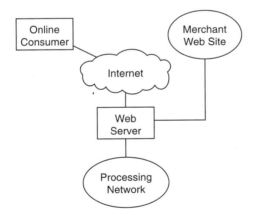

The e-commerce process works as follows:

1. A consumer uses a Web browser to connect to the home page of a merchant's Web site on the Internet.

2. The consumer browses the catalog of products featured on the site and selects items to purchase. The selected items are placed in the electronic equivalent of a shopping cart.

3. When the consumer is ready to complete the purchase of selected items, she provides a bill-to and ship-to address for purchase and delivery.

4. When the merchant's Web server receives this information, it computes the total cost of the order — including tax, shipping, and handling charges — and then displays the total to the customer.

5. The consumer can now provide payment information, such as a credit card number, and then submit the order.

6. When the credit card number is validated and the order is completed at the Commerce Server site, the merchant's site displays a receipt confirming the customer's purchase.

7. The Commerce Server site then forwards the order to a Processing Network for payment processing and fulfillment.

Tour of a Sample Site

This section contains the following topics:

- ◆ Requirements of a Good E-Commerce Site
- ◆ A Few E-Commerce Sites on the Net
- ◆ Practice: Visiting the Sample Site

Requirements of a Good E-Commerce Site

To attract online shoppers, it is necessary to keep the site simple and professional, ensure that pages download quickly, and sell goods that people want to buy online. You must also provide the following:

Promotional and Searchable Content

Companies online need to maintain product and service catalogs that display their offerings to shoppers in a clear and searchable format. Such catalogs should also promote special price and product offers.

Shopping Cart

Online stores should provide "shopping carts" into which shoppers can place their selections. This product selection feature should allow shoppers to add or remove products from their cart and indicate quantity and per unit cost of the items in the cart.

Shopper Management

Businesses need to engage both their customers and business partners who are visiting and purchasing via their site. To do this, businesses can gather information about shopper interests and what products consumers buy. The next step is to maintain a shopper profile, with a customer's purchase history and a record of his previous shopping carts' contents. Finally, businesses can assist shoppers after a purchase by providing receipts, answers to frequently asked questions, and information on product improvements.

Flexible Support for Payment

Both businesses and consumers need e-commerce sites that offer secure and flexible, Internet-based transactions. Effective e-commerce solutions should support online payment through credit cards, as well as offline payment methods, such as checks or cash.

Secure Transactions

E-commerce sites should have security features that control the access of consumers, business trading partners, and operators. Sites should also provide protection for shopper information that is transmitted over the Internet, such as passwords and credit card numbers.

Practice: Visiting the Sample Site

In this practice, you will visit the sample site and observe the following functionality:

- ◆ The product catalog
- ◆ The shopping cart
- ◆ Price promotions, cross-sell promotions, upsell promotions
- ◆ Registration of shoppers

- Searching by various parameters
- Completing purchase of an item
- Tracking orders
- The business-to-business feature

Note You will be able to create a site similar to the sample site by adding the functionality listed previously. To replicate the interface of the sample site, refer to Appendix A. You can modify the HTML code in the wizard-generated .asp (Active Server Pages) files to give your site the desired look and feel.

▶ **To access the sample site**

1. Start Microsoft Internet Explorer.
2. Type the URL address **http://Ecommerce/SampleSite**.

▶ **To browse the product catalog**

1. On the Five Lakes Publishing Home page, select a book section.
2. View the available books under this section.
3. Click **Home** on the navigation bar to view books in a different section.

▶ **To shop at the sample site**

1. Under **Book Sections**, on the Five Lakes Publishing Home page, click **Computers**.
2. On the Book Sections page, from the list of available computer books, click **Mastering Windows NT Server 4**. Notice the cross-sell product on the Product Information page.
3. On the Mastering Windows NT Server 4 Product Information page, click **BUY NOW** to add this product to your shopping cart.
4. On the Cart page, click **May we suggest a better book?** to see the associated upsell product.
5. On the Windows NT 4.0 MCSE Study Guide Product Information page, click **Update Cart** to replace Mastering Windows NT Server 4 with Windows NT 4.0 MCSE Study Guide.

6. On the Cart page, click **Continue Shopping** to add more products to your cart.

7. On the Computers Book Sections page, click **The C++ Programming Language** and **C++ Primer** to add them to your cart. Notice the discount on The C++ Programming Language book.

8. On the Cart page, next to C++ Primer, click **Delete**. Note that the discount on The C++ Programming Language is no longer applicable.

9. On the Cart page, click **Continue Checkout**.

10. On the Shipping page, type the shipping information and then click **Total**.

11. On the Payment page, type the credit card and billing information. You can use the following test credit card numbers:

    - American Express: 3111-111111-11117
    - Visa: 4111-1111-1111-1111
    - MasterCard: 5111-1111-1111-1118
    - Discover: 6111-1111-1111-1116

12. Click **PURCHASE** to submit the order. Note the order number generated on the Purchase Confirmation page.

▶ **To track your order**

1. On the Home page, on the navigation bar, click **Order Status**.

2. On the Order Status page, type your order number in the **Order Number** text box, and then click **Go**.

3. Note the status of your order.

▶ **To search for products**

1. On the Search page, from the **Search By** drop-down list, select **Category**.

2. In the **Value** text box, type **Databases**, and then click **Go**.

3. Note the search results.

▶ **To display orders received from business partners**

1. Access the sample site by typing the URL address **http://Ecommerce/SampleSite/default.asp?epartner_id=2**.

2. Shop at the sample site and complete the purchase of a product.

3. Access the Manager page by typing the URL address **http://Ecommerce/ SampleSite/Manager**.

4. On the Site Manager page, in the Transactions section, click **Orders**.

5. On the Order Manager page, click **Orders by ePartner**.

6. View the report.

A Few E-Commerce Sites on the Net

Microsoft Press

The Microsoft Press online store provides learning and training resources for all levels of PC users and professionals. This site offers books, CDs, self-paced training kits, and videos to accommodate different learning styles. Shoppers can browse through the catalog of books or use the search function to see a list of books by title, author, or subject. The site features "cross-sell" promotions, which suggest other items in which a shopper might be interested.

http://mspress.microsoft.com

Dell Computers

The Dell Computers online store allows shoppers to configure, price, and purchase customized desktop PCs, portables, and servers over the Internet. The online store reduces order costs and generates customized pricing and reports for corporate customers. After shoppers have placed an order, they can log onto the Dell site to find out the status of any order. Shoppers can use Dell's Order Watch system, which automatically sends the customer an e-mail notification after an order has been shipped. The site also offers extensive service and support features such as self-diagnostic tools, downloadable basic input/output (BIOS) files, drivers and utilities, and a public discussion area.

http://www.dell.com

Barnes and Noble

The Barnes and Noble online bookstore offers a large selection of book titles. Designed for easy navigation, the site also has a powerful search engine for fast results. The Barnes and Noble site provides book descriptions, reviews, and excerpts for all titles on the site. Shoppers can browse through specialty sections for gifts, magazines, and out-of-print and rare books. The site also offers shoppers features such as the option to send gift certificates or have their gifts wrapped.

http://www.barnesandnoble.com

Introduction to Commerce Server

This section contains the following topics:

◆ Overview of Commerce Server

◆ Commerce Server Platform Architecture

◆ Important Commerce Server Tools

Overview of Commerce Server

Commerce Server enables enterprises to build powerful and cost-effective solutions for engaging and transacting with customers and business partners online. The features and functionality of Commerce Server provide organizations with the ability to create an e-commerce site quickly and easily. Commerce Server supports business-to-consumer as well as business-to-business transactions:

◆ Business-to-consumer sites: Commerce Server provides tools and features for building business-to-consumer sites, including support for the shopping cart feature, promotions, cross-sells, secure payment, and order processing.

◆ Business-to-business sites: Commerce Server provides tools and features for building business-to-business sites, including support for purchase orders, order approval routing, and secure exchange of business information between trading partners.

Using Commerce Server, you can create, customize, and manage an e-commerce site.

Create an E-Commerce Site

You can quickly create a fully functional e-commerce site by using the Site Foundation Wizard and Site Builder Wizard. The Site Builder Wizard creates Active Server Pages (.asp) files based on the options that you choose. Sites generated by the wizard can be edited by using Microsoft Visual InterDev. The wizard creates a site that displays a catalog of your products, accepts orders, and integrates with your existing business systems. For more information, see Chapter 2, "Building a Site" on page 15.

Customize the E-Commerce Site

Commerce Server provides tools, COM objects, and samples that you can use to customize the way a site processes orders, integrates with existing business systems, and communicates with trading partners.

Manage the E-Commerce Site

The Site Builder Wizard generates a set of Web pages that are used for performing management tasks such as adding and deleting products, modifying the department structure, offering sales and promotions, checking orders, and so on. Changes are automatically reflected on the site's pages. Access to these Manager pages is restricted to the site operator and Microsoft Windows NT user accounts authorized by the site operator.

Commerce Server Platform Architecture

The following illustration shows the architecture of the Commerce Server platform.

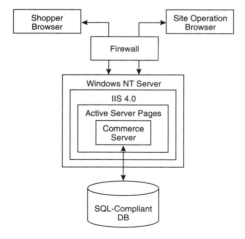

Commerce Server runs under the Windows NT Server operating system, which supports the security and performance requirements of Commerce Server.

Windows NT Server includes an integrated Web server, the Internet Information Server (IIS), which provides secure Web site administration for Internet sites using Commerce Server. In addition, IIS version 4.0 provides the ASP environment for developing Web-based applications and Microsoft ActiveX Data Objects (ADO) for dynamic database access from Commerce Server sites.

Commerce Server requires an ORACLE or SQL-compliant database and a database driver that is compatible with ODBC version 3.5 for data storage. A single Commerce Server site can have one or more databases, which can reside either on the same computer as the Commerce Server or on a separate computer connected by a local area network (LAN).

A Web browser is required to connect to a commerce site of this type.

Important Commerce Server Tools

Commerce Server contains a number of tools that make it easier to create a new or customized Commerce Server site. These tools include the Site Foundation Wizard, Site Builder Wizard, Pipeline Editor, and the Server Administration pages.

Site Foundation Wizard

The Site Foundation Wizard sets up the physical infrastructure of the site, including the directory structure for a new e-commerce site, virtual directories, site configuration files, Windows NT user account, and so on. After setting up the site foundation, the wizard generates a link to the new site's main Site Manager page, which provides access to the Site Builder Wizard.

Site Builder Wizard

The Site Builder Wizard provides a simple step-by-step interface that generates a fully functional e-commerce site quickly and easily. The wizard supports a variety of site options, including department hierarchies, products in multiple departments, variable numbers of product attributes, different registration models, price and cross-sell promotions, Microsoft Wallet payment options, and so on.

Pipeline Editor

The Pipeline Editor is used to customize the Order Processing Pipeline (OPP) of a site for complete integration with preexisting business systems. The OPP provides a series of processing stages defining the method in which orders are routed through the site. Each OPP stage consists of one or more pipeline components designed to perform some operation on the business object. Developers can add, move, and reconfigure the OPP components in the order suited to their commerce application.

Server Administration Pages

Server Administration pages are used for both local and remote administration of the server computer on which the e-commerce sites are hosted. Using this tool, the server administrator can access the Site Manager pages, open and close sites, create new sites, delete obsolete sites, and modify the properties of a site.

Review

The following review questions cover some of the key concepts taught in the chapter.

1. List five important requirements of a good e-commerce site.

2. What is the role of IIS in Commerce Server platform architecture?

3. What can you do with Commerce Server?

4. Which Commerce Server tool creates the physical directory structure of a new site?

Review Answers

1. Provide promotional and searchable content, flexible support for payment, secure transactions, shopping cart, and shopper management.

2. IIS provides secure Web site administration for Internet sites using Commerce Server. IIS also provides the ASP environment for developing Web-based applications and ActiveX Data Objects for dynamic access to the database from Commerce Server sites.

3. Using Commerce Server you can create, customize, and manage an e-commerce site.

4. The Site Foundation Wizard

Chapter 2:
Building a Site

Objectives

After completing this chapter, you will be able to:

- Create a foundation for a site by using the Site Foundation Wizard.
- Build the site by using the Site Builder Wizard and populate it with departments, products, and product attributes.
- Perform simple administrative tasks by using the Server Administration pages.

Creating a Site Foundation

In this section, you will learn to use the Site Foundation Wizard.

This section includes the following topics:

- What the Site Foundation Wizard Creates
- Prepare a Database for the Site
- Practice: Using the Site Foundation Wizard

What the Site Foundation Wizard Creates

The foundation for a site is created by using the Site Foundation Wizard. The foundation created by the wizard includes:

- The physical directory structure of the new site.
- The virtual directory.
- The site configuration files:
  - **Site_name\Config\Site.csc** for the site pages.
  - **Site_name\Manager\Config\Site.csc** for the Site Manager pages.
- The URL to Site Manager page.

Among other settings, the site configuration files store the connection string for the new site's database and the name of the Microsoft Windows NT account that has permission to access the site's Manager pages.

When the Site Foundation Wizard has created the foundation, it displays the URL for the new site's Manager page. At this point, the Manager page is blank except for a link that starts the Site Builder Wizard. Using the URL, the site operator can connect to the Manager page and run the Site Builder Wizard, which generates the Active Server Pages (ASP) files for the new site and the site's Manager pages.

Prepare a Database for the Site

The first step in creating a new Commerce Server site is to prepare a database for the site.

Creating the Site Database

The first step in preparing a database for the site is to create the database itself. This database will store information about the products offered at your site and the transactions that occur on your site.

To create a new database in SQL Server 7.0, you must determine the name of the database, its owner, its size, and the files that will be used to store it. Every database has one primary file that stores data and a transaction log that stores the log information used to recover the database. You can create databases by using Transact-SQL, SQL Server Enterprise Manager, or the Create Database Wizard, or by using SQL-DMO programmatically. For more information, see product documentation for Microsoft SQL Server 7.0.

Creating Database Logins

The next step in preparing a database for the site is to add login names for the site operators and site visitors to the SQL Server. You can create login names by using SQL Server Enterprise Manager. The site operator's login must have full permissions on the database, because the Site Builder Wizard uses this login name when it creates the database schema for the new site. The site visitor's login name has a restricted set of permissions, because the site visitor uses this login only to shop at the site.

Creating a Data Source Name (DSN)

The last step is to create a Data Source Name (DSN) by using the Microsoft Open Database Connectivity (ODBC) Data Source Administrator utility in Control Panel.

When you run the Site Foundation Wizard, you must provide a DSN, a database login name, and a password that enables the wizard to construct a connection string, which is used to connect to the new site's database.

Practice: Using the Site Foundation Wizard

In this practice, you will use the Site Foundation Wizard to create a foundation for a new site.

▶ **To access the Site Foundation Wizard**

1. Click the **Start** button, point to **Programs, Microsoft Site Server, Administration,** and then click **Site Server Service Admin (HTML).**

2. On the Site Server Web Administration page, click **Commerce.**

3. On the Getting Started with Site Server Commerce page, click **Server Administration.**

4. On the Server Administration page, click **Create.**

▶ **To create a site foundation with the Create New Site Foundation Wizard**

1. On the Create New Site Foundation Wizard - Select a Web Site page, select **Default Web Site,** and then click **Next.**

2. On the Select a Site Name page, type **DemoStore** into the **Short name** text box and **Demo Book Store** into the **Display name** text box. Then click **Next.**

3. On the Select a Directory Location page, click **Next** to accept the default directory.

4. On the Formulate a Database Connection String page, from the **Available DSNs** list box, select the DSN **DemoStore.** In the **Database login** text box, type **sa** leave the **Database password** text box blank, and then click **Next.**

5. On the Specify Manager Account page, click **Next** to use an existing account.

6. On the Select Windows NT Domain page, select the domain for your local computer and then click **Next.**

7. On the Select a Windows NT account page, select **Administrator** and then click **Next**.

8. On the Finish page, click **Finish**.

Leave the wizard in this state. The next demonstration continues from this point.

Creating a Site

In this section, you will learn to create and test a site.

This section contains the following topics:

◆ What the Site Builder Wizard Generates

◆ Practice: Creating and Testing a Site

What the Site Builder Wizard Generates

The Site Builder Wizard generates all the files and database tables for the new site and saves them on the Web server. The generated files and tables include the following:

◆ ASP files and database tables

◆ Site Manager pages

◆ The site's database schema

After the foundation for the new site has been created, the site operator can connect to the Manager page and run the Site Builder Wizard. Based on the options selected, the Site Builder Wizard generates the ASP files, database tables, and schema for the new site and its corresponding Site Manager pages; if required, it can also generate sample data and load it into the database. The wizard prefixes the site name to each table name. For example, if the site name is specified as **Test**, the new basket table is named **Test_basket**.

The following table lists and describes the default tables generated by the Site Builder Wizard.

Table Name	Description
Sitename_basket	Contains information about the items that a shopper has selected during a shopping session
Sitename_dept	Contains information about the various departments on the site
Sitename_dept_prod	Associates each product to a specific department
Sitename_product	Contains information on each product
Sitename_promo_cross	Contains information about the products for which cross-sell products exist
Sitename_promo_price	Contains information about the price discounts offered in a site
Sitename_receipt	Contains order information with order number as the primary key
Sitename_receipt_item	Associates each item to a specific order
Sitename_shopper	Contains personal details of visiting shoppers

Practice: Creating and Testing a Site

In this practice, you will:

- Build a site on the foundation by using Site Builder Wizard.
- Populate the site with a department and a product.
- Test the store by shopping for the product created.

▶ **To access the Site Builder Wizard**

1. On the Create New Site Foundation Wizard - Site Creation Complete page, click **http://localhost:80/DemoStore/manager/default.asp,** which is the URL to the new site's Manager page.
2. On the new site's Manager page, click **Commerce Site Builder Wizard.**

▶ **To create a site on the foundation with the Site Builder Wizard**

1. On the Welcome page, click **Next**.

2. On the Site Type page, click **Next** to create a custom site.

3. On the Merchant Information page, type information about the site that you are building, and then click **Next**.

4. On the Locale page, click **Next** to accept the default of **English (United States)**.

   The locale configures the new site to calculate taxes and to display currency, time, and address in the proper format.

5. On the Site Style page, set the navigation bar, font, background color, and button style to your preference, and then click **Next**.

6. On the Promotions page, select the **Price promotions** and **Cross-sell promotions** check boxes, and then click **Next**.

7. On the Features page, under Registration, accept the default **None**, and under Department Type, accept the default **Simple**. Make sure that under Product Searching, **Enabled** is selected, and then click **Next**.

8. On the Product Attribute Type page, click **Next** to accept **Static Attributes**.

9. On the Product Structure page, add **Author** as a single-valued custom field, and click **Next**.

10. On the Shipping & Handling page, select the **Enabled** check box for Handling charges, type **$2.00** as the cost for handling, and then click **Next**.

11. On the Tax: USA page, click **Enabled** for a tax on Georgia (**GA**) residents only. In the **Rate** box, type **5.0** and then click **Next**.

12. On the Payment Methods page, click **Next** to accept the default credit cards.

13. On the Order History page, click the **Retain order history and receipt information** check box, and then click **Next**.

14. On the Output Options page, next to the **Load Schema into Database** option, click **Enable**. Clear the **Generate Sample Data to file** option and then click **Finish** to create your site.

15. When the word "Done" appears at the bottom of the Shopper Site Pages list, click **Here is your manager site**.

▶ **To add a department and product to the new site**

Note If an unexpected HTTP application restart screen appears, click **Refresh** to clear it.

1. On the Site Manager page, in the Merchandising section, click **Departments**.

2. On the Departments page, click **Add New Department**.

3. On the New Department page, in the Dept Id field, type **1**, in the Name field, type **Computers**; in the Description field, type **The World of Computers**, and then click **Add Department**.

4. On the Departments page, notice that the first department has been created, and then click **Products**.

5. On the Products page, click **Add New Product**.

6. On the New Product page, type in the following parameters:

   a. Sku = **001**

   b. Name = **Windows NT 4.0 MCSE Study Guide**

   c. Description = **Just the minimum needed**

   d. List price = **$62.99**

   e. Author = **Alan R. Carter, Thomas C. Willingham**

7. Click **Add Product**.

8. On the Products page, click **Departments**.

9. On the Departments page, click **Manager**.

10. On the Site Manager page, in the System section, click **Shop Site**.

▶ **To test the store by shopping for the product that you have added**

1. On the opening page of the store, click the **Computers** department.

2. On the Computers department page, click **Windows NT 4.0 MCSE Study Guide**.

3. On the Product Information page, click **Add to Basket** to add this book to the shopping cart.

4. On the Shopping Basket page, click **Purchase**.

5. On the Shipping page, select **Overnight** as the shipping method, type in the ship-to information, and then click **Total**.

6. If a Security Information box appears, click **Yes** to release the shipping address to the Web.

7. On the Final Purchase Approval page, type in the credit card information and the bill-to information. You can use the following test credit card numbers:

   - American Express: 3111-111111-11117
   - Visa: 4111-1111-1111-1111
   - MasterCard: 5111-1111-1111-1118
   - Discover: 6111-1111-1111-1116

8. Click **Purchase** to submit the order.

9. On the Purchase Confirmation page, click the order number to view your receipt.

Working with the Server Administration Pages

The Server Administration pages are used to perform the following administrative tasks:

- Create new Commerce Server sites.
- Open, close, and delete Commerce Server sites.
- Modify the properties of a site, such as the database connection string of Commerce Server sites.
- Access the Site Manager pages.

▶ **To access the Server Administration page**

1. Start Microsoft Internet Explorer.

2. Type the URL **http://localhost/siteserver/admin/commerce** into the Internet Explorer address bar.

3. On the Getting Started with Site Server Commerce page, click **Server Administration**.

The following are displayed on the Server Administration page:

◆ A list of Commerce Server sites

◆ The version of Commerce Server that was used to create the site

◆ The site's status — open, closed, or invalid

◆ The name of the IIS virtual directory

◆ The Web site on which the site is located

Opening, Closing, and Deleting Sites

The Server Administration page is shown in the following illustration.

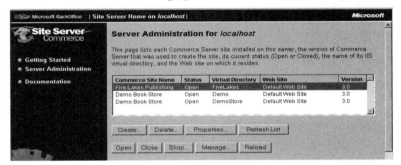

▶ **To open, close, or delete one or more Commerce Server sites**

1. On the Server Administration page, select the site or sites in the list of Commerce Server sites.

2. Click the **Open** button, **Close** button, or the **Delete** button.

   When you click **Delete,** a confirmation page appears on which you can specify whether you want to delete the site's files and database tables in addition to the site's virtual directory.

Modifying the Properties of a Site

By using the Server Administration pages, you can modify the following properties of a site, as shown in the illustration on the next page.

◆ Change the display name of a Commerce Server site.

◆ Add or remove a Windows NT user account.

◆ Add, remove, or edit named connections in the connection map.

A connection string consists of a DSN, a database login name, and a database password. You can create a name to represent each connection string and then store these named connections in the site's connection map.

◆ Specify security options for a Commerce Server site, such as the URL for the page that should be displayed when the site is closed.

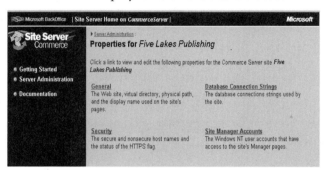

Managing a Site

By using the Site Manager page, you can:

◆ Add departments and products to your site.

◆ Edit a pipeline.

For more information, see Chapter 6, "Checking Out" on page 95.

◆ Add price and cross-sell promotions.

◆ Open and close a site.

◆ Reload a site.

Some modifications that you make to a site, such as changes to its connection strings, are not reflected in the site until you reload it. Reloading the site causes IIS to rerun the site's global.asa file, which picks up any changes.

The following illustration shows the Site Manager page.

Lab 2: Creating a New Commerce Server Site

Objectives

After completing this lab, you will be able to:

◆ Create a site foundation by using the Site Foundation Wizard.

◆ Build a site by using the Site Builder Wizard.

◆ Test the store by shopping at its site.

Before You Begin

Prerequisites

This lab assumes that Microsoft Site Server 3.0, Commerce Edition, has been installed on your computer successfully.

Before you begin this lab, you must be familiar with Microsoft Internet Explorer.

Estimated time to complete this lab: 30 minutes

Exercise 1: Using the Site Foundation Wizard

In this exercise, you will use the Site Foundation Wizard to create a foundation for the new site.

▶ **Access the Site Foundation Wizard**

1. Click the **Start** button, point to **Programs, Microsoft Site Server, Administration,** and then click **Site Server Service Admin (HTML).**

2. On the Site Server Web Administration page, click **Commerce.**

3. On the Getting Started with Site Server Commerce page, click **Server Administration.**

4. On the Server Administration page, click **Create.**

▶ **Create a site foundation with the Create New Site Foundation Wizard**

1. On the Create New Site Foundation Wizard - select a Web Site page, select **Default Web Site,** and then click **Next.**

2. On the Select a Site Name page, type **FiveLakes** into the **Short Name** text box and **Five Lakes Publishing** into the **Display name** text box. Then click **Next.**

Note The short name cannot contain spaces, must begin with an alphabetic character, and can have a maximum of 12 characters.

3. On the Select a Directory Location page, click **Next** to accept the default directory.

4. On the Formulate a Database Connection String page, in the **Available DSNs** list box, select the DSN **FiveLakes.** In the **Database login** text box, type **sa,** leave the **Database password** text box blank, and then click **Next.**

5. On the Specify Manager Account page, click **Next** to use an existing account.

6. On the Select Windows NT Domain page, select the domain for your local computer, and then click **Next.**

7. On the Select a Windows NT account page, select **Administrator,** and then click **Next.**

8. On the Finish page, click **Finish.**

Exercise 2: Using the Site Builder Wizard

In this exercise, you will use the Site Builder Wizard to build a site on the foundation.

▶ **Access the Site Builder Wizard**

1. On the Create New Site Foundation Wizard - Site Creation Complete page, click **http://localhost:80/FiveLakes/manager/default.asp**, which is the URL to the new site's Manager page.

2. On the new site's Manager page, click **Commerce Site Builder Wizard**.

▶ **Create a site on the foundation with the Site Builder Wizard**

1. On the Welcome page, click **Next**.

2. On the Site Type page, click **Next** to create a custom site.

Note A warning — "No copy template sites installed" — is displayed, because the sample sites included with Commerce Server are not installed.

3. On the Merchant Information page, type information about the site that you are building, and then click **Next**.

4. On the Locale page, click **Next** to accept the default of **English (United States)**.

5. On the Site Style page, set the navigation bar, font, background color, and button style to your preference, and then click **Next**.

6. On the Promotions page, select the **Price promotions** and **Cross-sell promotions** check boxes, and then click **Next**.

7. On the Features page, under Registration, accept the default **None**. Under Department Type, accept the default **Simple**. Make sure that under Product Searching, **Enabled** is selected, and then click **Next**.

8. On the Product Attribute Type page, click **Next** to accept **Static Attributes**.

9. On the Product Structure page, in the **Custom** text box, type **Author**, from the **Type** drop-down list box, select **Single Valued**, and then click **Add**. Similarly, add Publisher, Edition, and Category as single-valued custom fields, and then click **Next**.

10. On the Shipping & Handling page, ensure that **Overnight** and **2nd Day** are selected as the shipping methods, select the **Enabled** check box for Handling charges, type **$2.00** as the cost for handling, and then click **Next**.

11. On the Tax: USA page, click **Enabled** for a tax on Georgia (**GA**) residents only. In the **Rate** box, type **5.0** and then click **Next**.

12. On the Payment Methods page, click **Next** to accept the default credit cards.

13. On the Order History page, click the **Retain order history and receipt informa- tion** check box, and then click **Next**.

14. On the Output Options page, clear the **Generate Schema to file** and **Generate Sample Data to file** check boxes. This is done because the site database is already installed on your machine and the tables have been populated with sample data.

15. Click **Finish** to create your site.

16. When the word "Done" appears at the bottom of the Shopper Site Pages list, click **Here is your shopping site**.

Exercise 3: Testing the Store

In this exercise, you will test the store by shopping at its site.

▶ **Test the store by shopping for the products in it**

1. Note that the initial user interface screen for the store displays the font and background settings that you requested in the Site Builder Wizard. On the opening page of the store, click the **Computers** department.

2. On the Computers department page, click **Windows NT 4.0 MCSE Study Guide**.

3. On the Product Information page, click **Add to Basket** to add this book to the shopping cart.

4. On the Shopping Basket page, click **Purchase**.

5. On the Shipping page, select **Overnight** as the shipping method, and then click **Add address**.

6. In the **Add a New Address** dialog box, type your personal details and then click **OK**. Ensure that the country is specified as United States.

7. On the Shipping page, click **Total**.

8. If a **Security Information** dialog box appears, click **Yes** to release the shipping address to the Web.

9. On the Final Purchase Approval page, click **Add card**, and from the available list select a credit card type.

10. In the **Add a New Credit Card** dialog box, click **Next**.

11. In the **Credit Card Information** dialog box, type your credit card information and then click **Next**. You can use the following test credit card numbers:

    - American Express: 3111-111111-11117
    - Visa: 4111-1111-1111-1111
    - MasterCard: 5111-1111-1111-1118
    - Discover: 6111-1111-1111-1116

12. In the **Credit Card Billing Address** dialog box, from the **Billing address** drop-down list box select a billing address or specify a different billing address by clicking **New address**.

13. Click **Next**.

14. In the **Credit Card Password** dialog box, type your credit card password in the **Password** and **Confirm password** text boxes, and then click **Finish**.

15. On the Final Purchase Approval page, click **Purchase**.

16. In the **Password** text box, re-type your credit card password and then click **OK**.

17. On the Purchase Confirmation page, click the order number to view your receipt.

Review

The review questions cover some of the key concepts discussed in this chapter.

1. What are the names of the site configuration files, and what kind of configuration data do they contain?

2. What is the best way to test a newly created site?

3. What does the Site Builder Wizard do?

4. What does the database table Sitename_basket contain?

Review Answers

1. The site configuration file for the site pages is Site_name\Config\Site.csc and the file for the Site Manager pages is Site_name\Manager\Config\Site.csc. The site configuration files store the connection string for a site's database and the name of the Windows NT account that has permission to access the site's Manager pages.

2. The best way to test a site setup is to enter the site as a shopper.

3. The Site Builder Wizard generates the ASP files, database schema, and tables for the new site, as well as its corresponding Site Manager pages.

4. The Sitename_basket table contains information about the items that a shopper has selected during a shopping session.

Chapter 3:
Enhancing the Product Catalog

Objectives

After completing this chapter, you will be able to:

◆ Describe Commerce Server objects.

◆ Modify product catalog pages generated by the Site Builder Wizard to display custom attributes.

◆ Add product search capability to the site.

◆ Implement cross-sell functionality in the site.

Introducing Commerce Server Objects

In this section, you will learn about standard Commerce Server Objects and Global.asa.

This section includes the following topics:

◆ Commerce Server Objects
  • The Page object
  • The QueryMap object

◆ Understanding the Global.asa File

Installing Commerce Server registers Commerce Server objects on a system, which are Microsoft ActiveX Server objects. These objects provide an extensive set of services, including:

◆ Storing customer and purchase information for the current shopping session.

◆ Storing receipts and order information in a database.

◆ Defining queries to retrieve information from a site database.

◆ Formatting HTML page items.

◆ Retrieving values from a URL query string and converting the values to specific data types.

Commerce Server objects support methods and properties that provide these services. On instantiating a Commerce Server object, you can call its methods and properties from within Microsoft Visual Basic Scripting Edition or Microsoft Jscript server-side code that runs on a Commerce Server site.

The following table lists and describes a few Commerce Server objects used in a Commerce Server site.

Object	Description
Page	Provides methods to format HTML page items, generate URL strings, and retrieve values from a URL query string and convert the values to specific data types.
QueryMap	Contains multiple query descriptions to retrieve information from a site database.
OrderForm	Supports the in-memory storage of shopper and purchase information for the current shopping session. For more information on the **OrderForm** object, see Chapter 4, "Managing a Shopping Cart," on page 51.
Dictionary	Provides for the in-memory storage of name/value pairs.
SimpleList	General-purpose list of variants.
DBStorage	Supports mapping **Dictionary** and **SimpleList** objects to and from a database, for the storage and retrieval of order information. For more information on the **DBStorage** object, see Chapter 4, "Managing a Shopping Cart," on page 51.
StandardSManager	Facilitates the creation, deletion, and retrieval of shopper IDs. For more information on the **StandardSManager** object, see Chapter 4, "Managing a Shopping Cart," on page 51.

The Page Object

The **Page** object is a Commerce Server object that is usually created on every ASP page displayed in the shopping process. The Site Builder Wizard in Commerce Server provides the following definition of a **Page** object in i_shop.asp, which is a wizard-generated .asp file:

```
set mscsPage = Server.CreateObject("Commerce.Page")
```

The **Page** object supports methods that make it possible to easily format HTML page items, generate URL strings, retrieve values from a URL query string, and convert the values to given data types based on a local value.

The following table lists the frequently used **Page** object methods in the .asp files of the Five Lakes Publishing sample site.

Method	Description	Example

HTMLEncode	Applies HTML encoding to a specified text string. Characters in the string such as "<" and "&" that have special meanings in HTML are converted to their HTML equivalents, such as < and & so that they are displayed correctly by a client browser.	The following code in dept.asp invokes the mscsPage.**HTMLEncode** method to HTML encoding to the department name so that it can be displayed correctly by the shopper's browser:
		`<title><%= displayname%> _`
		`:Department: _`
		`'<%=mscsPage.HTMLEncode _`
		`(dept_name)%>' </title>`

GetShopperID	Returns the shopper ID for the current shopper from a URL query string or a cookie, depending on the initialization mode of a Commerce Server site.	The following code in i_shop.asp file, which is included in basket.asp, retrieves the shopper ID from the URL. The script in basket.asp uses the shopper ID to extract the shopper's cart items from the database.
		`mscsShopperID= _`
		`mscsPage.GetShopperID`

table continued on next page

Method	Description	Example

PutShopperID	Writes the specified shopper ID to a cookie or stores it in a URL, depending on the initialization mode of a Commerce Server site.	The following code in i_shop.asp file, which is included in basket.asp, stores the specified shopper ID in the URL. The script in basket.asp uses the shopper ID to associate every item in the cart with the specified shopper ID.
		
		`mscsPage.PutShopperID _`
		`(mscsShopperID)`

RequestString	Retrieves a value from a URL query string or form post variable and based on the specified locale, processes it. This processing may involve removing carriage returns, removing leading and trailing spaces, checking the string length against a specified range, and validating the string based on the specified or default locale.	The following code in product.asp retrieves a Product ID from the URL. The script in product.asp uses the Product ID to retrieve information about a product from the database.
		
		`sku=mscsPage.RequestString _`
		`("sku")`

RequestNumber	Retrieves a value from a URL query string or form post variable and converts it to a number based on the specified or default locale. Optionally, **RequestNumber** checks the converted number against the specified range and validates it based on the specified locale.	The following code in dept.asp retrieves the department ID from the URL. The script in dept.asp uses the department ID to display products in the department.
		
		`dept_id = _`
		`mscsPage.RequestNumber _`
		`("dept_id","0")`

Option	Generates an OPTION item in an HTML form selection list and assigns it a value and selection state.	The **mscsPage.Option** method in payment.asp generates an HTML selection field to enable a shopper to select the expiration year of the credit card. For the implementation

table continued on next page

Method	Description	Example
Option (cont.)		of the **Option** method, see the payment.asp file of the Five Lakes Publishing sample site in Appendix A.

The QueryMap Object

Commerce Server uses ActiveX Data Objects for data storage and retrieval from the RDBMS.

Creating a QueryMap Object

Commerce Server sites use database queries to retrieve information from the database. Query statements are collectively stored in a QueryMap. Each query in the QueryMap is specified by means of a query description.

A query description includes at least one property called **SQLCommand**. The **SQLCommand** property is set to a SQL statement that will retrieve information from the site database. For more information on defining SQL statements, see Microsoft SQL Server 7.0 Books Online.

A **QueryMap** object is created in the Application_OnStart subroutine in the site's global.asa file (configuration file for each Commerce site) as follows:

```
set MSCSQueryMap = Server.CreateObject ("Commerce.Dictionary")
```

Adding Queries to a QueryMap Object

A query description is added to the **MSCSQueryMap** object as follows:

```
set MSCSQueryMap.departments = Server.CreateObject _
("Commerce.Dictionary")
```

Next, the SQLCommand property of departments is set to a SQL statement as follows:

```
set MSCSQueryMap.departments.SQLCommand = "select dept_id, _
dept_name from <Sitename>_dept where dept_id = :1"
```

where : "1" in the SQL statement serves as a parameter that can be replaced with a value when the **QueryMap** object is used.

For more information on how query descriptions are added to a **QueryMap** object in the global.asa file of the Five Lakes Publishing sample site, see Appendix A.

Understanding the Global.asa File

Each Commerce Server site contains a global.asa, a configuration file that stores event scripts and objects used by the application. The objects are created as Application objects in global.asa, so that they can be accessed from within any page in the site.

In global.asa, the following objects are created and initialized.

Object	Description
FileDocument	Reads and writes configuration information to and from the site configuration file (site.csc) and the Site Dictionary.
Site Dictionary	Contains the configuration data.
QueryMap Dictionary	Contains description of SQL queries used by the site.
MessageManager	Stores messages used by pipeline components.
StandardSManager	Initializes the application mode to cookie, url, cookieurl, or urlcookie.
DataFunctions	Formats and converts values based on a specific locale, as well as performs validation checks on values passed to the pipeline or saved to the database.

For more information on how objects are created in the global.asa file of the Five Lakes Publishing sample site, see Appendix A.

Modifying Wizard-Generated Catalog Pages

In this section, you will learn about:

◆ What the Wizard Generates
◆ Customizing Product Catalog Pages

Commerce Server sites are designed to contain catalog pages that display departments and their products. Catalog pages are created as standard Active Server Pages (ASP) files that run queries on the product database using Microsoft ActiveX Data Objects (ADO).

For more information on Active Server Pages, see Introducing Active Server Pages in the Product Documentation of Windows NT 4.0 Option Pack.

What the Wizard Generates

Commerce Server organizes products within departments.

The following table describes the elements created and included by the Site Builder Wizard for catalog presentation.

Element	Location	Description
Department table	Site database	Contains information on the various departments present in your site.
Department-Product table	Site database	Contains information, that associates each product to a specific department.
Product table	Site database	Contains information on the various products present in your site.
Query descriptions	Global.asa	Defines queries to extract department and product information from the site database.
Scripts in .asp files dept.asp and product.asp	Default.asp, and display the catalog.	Contains code to execute queries

Customizing Product Catalog Pages

Commerce Server allows you to modify wizard-generated catalog pages. For example, in the Five Lakes Publishing sample site, the default catalog generated by the wizard will display only the title, description, and price for each book. To display custom attributes such as author, edition, and publisher, you will need to modify:

◆ The query description **product_by_sku** in global.asa to include author, edition, and publisher attributes in the select statement as follows:

```
set MSCSQueryMap.product_by_sku = AddQuery _
("SELECT pf.sku, pf.name, pf.description, _
   pf.list_price, pf.sale_price, pf.sale_start, _
   pf.sale_end, pf.image_file, pf.image_width, _
   pf.image_height, pf.author, pf.edition, pf.publisher, _
   dept.dept_id, dept.dept_name _
FROM <Sitename>_product pf, <Sitename>_dept_prod _
   deptprod, <Sitename>_dept dept _
WHERE pf.sku = :1 and pf.sku = deptprod.sku and _
   dept.dept_id = deptprod.dept_id AND _
   dept.dept_id = :2")
```

◆ The script in product.asp to display author, edition, and publisher on the Product page along with other attributes as follows:

```
REM — get author, edition, and publisher fields from recordset
author = rsProduct("author").value
edition = rsProduct("edition").value
publisher = rsProduct("publisher").value

REM — display the fields in HTML format
<P><%=mscsPage.HTMLEncode(author) %>
<P><%=mscsPage.HTMLEncode(edition) %>
<P><%=mscsPage.HTMLEncode(publisher) %>
```

Adding Product Search Capability

This section contains the following topics:

◆ Adding Search Capabilities

◆ Practice: Implementing Search by Various Parameters

Adding Search Capabilities

As you saw in the previous chapter, the Site Builder Wizard provides an option to enable product search capabilities on your site. This enables shoppers to look for products in the site that match a specified keyword. The search page (find.asp) can be extensively tailored to the needs of your shoppers and to the information that is available on your catalog.

For example, to enhance the search capabilities of the Five Lakes Publishing sample site, you can allow shoppers to look for books by specifying an author, publisher, or book category, as shown in the illustration below.

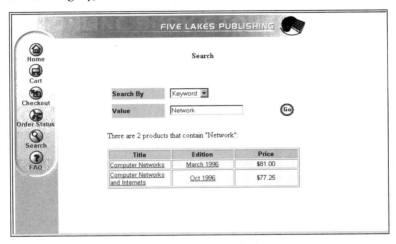

The find.asp file can be modified to include:

◆ A list of search options to be displayed on the page.

◆ SQL queries with conditions based on the search option selected.

Practice: Implementing Search by Various Parameters

In this practice, you will add search options to your site that will enable shoppers to look for specific books.

▶ **Open an .asp file using Microsoft Visual InterDev 6.0**

1. On the **Start** menu, click **Programs, Microsoft Visual InterDev 6.0.**

2. On the New Project page, type **FiveLakes** as your project name, accept the default location, and then click **Open.**

3. In step 1 of the Web Project Wizard, enter **localhost** in the **What server do you want to use?** drop-down list box, select **Master mode**, and then click **Next.**

4. In step 2 of the Web Project Wizard, select the **Connect to an existing Web application on localhost** option button, select **FiveLakes** from the **Name** drop-down list box, and then click **Finish**.

If you are asked, install the scripting library.

5. In the Project Explorer window, double-click **global.asa** to modify the code in this file.

▶ **Define query descriptions in global.asa**

1. In the **InitQueryMap** function, add the following query descriptions to retrieve product information from the site database for a specific keyword or category.

```
set MSCSQueryMap.find_by_keyword = AddQuery _
("SELECT p.sku, p.name, p.list_price, dp.dept_id _
FROM FiveLakes_product p, FiveLakes_dept_prod dp _
WHERE p.name like '%:1%' AND p.sku = dp.sku _
  order by p.name")

set MSCSQueryMap.find_by_keyword = AddQuery _
("SELECT p.sku, p.name, p.category, p.list_price, _
  dp.dept_id _
FROM FiveLakes_product p, FiveLakes_dept_prod dp _
WHERE p.category = ':1' AND p.sku = dp.sku _
  order by p.name")
```

2. On the **File** menu, click **Save global.asa**, and then click **Close**.

▶ **Display search options on the Search page**

1. Double-click **find.asp** in the Project Explorer window.

2. Scroll to the form tag in find.asp and add the following code below the line that reads "**Find:**" to:

   a. Display a list of two search options – Keyword and Category.

   b. Store the selected option in a variable named **search_by** and the search value in a variable named **strFindSpec**.

```
<%
search_by = trim(mscsPage.RequestString("sselect"))
strFindSpec = mscsPage.RequestString("find_spec")
%>
<td width="125%" colspan="2"><select name="sselect" _
size="1" tabindex="20">

<%= mscsPage.Option("Keyword", search_by) %>Keyword
<%= mscsPage.Option("Category", search_by) %>Category
</select></td>
```

▶ **Execute an appropriate query that will search the database**

1. Scroll to the following line of code in find.asp that defines a query for retrieving product information for a specified keyword whose value is stored in a variable **safeFindSpec**.

```
cmdTemp.CommandText= _
  "SELECT p.sku, p.name, p.list_price, dp.dept_id _
FROM FiveLakes_product p, FiveLakes_dept_prod dp _
WHERE p.name like '%" & safeFindSpec & "%' _
  AND p.sku = dp.sku order by name"
```

2. Replace this line with the following code to check the content of the variable **search_by** and assign the appropriate query description value to a variable **sqlText** depending on its content:

```
if search_by = "Keyword" then
    sqlText = MSCSQueryMap.find_by_keyword.SQLCommand
elseif search_by = "Category" then
    sqlText = MSCSQueryMap.find_by_category.SQLCommand
end if

sqlText = Replace(sqlText, ":1", safeFindSpec)
cmdTemp.CommandText = sqlText
```

3. On the **File** menu, click **Save find.asp**, and then click **Close**.

▶ **Search for products on the site**

1. Start Microsoft Internet Explorer and type the URL http://localhost/FiveLakes in the address bar of Internet Explorer.

2. On the site Home page, click **Find**.

3. On the Find page, select **Category** from the drop-down list box next to **Find**.

4. Type **Databases** in the text box provided for search value, and then click **Find**.

5. Notice the search results.

Implementing Cross-Sell

This section contains the following topics:

◆ What the Site Builder Wizard Generates

◆ Using Promotions Wizard

Cross-sell promotions encourage shoppers to consider purchasing a related product. For example, in the Five Lakes Publishing sample site, the Product page for Essential Windows NT System Administration promotes Mastering Windows NT Server 4 as a related product.

What the Site Builder Wizard Generates

The Site Builder Wizard includes the following elements for cross-sell promotions:

◆ A Cross-Sell Promotions table (<Sitename>_promo_cross), which specifies which related product is to be cross-promoted.

◆ A script in the Product page (product.asp), which executes a query to retrieve cross-sell items. The script also displays the related products under the heading "See Also" on the Product page.

The Cross-Sell Promotions Table

The <Sitename>_promo_cross table contains two columns: Sku and Related_sku. Sku is the Product-ID for which related products exist. Related_sku is the Product-ID of the product that will appear under the heading "See Also" on the Product page.

The Product Page

The following script in product.asp retrieves information on related products from the Cross-Sell Promotions table and displays it on the Product page.

```
<%
REM get related products (if any):
cmdTemp.CommandText = Replace("SELECT prod.sku, _
  prod.name, deptprod.dept_id _
FROM <Sitename>_promo_cross promo_cross, _
  <Sitename>_product prod, demo_dept_prod deptprod _
WHERE promo_cross.sku = :1 and prod.sku = deptprod.sku _
  and promo_cross.rel_sku = prod.sku", ":1", quoted_sku)

Set rsRelated = Server.CreateObject("ADODB.Recordset")
rsRelated.Open cmdTemp, , adOpenForwardOnly, adLockReadOnly

REM display up to 5 related products:
if Not rsRelated.EOF then
%>
  <BR>
  <B>See Also</B>
  <%
  nRelated = 0
  set skuField = rsRelated("sku")
  set nameField = rsRelated("name")
  set dept_idField = rsRelated("dept_id")
  do while Not (rsRelated.EOF Or nRelated >= 5)
    %><BR>
    <A HREF="<% = baseURL("product.asp") & _
    mscsPage.URLShopperArgs("sku", skuField.value, _
    "dept_id", dept_idField.value) %>"> <% = _
    mscsPage.HTMLEncode(nameField.value) %> </A>
    <%
    nRelated = nRelated + 1
    rsRelated.MoveNext
  loop %>
<% end if %>
```

Using Promotions Wizard

The Promotions Wizard of Commerce Server enables you to add, edit, and delete related products on your site, as shown in the following illustration.

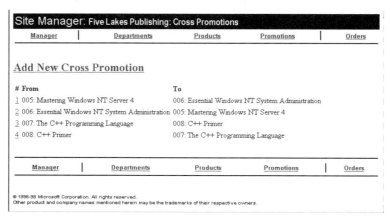

To add related products to the Cross-sell Promotions table

1. Use your browser to navigate to the Site Manager page.

2. On the Site Manager page, click **Promotions**.

3. On the Promotions Manager page, click **Cross Promotions**.

4. On the Cross Promotions page, click **Add New Cross Promotion**.

To edit or delete an existing promotion

1. Use your browser to navigate to the Site Manager page.

2. On the Site Manager page, click **Promotions.**

3. On the Promotions Manager page, click **Cross Promotions**.

4. On the Cross Promotions page, click the name of the cross promotion you want to edit or delete.

Lab 3: Customizing Product Catalog Pages

Objectives

After completing this lab, you will be able to:

◆ Create a customized catalog for your site.

◆ Add the Cross-sell functionality to your site using the Promotions Wizard.

Before You Begin

Prerequisites

This lab assumes that you have successfully created a site using the Site Builder Wizard.

Before you begin this lab, you must have the following prerequisites:

◆ Basic knowledge of HTML and ASP scripting

◆ Familiarity with Microsoft Internet Explorer and Microsoft Visual InterDev 6.0

Estimated time to complete this lab: 30 minutes

Exercise 1: Modifying Catalog View

In this exercise, you will modify the global.asa and product.asp files to display custom attributes on the Product page because the wizard does not display static attributes on the Product page by default.

▶ **Open the global.asa file using Microsoft Visual InterDev 6.0**

If you completed the practice in this chapter, start Microsoft Visual InterDev, open the project that you created there, and then open global.asa.

1. On the **Start** menu, and click **Microsoft Visual InterDev 6.0**.

2. On the New Project page, type **FiveLakes** as your project name, specify the location, and then click **Open**.

3. In step 1 of the Web Project Wizard, select **localhost** from the **What server do you want to use?** drop-down list box, select **Master mode**, and then click **Next**.

4. In step 2 of the Web Project Wizard, select the **Connect to an existing Web application on localhost** option button, select **FiveLakes** from the **Name** drop-down list box, and then click **Finish**.

5. In the Project Explorer window, double-click **global.asa** to modify the code in this file.

> **Note** Every time you open an ASP for the first time in Microsoft Visual InterDev, click **Get Working Copy** to retrieve a write-enabled copy for editing.

▶ **Modify the QueryMap in global.asa**

1. In the **InitQueryMap** function, modify the query description **product_by_sku** to include pf.author, pf.publisher, and pf.edition in the select statement as follows:

```
set MSCSQueryMap.product_by_sku = AddQuery _
("SELECT pf.sku, pf.name, pf.description, _
    pf.list_price, pf.sale_price, pf.sale_start, _
    pf.sale_end, pf.image_file, pf.image_width, _
    pf.image_height, pf.author, pf.edition, pf.publisher, _
    dept.dept_id, dept.dept_name _
FROM FiveLakes_product pf, FiveLakes_dept_prod _
    deptprod, FiveLakes_dept dept _
WHERE pf.sku = :1 and pf.sku = deptprod.sku and _
    dept.dept_id = deptprod.dept_id and _
    dept.dept_id = :2")
```

2. On the **File** menu, click **Save global.asa**, and then click **Close**.

▶ **Display custom attributes on the Product Information page**

1. Double-click **product.asp** in the Project Explorer window.

2. In product.asp, look for the line **REM – get fields from recordset** and insert the following code below it:

```
author=rsProduct("author").value
publisher=rsProduct("publisher").value
edition=rsProduct("edition").value
```

3. Scroll down to the HTML section of product.asp.

4. Below the line of code that reads as follows:

```
<P><%=mscsPage.HTMLEncode(description)%>
```

Add the following code to display author, publisher, and edition using HTML tags:

```
<P>
<P><FONT SIZE="4"><B>Author</B></FONT>
<P><%= mscsPage.HTMLEncode(author) %>
<P><FONT SIZE="4"><B>Publisher</B></FONT>
<P><%= mscsPage.HTMLEncode(publisher) %>
<P><FONT SIZE="4"><B>Edition</B></FONT>
<P><%= mscsPage.HTMLEncode(edition) %>
<P>
<P>
```

5. On the **File** menu, click **Save product.asp**, and then click **Close**.

▶ **View custom attributes on the Product Information page**

1. Start Microsoft Internet Explorer and type **http://localhost/FiveLakes** in the address bar of Internet Explorer.

2. On the site Home page, click **Computers**.

3. On the Department: Computers page, click **Essential Windows NT System Administration**.

4. On the Product: Essential Windows NT System Administration page, notice the author, publisher, and edition being displayed.

Exercise 2: Implementing Cross-Sell

In this exercise, you will use the Promotions Wizard to add Cross-Sell products.

▶ **Access the Promotions Wizard**

1. Start Microsoft Internet Explorer and type **http://localhost/FiveLakes/manager** in the address bar of Internet Explorer.

2. On the Site Manager page, in the **Merchandising** section, click **Promotions**.

3. On the Promotions page, click **Cross Promotions**.

▶ **Add Cross Promotions**

1. On the Cross Promotions page, click **Add New Cross Promotion**.

2. On the New Cross Promotions page, select **Computer Networks** from the **Product** list box.

3. Select **Computer Networks and Internet** from the **Related Product** list box.

4. Click **Add Cross Promotion**.

▶ **View the Cross-sell product on the Product page**

1. On the Site Manager page, in the System section, click **Shop Site**.

2. On the site Home page, click **Computers**.

3. On the Department: Computers page, click **Computer Networks**.

4. On the Product: Computer Networks page, notice Computer Networks and Internet under the heading **See Also**.

Review

The review questions cover some of the key concepts taught in the chapter.

1. What is the role of Global.asa in a Commerce Server site?

2. What is the advantage of adding search capabilities to your site?

3. Why is it a good idea to display related products on the site?

Review Answers

1. Each Commerce Server site contains a configuration file named global.asa that initializes the site by creating objects such as FileDocument and QueryMap, which are used by a Commerce Server site.

2. Adding search capabilities will make it easy for shoppers to look for specific information in the catalog.

3. Displaying related products on a site encourages shoppers to look at other products available on a site and consider purchasing them.

Chapter 4:
Managing a Shopping Cart

Objectives

After completing this chapter, you will be able to:

◆ Explain the need for identifying shoppers in a site.

◆ Generate a shopper ID and assign it to a shopping session.

◆ Add, remove, and update items in a shopping cart.

◆ Use Promotions Wizard to add price discounts and special offers on products.

◆ Implement the Upsell functionality.

Managing a Shopping Session

This section includes the following topics:

◆ Identifying Shoppers Through a Shopper ID

◆ Generating and Storing Shopper IDs

Identifying Shoppers Through a Shopper ID

Need for Identifying Shoppers

During a visit to a Commerce Server site, a shopper navigates through a number of pages, browsing the product catalog, adding, updating, and removing items from a shopping cart. The contents of a shopping cart are saved and retrieved from the site database. As a shopper moves from one page to another, the site must be able to identify the shopper to connect the shopper with the shopping cart data.

What Is a Shopper ID?

A Commerce Server site keeps track of shoppers by assigning each shopper a unique shopper ID. A shopper ID is a random, unique, 32-character string generated by

Commerce Server to keep track of a shopper's order. The site uses this ID to maintain orders in the site database.

Generating and Storing Shopper Ids

A Commerce Server site can save a shopper ID from page to page either in a cookie or in the URL.

Storing a Shopper ID in a Cookie

A cookie is a small file (approximately 1 KB) that contains information about a shopper and is stored on the shopper's computer. When a shopper connects to a site for the first time, the shopper ID and site address is stored as a cookie on the hard disk of the shopper's computer. When the shopper moves to a new page on the site, a script in the new page retrieves the shopper ID from the cookie.

Storing a Shopper ID in the URL

Another method of saving a shopper ID across pages is by storing it in the URL, so that when a shopper moves from one page to another, the script in the page can extract the shopper ID from the URL. However, to save a shopper ID in this fashion, you must initialize an Application MSCSSIDUrlKey variable to identify the key that will appear in the name/value pair that is stored in the URL.

For example, in the Five Lakes Publishing sample site, the following code in global.asa initializes the Application MSCSSIDUrlKey variable to **mscssid**.

```
Application ("MSCSSIDUrlKey") = "mscssid"
```

A call to the **Page** object's SURL or URL method, to move to a new page, will generate the URL as:

```
http://host- _
name/site/newpage.asp?mscssid=TDPLPE10ULSH2J2400G09V85SGAHDJQB
```

Creating Shopper IDs Using StandardSManager

Commerce Server uses the **Page** object **GetShopperID** and **PutShopperID** methods to retrieve and store shopper IDs. These methods store and retrieve shopper IDs either from a cookie or the URL, depending on how the **StandardSManager** object has been initialized in global.asa. **StandardSManager** is a Commerce Server object that supports methods to create, delete, and retrieve shopper IDs.

You can initialize a **StandardSManager** object to the cookie mode as follows:

```
set mscsShopperManager _
     =Server.CreateObject("Commerce.StandardSManager")
call mscsShopperManager.InitManager(sitename,"cookie")
```

The following table describes initialization modes of the **StandardSManager** object.

Mode	Description
Cookie	Stores and retrieves a shopper ID from a cookie.
url	Stores and retrieves a shopper ID from the URL.
Cookieurl	Stores a shopper ID in a cookie and as part of the URL. Retrieves a shopper ID from the cookie. If the cookie is not found, the shopper ID is retrieved from the URL.
Urlcookie	Stores a shopper ID in a cookie and as part of the URL. If the shopper ID is not passed in the URL, it is retrieved from a cookie.

The design of your site will dictate when a shopper ID is generated. You can generate a shopper ID as soon as a shopper enters your site or when a shopper adds an item to the shopping cart. For example, in the Five Lakes Publishing sample site, a shopper ID is generated immediately after a shopper connects to the site.

The following code in i_shop.asp, which is included in most of the pages, creates a shopper ID if it does not exist:

```
mscsShopperID=mscsPage.GetShopperID
if IsNull(mscsShopperID) then
  mscsShopperID=mscsShopperManager.CreateShopperID()
  mscsPage.PutShopperID(mscsShopperID)
end ifAdding Items to a Shopping Cart
```

Adding Items to a Shopping Cart

This section contains the following topics:

◆ Using the **OrderForm** Object

◆ Understanding the **DBStorage** Object

◆ Adding an Item to the Shopping Cart

Using the OrderForm Object

A shopper who visits your site selects items to purchase in a way that is similar to a shopper walking into a physical store, collecting items in a shopping cart. In a Commerce Server site, a shopper moves from one page to another collecting items in a virtual shopping cart called an order form.

The following illustration shows how the **OrderForm** object is used.

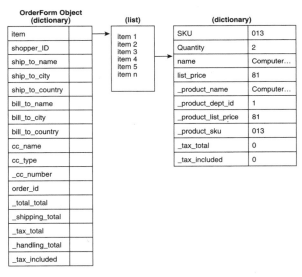

An order form consists of a set of Dictionary (a list of name/value pairs) objects and SimpleList (an array of variants) objects that provide for the in-memory storage of shopper and purchase information such as shopper ID, items selected for purchase, shipping and billing information, payment information, and various data generated by pipeline components.

Creating an OrderForm object

An **OrderForm** object is created as follows:

```
set mscsOrderForm = Server.CreateObject("Commerce.OrderForm")
```

The following table lists the methods supported by an **OrderForm** object.

Method	Description
AddItem	Adds an item to the order form.
ClearOrderForm	Clears the entire **OrderForm** object.
ClearItems	Clears the items collection from the order form.

Commerce Server sites store the contents of an order form in an order form table in the site database. This table, called <Sitename>_basket, contains information of all the shopping carts currently being used by shoppers. Permanent records of completed orders are stored in the <Sitename>_receipt and <Sitename>_receipt_item tables.

Not all of the values in the **OrderForm** object are stored in the site database. Those values whose name begins with an underscore ("_") appear only in the **OrderForm** object and are not saved in the order form table for orders in progress. These values are saved instead to the site's receipt table when the purchase is finalized.

Managing an OrderForm Object

An **OrderForm** object is created, loaded, modified, and stored in the site database on a page-by-page basis. As a shopper adds or removes items from the order form, the revised order form data is saved in the database. When the shopper moves to a new page using the shopper ID, the order form values are retrieved from the database and a new **OrderForm** object is created by using these values.

Understanding the DBStorage Object

Information contained in the **OrderForm** object is loaded and saved in the site database by means of a **DBStorage** object.

A **DBStorage** object is a Commerce Server object that is used to create a data object (Dictionary/SimpleList) that serves as an interface between the site database and the

OrderForm object. The **DBStorage** object provides methods for reading and writing order form values from the site database, as illustrated below.

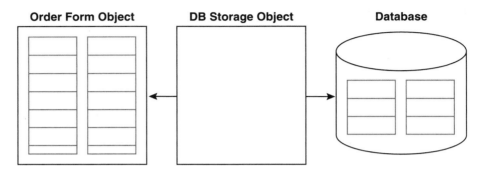

A **DBStorage** object can be created as follows:

```
set mscsOrderFormStorage = _
    Server.CreateObject("Commerce.DBStorage")
```

A **DBStorage** object must be initialized to establish a link to the site database and to identify the type of object to be read or written. When you initialize a **DBStorage** object, you specify:

◆ The datasource that connects to the site database.

◆ The table that will contain the order form information.

◆ The column to be used as the primary key.

◆ The object in which data will be stored or retrieved by the **DBStorage** object.

◆ The column in which the order form values are stored in an encoded format.

◆ The column to store the date when the data is changed.

A **DBStorage** object can be initialized as follows:

```
call mscsOrderFormStorage.InitStorage(mscsDataSource, _
    <Sitename>_basket, "shopper_ID", "Commerce.OrderForm", _
    "marshalled_order", "date_changed")
```

Most of the order form data is stored in the database as a single binary object, usually in the **marshalled_order** field. Queries cannot be run directly on information stored in a binary object. To execute queries on order form data, you can add columns to the table that contains order form data. If a column name exactly matches the name of an entry on the order form, the **DBStorage** object automatically saves the value for that entry into the column of the same name. For example, if your table contains a column named ship_to_country, the **DBStorage** object saves the value in the ship_to_country entry of the order form into that column.

Adding an Item to the Shopping Cart

Commerce Server retrieves a shopper's existing shopping cart data from the database before adding a new item, as illustrated below.

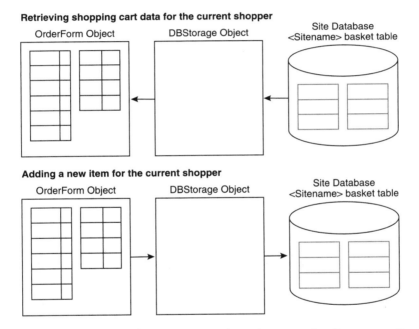

Retrieving shopping cart data for the current shopper

OrderForm Object   DBStorage Object   Site Database
                                            <Sitename> basket table

Adding a new item for the current shopper

OrderForm Object   DBStorage Object   Site Database
                                            <Sitename> basket table

When a shopper adds an item to a shopping cart, the Commerce Server site executes the following steps to add the item to the site database.

1. A **DBStorage** object is created and initialized to access the site database.

2. The **DBStorage.GetData** method is invoked to retrieve the shopping cart data for the current shopper. Assuming the shopping cart exists, it is returned as an **OrderForm** object by the **GetData** method. If it does not exist, the site creates a new **OrderForm** object.

3. The item is added to the order form by using the **AddItem** method of the **OrderForm** object.

4. If the shopping cart does not exist and a new **OrderForm** object is created, the data is inserted in the site database by using the **DBStorage.InsertData** method. If the order form already exists in the site database, the revised data is updated by using the **DBStorage.CommitData** method.

The following ASP code implements the steps to add an item to the <Sitename>_basket table that maintains shopping cart data:

```
REM - Create and initialize a DBStorage object
set mscsOrderFormStorage = _
  Server.CreateObject("Commerce.DBStorage")
call mscsOrderFormStorage.InitStorage(mscsDataSource,_
  <Sitename>_basket, "shopper_ID", "Commerce.OrderForm", _
  "marshalled_order", "date_changed")

REM - Create and initialize an OrderForm object
created = 0
set mscsOrderForm = mscsOrderFormStorage.GetData(null, _
  mscsShopperID)
if IsEmpty(mscsOrderForm) then
  set mscsOrderForm = _
     Server.CreateObject("Commerce.OrderForm")
  mscsOrderForm.shopper_ID = mscsShopperID
  created=1
end if

REM -- Add the item to the shopping cart
call mscsOrderForm.AddItem(product_sku, product_qty, 0)

REM - Update the site database
if created = 0 then
  call mscsOrderFormStorage.CommitData(NULL, mscsOrderForm)
else
  call mscsOrderFormStorage.InsertData(NULL, mscsOrderForm)
end if
```

A Commerce Server site created by using the Site Builder Wizard posts data to xt_orderform_additem.asp when a shopper clicks **Add to Basket.** The script in xt_orderform_additem.asp saves the data in the OrderForm and updates the database.

For the complete code of xt_orderform_additem.asp created in the Five Lakes Publishing sample site, see Appendix A.

Displaying, Updating, and Removing Items

This section contains the following topics:

◆ Updating Items in a Shopping Cart

◆ Removing Items from a Shopping Cart

◆ Displaying a Shopping Cart

Updating Items in a Shopping Cart

A shopper may want to make changes in the shopping cart. For example, in the Five Lakes Publishing sample site, the shopper can modify the quantity of all items in the shopping cart. Once the shopper has made the changes, the site database needs to be updated with the new values.

A Commerce Server site executes the following steps to update the database with details of the modified item.

1. A **DBStorage** object is created and initialized to access the site database.

2. The **DBStorage.GetData** method is invoked to retrieve the shopping cart data for the current shopper into an **OrderForm** object.

3. The modified values entered by the shopper are updated in the order form.

4. The revised order form data is stored in the site database by using the **DBStorage.CommitData** method.

Assuming that a shopper has modified the quantity of an item in the shopping cart, the following ASP code implements the steps to update the site database:

```
REM - Create and initialize a DBStorage object

set mscsOrderFormStorage = _
  Server.CreateObject("Commerce.DBStorage")
```

code continued on next page

code continued from previous page

```
call mscsOrderFormStorage.InitStorage(mscsDataSource, _
  <Sitename>_basket, "shopper_ID", "Commerce.OrderForm", _
  "marshalled_order", "date_changed")

REM - Create and initialize an OrderForm object
set mscsOrderForm = mscsOrderFormStorage.GetData(null, _
  mscsShopperID)

REM - Retrieve the Items list from the order form
set items = mscsOrderForm.Items

REM - For every item in the shopping cart page, starting
REM - with the last item
for index = mscsOrderForm.Items.count - 1 to 0 step -1
  REM - Retrieve an item
  set item = items(index)
  REM - Retrieve the new quantity value from the shopping
  REM - cart page
  new_quantity=mscsPage.RequestNumber("qty_" & CStr(index), _
      item.quantity,0,999)
  if new_quantity = 0 then
      call mscsOrderForm.Items.Delete(index)
  else
      item.quantity = new_quantity
  end if
  REM -- Update the shopping cart table
  call mscsOrderFormStorage.CommitData(null, mscsOrderForm)
next
```

The Site Builder Wizard generates xt_orderform_editquantities.asp, which contains the script for updating every row in the <Sitename>_basket table whose quantity has been modified by the shopper.

For the complete code of xt_orderform_editquantities.asp created in the Five Lakes Publishing sample site, see Appendix A.

Removing Items from a Shopping Cart

A shopper can remove an item from the shopping cart. This requires the deletion of the item from the **OrderForm** object.

A Commerce Server site executes the following steps to delete an item from the **OrderForm** object and update the site database.

1. A **DBStorage** object is created and initialized to access the site database.

2. The **DBStorage.GetData** method is invoked to retrieve the shopping cart data for the current shopper into an **OrderForm** object.

3. The item is deleted from the **OrderForm** object.

4. The revised order form data is stored in the site database by using the **DBStorage.CommitData** method.

The following ASP code deletes an item from the **OrderForm** object and updates the site database:

```
REM - Create and initialize a DBStorage object
set mscsOrderFormStorage = _
  Server.CreateObject("Commerce.DBStorage")
call mscsOrderFormStorage.InitStorage(mscsDataSource,_
  <Sitename>_basket, "shopper_ID", "Commerce.OrderForm", _
  "marshalled_order", "date_changed")

REM - Create and initialize an OrderForm object
set mscsOrderForm = mscsOrderFormStorage.GetData(null, _
  mscsShopperID)

REM - Delete the item in the shopping cart
call mscsOrderForm.Items.Delete(index)

REM -- Update the shopping cart table
call mscsOrderFormStorage.CommitData(null, mscsOrderForm)
```

The Site Builder Wizard generates xt_orderform_delitem.asp, which contains the script for deleting a specific item in the <Sitename>_basket table. This script is executed when a shopper removes an item from the shopping cart.

For the complete code of xt_orderform_delitem.asp created in the Five Lakes Publishing sample site, see Appendix A.

Displaying the Shopping Cart

When a shopper adds, updates, or deletes items in the order form, the site redirects the shopper to the shopping cart page to view the new contents.

A Commerce Server site executes the following steps to retrieve items selected for purchase by the current shopper.

1. A **DBStorage** object is created and initialized to access the site database.

2. The **DBStorage.GetData** method is invoked to retrieve the shopping cart data for the current shopper into an **OrderForm** object.

3. The order form data is displayed on the shopping cart page.

The following ASP code retrieves order form values from the <Sitename>_basket table:

```
REM - Create and initialize a DBStorage object
set mscsOrderFormStorage = _
  Server.CreateObject("Commerce.DBStorage")
call mscsOrderFormStorage.InitStorage(mscsDataSource, _
  <Sitename>_basket, "shopper_ID", "Commerce.OrderForm", _
  "marshalled_order", "date_changed")

REM - Create and initialize an OrderForm object
set mscsOrderForm = mscsOrderFormStorage.GetData(null, _
  mscsShopperID)
```

The basket.asp file generated by the Site Builder Wizard contains the code to display items on the shopping cart page.

For the complete code of basket.asp created in the Five Lakes Publishing sample site, see Appendix A.

Implementing Price Promotions

This section contains the following topics:

♦ Understanding Price Promotions

♦ Using the Promotions Wizard

♦ Practice: Implementing Price Promotions

Understanding Price Promotions

A Commerce Server site may want to offer price promotions on products.

What Is a Price Promotion?

A price promotion applies price discounts and special offers based on the purchase of products in an order. For example, in the Five Lakes Publishing sample site, a shopper gets a discount of $5 on Programming Visual C++ if the shopper purchases Mastering Windows NT Server 4.

Types of Price Promotions

Commerce Server enables you to implement different types of price promotions, as shown in the following table.

Price Promotion	Description
Cross Line-Item Discount	Buy one product and get another product at a discount.
Cross-Department Discount	Buy one product and get a product from a specified department at a discount.
Two for the Price of One	Buy two of a specified product for the price of one.
Targeted Quantity Discount	Buy a specified number of units of a specified product and get a discount on the order.
Total Order Percentage Discount	Place an order of more than a specified total price and receive a specified percentage discount on the total order.

Using Promotions Wizard

The Promotions Wizard of Commerce Server enables you to include price promotions in your site.

▶ **To add a price promotion**

1. Go to the Site Manager page by using your Web browser.

2. On the Site Manager page, click **Promotions**.

3. On the Promotion Manager page, click **Price Promotions**.

The Price Promotions page enables you to include price promotions based on:

◆ Quantity of a specific product

◆ Amount of purchase, quantity of product(s), or products that match a specific criteria

▶ **To enable price promotions based on quantity of a specific product**

1. On the Price Promotions page, select one of the following categories from the **Add Special Promotion** drop-down list box and click **Add**.

Category	Description
Buy x get y at z% off	Applies a percentage discount based on the quantity of a specific product.
Buy x get y at $z off	Applies a cash discount based on the quantity of a specific product.
Buy 2 x for the price of 1	Applies a discount of one unit on the purchase of two units of a specific product.

2. Enter values for the following fields that appear on the New Price Promotions page.

Field	Description
Promo Name	A name to identify the price promotion.
Status	(On/Off) A field that indicates whether the price promotion is enabled.
Rank	A priority value between 10 and 100 where 10 is the highest priority value. The promotion with the highest priority will be used for a product on which multiple promotions apply.
Start date	A date on which promotion is to take effect.
End date	A date on which the promotion is to end.
Buy	A field that indicates the product and the quantity of the product for which the promotion is applied.

table continued on next page

Field	Description
Get	A field that indicates the product and the quantity of the product on which the promotion is applied.
At	A numeric value representing cash/percentage discount to be applied.

3. Click **Add Price Promotion** to add the promotion to the list of price promotions.

▶ **To enable price promotions based on amount of purchase, quantity of product(s), or products that match a specific criteria**

1. On the Price Promotions page, click **Add New Price Promotion**.

2. Enter values for the following fields that appear on the New Price Promotions page.

Field	Description
Promo Name	A name to identify the price promotion.
Description	A description of the price promotion.
Status	(On/Off) A field that indicates whether the price promotion is enabled.
Rank	A priority value between 10 and 100 where 10 is the highest priority value. The promotion with the highest priority will be used for a product on which multiple promotions apply.
Start date	A date on which promotion is to take effect.
End date	A date on which the promotion is to end.
Buy	A field that indicates the quantity or value of purchase of specific product(s) for which the promotion will be available. It includes a pair of option buttons that indicate whether the promotion is based on a specific product(s) or all products.

table continued on next page

Field	Description
Get	A field that indicates the quantity of specific product(s) offered by the promotion. It includes a drop-down list box that determines whether the promotion can apply to the product purchased or only to additional products and a pair of option buttons to indicate whether the promotion is applicable on specific product(s) or all products.
At	A field that indicates the discount in percentage or money amount.

3. Click **Add Price Promotion** to add the promotion to the list of price promotions.

Practice: Implementing Price Promotions

In this practice, you will use the Promotions Wizard to add price promotions.

▶ **Access the Promotions Wizard**

1. Start Microsoft Internet Explorer and type the URL **http://localhost/FiveLakes/ manager** in the address bar of Internet Explorer.

2. On the Site Manager page, in the **Merchandising** section, click **Promotions**.

3. On the Promotion Manager page, click **Price Promotions**.

▶ **Add price promotions**

1. On the Price Promotions page, click **buy x get y at $z off** in the Add Special Promotion drop-down list box and click **Add**.

2. On the New Price Promotion page, type the Promo name as **Promotion for Computer Section**.

3. Select **ON** from the **Status** drop-down list box and the select **10** from the **Rank** drop-down list box.

4. Type two different dates in the **Start date** and the **End date** fields in the following format: mm/dd/yyyy.

5. In the **Buy** field:

    a. Click **Mastering Windows NT Server 4** in the drop-down list box within the Buy field.

    b. Type the quantity as **1** in the text box within the Buy field.

6. In the **Get** field:

    a. Select **Programming Visual C++** from the list box within the Get field.

    b. Type the quantity as **1** in the text box within the Get field.

    c. Click **$5 OFF** in the **at** drop-down list box.

7. Click **Add Price Promotion**.

▶ **View the price promotion on the shopping cart page**

1. On the Site Manager page, in the **System** section, click **Shop Site**.

2. On your site Home page, click **Computers**.

3. On the Department: Computers page, click **Mastering Windows NT Server 4**.

4. On the Product: Mastering Windows NT Server 4 page, click **Add to Basket**.

5. Return to the home page.

6. Repeat steps 2 to 4 to add **Programming Visual C++** to the shopping cart.

7. Notice the discount value, on the shopping cart page.

Implementing Upsell

This section contains the following topics:

♦ Understanding Upsell

♦ Creating the Upsell Table

♦ Retrieving Upsell information

♦ Adding an Upsell Item

Understanding Upsell

An Upsell promotion encourages shoppers to buy a more expensive item instead of the one in the shopping cart.

What Is an Upsell Promotion?

If an item in the shopping cart has an Upsell item with it, the script in basket.asp displays an Upsell text prompt on the shopping cart page. The Upsell text prompt is a link that enables the shopper to view the Upsell item information. If the shopper decides to buy, the Upsell item replaces the item in the shopping cart. For example, in the Five Lakes Publishing sample site, if a shopper orders Mastering Windows NT Server 4, the shopping cart page suggests Windows NT 4.0 MCSE Study Guide instead.

Elements for Implementing Upsell

To implement an Upsell promotion in your site, you need to include the following elements.

◆ An Upsell promotion table in the site database that specifies which product is to be associated with a given product.

◆ A query description in global.asa to retrieve data from the Upsell promotion table.

◆ A script in basket.asp that executes a query to retrieve the Upsell item, if any.

◆ A variation of the Product page to display the Upsell item, if any.

◆ A .asp file that executes a script to replace the existing item with the promoted item.

Creating the Upsell Table

The Upsell table must contain a record for every item that has a related item, as shown in the following illustration.

The <Sitename>_promo_upsell Table

Sku	Upsell_sku	Description
002	001	May we suggest a better book?
003	001	May we suggest a better book?
005	004	May we suggest a better book?
006	004	May we suggest a better book?
009	012	May we suggest a better book?
010	012	May we suggest a better book?

The following table lists the attributes of the <Sitename>_promo_upsell table.

Attribute	Description
Sku	Product-ID of the product for which an Upsell item exists.
Upsell_sku	Product-ID of the item that will be promoted.
Description	Upsell text prompt that will appear as a link on the shopping cart page.

Retrieving Upsell Information

Once a shopper has selected an item and added it to the shopping cart:

1. The Upsell item for the selected item must be retrieved from the site database.

2. An Upsell text prompt must be displayed as a link on the shopping cart page, which will enable the shopper to view the Upsell item information.

You can add the following query to global.asa to retrieve data from the Upsell promotion table:

```
set MSCSQueryMap.related_products_upsell = AddQuery _
("select sku, upsell_sku, description _
from <Sitename>_promo_upsell where sku = :1")
```

The following script in basket.asp executes the related_products_upsell query for a shopping cart item for which Upsell items exist. The script also displays the Upsell text prompt that serves as a link to a page that displays Upsell item information.

```
<%
REM - Execute the upsell query to retrieve the upsell item
REM - for an item in the shopping cart
cmdTemp.CommandText=Replace(MSCSQueryMap. _
  related_products_upsell.SQLCommand,":1",lineitem.sku)
set rsUpsell = Server.CreateObject("ADODB.Recordset")
rsUpsell.Open cmdTemp, , adOpenKeyset, adLockReadOnly
If  rsUpsell.recordcount > 0 then
  REM - For every item in the shopping cart table
  do while not rsUpsell.EOF
      REM - Check if the Upsell item already exists in the _
      Shopping cart
```

code continued on next page

code continued from previous page

```
            set checkitem = mscsOrderForm.items
            inbasket = 0
            for each row_checkitem in checkitem
              if row_checkitem.sku =
                rsUpsell("upsell_sku").Value then
                inbasket = 1
              end if
            next

            REM - Display Upsell text prompt and redirect
            REM - shopper to product_alt.asp
            if Cbool(inbasket = 0) then %>
              <a HREF="<%=mscsPage.URL("product_alt.asp","sku", _
              rsUpsell("upsell_sku").Value, "index", ilineitem, _
              "quantity", orderformitems.quantity, "dept_id", _
              orderformitems.[_product_dept_id])%>"> <% = _
              rsUpsell("description")%> </a>
            <%end if

            REM - Retrieve the next item from the shopping cart table
            rsUpsell.MoveNext
        loop
      end if %>
```

For the complete code of basket.asp created in the Five Lakes Publishing sample site, see Appendix A.

Adding an Upsell Item

When a shopper clicks the Upsell text prompt that appears as a link on the shopping cart page, the shopper is redirected to a page that displays the Upsell item information.

In the Five Lakes Publishing sample site, the shopper is redirected to product_alt.asp file that retrieves the Upsell item information from the site database information and displays it on a new page. If the shopper decides to buy, the Upsell item replaces the item on the shopping cart page. In other words, the item already present in the shopping cart is deleted from the order form and the Upsell item is added to the order form. The product_alt.asp file in the Five Lakes Publishing sample site posts data to another .asp file (xt_orderform_edititem) that deletes the shopping cart item and inserts the Upsell item in the site database.

 Note The product_alt.asp and xt_orderform_edititem.asp files in the Five Lakes Publishing sample site are not wizard-generated files. These files have been created to provide the Upsell functionality in the site.

▶ To retrieve and display Upsell item information

1. Define a query to retrieve the Upsell item information from the <Sitename>_product table.
2. Execute the query when the shopper clicks the Upsell text prompt on the shopping cart page.
3. Redirect the shopper to the page that displays the Upsell item information.

▶ To update the site database with the Upsell item

1. Delete the item the shopper wants to replace from the order form.
2. Add the Upsell item to the order form.

For the complete code of product_alt.asp and xt_orderform_edititem.asp created in the Five Lakes Publishing sample site, see Appendix A.

Lab 4: Implementing Upsell

Objectives

After completing this lab, you will be able to:

◆ Modify the shopping cart page to include the Upsell functionality.
◆ Update the site database with the Upsell item.

Before You Begin

Prerequisites

This lab assumes that you have successfully created a site using the Site Builder Wizard, added departments and products to your site, and completed Lab 3, "Customizing Product Catalog Pages."

Before you begin this lab, you must have the following prerequisites:

◆ Basic knowledge of Microsoft SQL Server 7.0, HTML, and ASP scripting

◆ Familiarity with Microsoft Internet Explorer and Microsoft Visual InterDev 6.0

Estimated time to complete this lab: 30 minutes

Exercise 1: Adding a Row in the Upsell Table

In this exercise, you will insert a row in the Upsell table in the site database.

▶ **Insert a row in the Upsell table**

1. On the Start menu, point to Programs, Microsoft SQL Server 7.0, and then click Query Analyzer.

2. In the Connect to SQL Server dialog box, select the Use SQL Server authentication option button, type **sa** in the Login Name text box, leave the Password text box blank, and then click OK.

> **Note** You do not need to select the Server name because it is selected by default.

3. In the **New query** dialog box, select the **FiveLakes** database from the **DB** drop-down list box.

4. Type the following SQL statement into the Query window to make **Budgeting: Profit Planning and Control** an Upsell item for **Essentials of Business Budgeting.**

```
insert into FiveLakes_promo_upsell values ("017", _
"018", "May we suggest a better book?")
```

5. Press F5 to execute the query.

   The result should show "1 row(s) affected".

6. Close the Query Analyzer.

Exercise 2: Modifying the Cart Page

In this exercise, you will display Upsell information on the shopping cart page.

▶ **Define a query description in global.asa**

1. In Microsoft Visual InterDev 6.0, open the FiveLakes project and then double-click **global.asa** in the Project Explorer window.

2. In the **InitQueryMap** function, add the following query to retrieve data from the FiveLakes_promo_upsell table:

   ```
   set MSCSQueryMap.related_products_upsell = AddQuery _
   ("select sku, Upsell_sku, description _
       from FiveLakes_promo_upsell _
       where sku = ':1'")
   ```

3. On the **File** menu, click **Save global.asa**, and then click **Close**.

▶ **Modify script in basket.asp**

1. Double-click **basket.asp** in the Project Explorer window.

2. After the lines of code that read as follows:

   ```
   <IMG SRC="<%= "/" & siteRoot _
   %>/manager/MSCS_Images/buttons/btnremove1.gif" _
   BORDER="0" ALT="Delete item">
   </A>
   </TD>
   </TR>
   ```

   a. include the following code:

   ```
   <% REM - Create Recordset, execute Query
           cmdTemp.CommandText=Replace _
      (MSCSQueryMap.related_products_upsell.SQLCommand,":1", _
   Replace(lineitem.sku, "'", "''"))
   ```

   code continued on next page

code continued from previous page

```
set rsUpsell = Server.CreateObject("ADODB.Recordset")
rsUpsell.Open cmdTemp, , adOpenKeyset, adLockReadOnly

if  rsUpsell.recordcount > 0 then
  while not rsUpsell.EOF
      set checkitem = mscsOrderForm.items
    inbasket = 0
    for each row_checkitem in checkitem
  if row_checkitem.sku = _
    rsUpsell("Upsell_sku").Value then
      inbasket = 1
    end if
    next

    if Cbool(inbasket = 0) then %>
      <tr>
      <td colspan="1">  </td>
      <td colspan="5">
      <a HREF="<% = mscsPage.URL("product_alt.asp", _
      "sku",rsUpsell("Upsell_sku").Value , "index", _
      ilineitem, "quantity", lineItem.quantity, _
      "dept_id", lineItem.[_product_dept_id]) _
      %>"><font face="Arial" size="2" COLOR="#FF0000"
      >***<% = rsUpsell("description")
      %>***</font></a>
      </td>
      </tr>

    <%end if
    rsUpsell.MoveNext
Wend
end if %>
```

3. On the **File** menu, click **Save basket.asp,** and then click **Close.**

Exercise 3: Adding an Upsell Item to the Database

In this exercise, you will display Upsell information on the shopping cart page and add the Upsell item to the site database.

► **Create a new .asp file in the site directory**

1. In Microsoft Visual InterDev 6.0, open the product.asp file.

2. On the **File** menu, click **Save product.asp As** to save the file as product_alt.asp.

► **Display Upsell item information**

1. In the product_alt.asp file, below the lines of code that read as follows:

```
sku = mscsPage.RequestString("sku")
quoted_sku = "'" & Replace(sku,"'","''") & "'"
```

add the following code to retrieve the index and dept_id from the URL:

```
index = Request.QueryString("index")
dept_id = mscsPage.RequestNumber("dept_id")
```

2. Locate the following code:

```
<FORM METHOD = POST ACTION = _
"<%=pageSURL("xt_orderform_additem.asp")%>">
```

3. Modify the code to post the form contents to xt_orderform_edititem.asp instead of xt_orderform_additem.asp using the **pageSURL** function as follows:

```
<FORM METHOD=POST ACTION= _
"<%= pageSURL("xt_orderform_edititem.asp") %> _
index=<%=index%>">
```

4. On the **File** menu, click **Save product_alt.asp,** and then click **Close.**

► **Replace the cart item in the database with the Upsell item**

1. Open the xt_orderform_additem.asp file.

2. On the **File** menu, click **Save xt_orderform_additem.asp As** to save the file as xt_orderform_edititem.asp.

3. In the xt_orderform_edititem.asp file, add the following code above the include statements to allow execution of response.redirect and response.write statements:

```
<% Response.Buffer = true %>
```

4. Include the following code before the line **REM – retrieve quantity:** in the **OrderFormAddItem** function:

```
if mscsOrderForm.Items.Count > 0 then
  index = Request.QueryString("index")
  call mscsOrderForm.Items.Delete(index)
  call mscsOrderFormStorage.CommitData(NULL, _
  mscsOrderForm)
end if
```

5. On the **File** menu, click **Save xt_orderform_edititem.asp,** and then click **Close.**

▶ **View Upsell Information**

1. Start Microsoft Internet Explorer and type **http://localhost/FiveLakes** in the address bar of Internet Explorer.

2. On your site Home page, click **Business.**

3. On the Department: Business page, click **Essentials of Business Budgeting.**

4. On the Product: Essentials of Business Budgeting page, click **Add to Basket.**

5. Click on the Upsell text prompt "**May we suggest a better book?**" on the shopping cart page. This will take you to the Budgeting: Profit Planning and Control Product page.

6. On the Product: Budgeting: Profit Planning and Control page, click **Add to Basket.**

7. Notice that Essentials of Business Budgeting on the cart page has been replaced with Budgeting: Profit Planning and Control.

Review

The review questions cover some of the key concepts taught in the chapter.

1. What is the role of an OrderForm object and a DBStorage object in the shopping process?

2. Explain the need for creating a shopper ID.

3. What change do you need to make in global.asa to store shopper IDs in the URL?

4. How is Upsell functionality different from cross-sell?

Review Answers

1. An OrderForm object contains shopping cart data and a DBStorage object reads and writes order form values in the site database.

2. A shopper ID is used by Commerce Server to associate the shopping cart items and the order with a specific shopper.

3. The StandardSManager object in global.asa must be initialized to the url mode to store shopper IDs in the URL.

4. Upsell functionality encourages a shopper to buy a more expensive product after the shopper has selected an item for purchase, whereas cross-sell encourages a shopper to see related products while browsing the product catalog pages.

Chapter 5:
Processing Orders

Objectives

After completing this chapter, you will be able to:

- Explain what an Order Processing Pipeline (OPP) is.
- Explain how an OPP works.
- List the types of OPP.
- Set up error handling to process errors that occur when the OPP is running.
- Describe the 14 stages of the Plan pipeline.

Understanding Order Processing

This section includes the following topics:

- How Does OPP Work?
- What Are the Types of OPP?
- How to View Pipeline Configuration Files?

Commerce Server sites process orders by placing the information about the order in an **OrderForm** object and then executing a series of software components that perform operations on the order form. These operations include computing tax or shipping costs for an order and writing an order to receipt storage. The software components that perform these operations are Component Object Model (COM) objects designed to be executed within a Commerce Server pipeline.

Understanding Pipelines

A pipeline defines and links a series of stages, each containing pipeline components, and runs them in sequence. You can customize your Commerce Server application by adding, removing, and configuring the components in each stage.

Commerce Server has two pipeline models:

◆ **Order Processing Pipeline (OPP)** Processes sales order by performing checks on the order form information and verifying payment.

◆ **Commerce Interchange Pipeline** Enables the secure exchange of business data objects, such as purchase orders and shipping notices, between business trading partners.

How Does OPP Work?

The OPP, shown below, addresses the need for compartmentalization by:

◆ Dividing the processing of orders into stages

◆ Ensuring that every component is reading from and writing to same OrderForm to next component in the pipeline

◆ Passing OrderForm to next component in the Pipeline

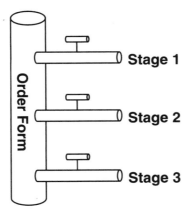

The following are the tasks performed by the OPP.

◆ The OPP divides the processing of orders into stages and determines the sequence in which work is performed. Stages describe a category of work and each stage in a pipeline consists of zero or more components that run in sequence.

◆ The OPP coordinates the work of components by ensuring that every component in an OPP is reading from and writing to the same **OrderForm** object.

♦ After each component in the OPP has performed its work on the **OrderForm,** the OPP passes the **OrderForm** to the next component in the pipeline.

What Are the Types of OPP?

Commerce Server has five basic types of OPPs.

Business-to-Consumer Pipelines

The business-to-consumer OPPs are used in e-commerce sites designed for retail shopping. The following table lists and describes the business-to-consumer pipelines.

Pipeline	Function
Product	Runs OPP components that compute price and discount information on individual products.
Plan	Runs OPP components that display order total, including promotional discounts, taxes, shipping, and handling charges to the shopper.
Purchase	Runs OPP components that validate the shopper's payment, perform the actual purchase transaction, and write an order to database storage.

Note The site generated by the Site Builder Wizard uses only the Plan and Purchase pipelines to process an order. The Plan pipeline contains components that compute tax, shipping, and handling charges in addition to the components of the Product pipeline.

Business-to-Business Pipelines

The business-to-business OPPs are used in e-commerce sites designed for creation and exchange of purchase orders between business trading partners. The table on the following page lists and describes the business-to-business pipelines.

Pipeline	Function
Corporate Purchasing Plan	Runs OPP components that compute the order total, including promotional discounts, taxes, shipping and handling charges. This pipeline is analogous to the Plan pipeline used in business-to-consumer sites.
Corporate Purchasing Submit	Runs OPP components that validate the purchase order requisition, transfer the purchase order to the vendor, and write the order to database storage. This pipeline is analogous to the Purchase pipeline used in business-to-consumer sites.

Viewing Pipeline Configuration Files

The pipeline components along with their properties are saved in a pipeline configuration (.pcf) file. This file is created in the /Config folder of a custom site created by the Site Builder Wizard. For example, Plan.pcf contains the Plan pipeline configuration.

The following illustration shows how to view the configuration files using the Pipeline Editor.

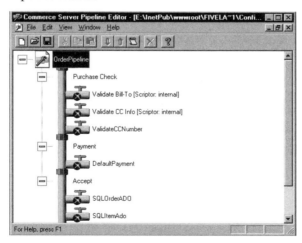

You can create, modify, and view the configuration files of sites by using the Pipeline Editor. Alternatively, you can configure the pipelines of a specific site by using the Site Manager page.

Using the Pipeline Editor

The Pipeline Editor displays a tree, outlining the stages implemented by the default OPP, and the components that can be used in each stage of processing. Stages and components are executed by the OPP in the order in which they are included in the tree.

The Pipeline Editor can be run either in **standard mode** or **expert mode**. To run the Pipeline Editor in **standard mode**, use one of the following methods:

◆ On the **Start** menu, point to **Programs, Microsoft Site Server, Commerce,** and then click **Pipeline Editor**.

◆ Invoke PipeEditor.exe from the command prompt.

To run the Pipeline Editor in **expert** mode, invoke PipeEditor.exe from the command prompt as follows:

```
PipeEditor.exe /e
```

Running the Pipeline Editor in **expert mode** provides you with the additional functionality to:

◆ Create a custom pipeline without using a pre-configured template file.

◆ Insert, move, and delete pipeline stages.

◆ Cut, copy, and paste a stage including its components.

◆ View the required components that are not displayed in the standard mode.

Using the Site Manager Page

By using the Site Manager page, you can configure the pipelines of a specific site to:

◆ Insert, edit, or delete components in a stage.

◆ Change the order in which the components will be executed within a stage.

Running the Order Processing Pipeline (OPP)

In this section, you will learn about the steps to be performed in order to run an OPP and handle errors.

This section contains the following topics:

◆ Process Overview

◆ Error Handling

Process Overview

The order processing steps are shown in the following illustration.

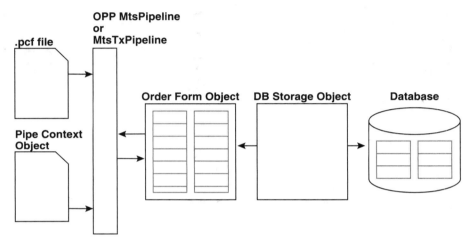

The **OrderForm** object and its corresponding table in the database maintain information about an order throughout a shopping session. Whenever computations need to be performed on the order, the **OrderForm** object is passed to the OPP. The OPP then performs appropriate verifications and computations, and stores updated values into the **OrderForm**.

The following procedure explains the steps that are performed in order to run an OPP. The i_util.asp file contains the script to run an OPP and is executed whenever the order form needs to be processed.

▶ **To run an OPP**

1. Create a **DBStorage** object for order form data, and then initialize the object as follows:

```
Set orderFormStorage = _
Server.CreateObject("Commerce.DBStorage")

Call orderFormStorage.InitStorage _
(MSCSSite.DefaultConnectionString, "<Sitename>_basket", _
"shopper_id", "Commerce.OrderForm", "marshalled_basket", _
"date_changed")
```

2. Read the order form data by using the current shopper ID and store it into a new **OrderForm** object as follows:

```
created = 0
On Error Resume Next
Set orderForm = orderFormStorage.GetData (null, _
mscsShopperID)
On Error Goto 0
if IsEmpty(orderForm) then
    set orderform = _
        Server.CreateObject("Commerce.OrderForm")
    orderForm.shopper_id = mscsShopperID
    created = 1
end if
```

3. Create and configure a pipe context as shown in the following code. The **PipeContext** object is a Dictionary object containing a group of initialized objects that store information needed by the OPP.

```
Set pipeContext = Server.CreateObject("Commerce.Dictionary")
Set pipeContext("MessageManager") = MSCSMessageManager
Set pipeContext("DataFunctions") = MSCSDataFunctions
Set pipeContext("QueryMap") = MSCSQueryMap
Set pipeContext("ConnectionStringMap") = _
    MSCSSite.ConnectionStringMap
pipeContext("SiteName") = displayName
pipeContext("DefaultConnectionString") = _
    MSCSSite.DefaultConnectionString
pipeContext("Language") = "USA"
```

4. Create the pipeline as follows:

```
Set pipeline = Server.CreateObject("Commerce.MtsPipeline")
```

5. Load the appropriate pipeline configuration file into the pipeline by using the **LoadPipe** method as follows:

```
Call pipeline.LoadPipe("e:\inetpub\wwwroot\<Sitename>\plan.pcf")
```

6. Run the pipeline by using the **Execute** method, specifying both the **OrderForm** object and the **PipeContext** object, as follows:

```
errorLevel = pipeline.Execute(1, orderForm, pipeContext, 0)
```

The syntax of the **Execute** method is:

```
MtsPipeline.Execute (Mode, Object, PipeContext, Reserved)
```

The following table explains the parameters of the **Execute** method.

Parameter	Description
Mode	Specifies the mode in which to execute the stages in the pipeline. This parameter is included for backward compatibility with sites created in Commerce Server 2.0.
Object	Specifies the data object to be processed by the components in the pipeline.
PipeContext	Specifies the PipeContext object.
Reserved	This value is not used and must be set to zero.

7. Save the **OrderForm** back to the order form table in the database if running the pipeline made any changes to the order form data.

```
if created then
    Call mscsOrderFormStorage.InsertData(null, _
mscsOrderForm)
else
    Call mscsOrderFormStorage.CommitData(null, _
mscsOrderForm)
end if
```

For the complete code of i_util.asp in the Five Lakes Publishing sample site, see Appendix A.

Error Handling

Error handling in Commerce Server revolves around the OPP's interaction with the **OrderForm, MtsPipeline** or **MtsTxPipeline** object, and the **MessageManager** object.

You pass an initialized **OrderForm** object to the OPP by calling the pipeline's **Execute** method. As the **OrderForm** is passed through various stages of the OPP, the components associated with each stage read and write values to and from the **OrderForm**. The collections _Basket_Errors and _Purchase_Errors, which are members of the **OrderForm** object, store strings that describe error conditions detected by the OPP while processing elements of the **OrderForm**. The OPP gets these strings from the MessageManager.

The MessageManager

The MessageManager is a site's central repository of locale-based error messages. Each message stored in the MessageManager consists of a string describing the error condition and a string identifier. The MessageManager uses the **AddMessage** method to create the association between string identifier and string message.

For example, if the OPP is unable to validate a credit card in the **OrderForm,** the pipeline retrieves the string associated with the message ID pur_badcc from the MessageManager. The OPP then writes the string to the OrderForm's Purchase_Errors collection. When the **Execute** method that initiated the pipeline returns, the strings in this collection can be used to provide site users with a description of errors that occurred during order processing.

▶ **To set up error handling**

1. A MessageManager component is created in the global.asa file as follows:

```
REM - Create a message manager for use by the pipeline
Set MSCSMessageManager = _
Server.CreateObject("Commerce.MessageManager");
```

2. The MessageManager's **AddMessage** method is called to add a group of messages to the MessageManager as follows:

```
call MSCSMessageManager.AddMessage("pur_out_of_stock", _
```

code continued on next page

code continued from previous page

```
                "At least one item is out of stock.")
        call MSCSMessageManager.AddMessage("pur_badsku", _
                "Please note that one or more items were removed from _
                your basket because the product is no longer sold.")
        call MSCSMessageManager.AddMessage("pur_noitems", _
                "An order must have at least one item.")
        call MSCSMessageManager.AddMessage("pur_badpayment", _
                "There was a problem authorizing your credit. Please _
                verify your payment information or use a different card.")
        call MSCSMessageManager.AddMessage("pur_badcc", _
                "The credit card number you provided is not valid. Please _
                verify your payment information or use a different card.")
```

3. MessageManager is initialized as an Application variable named **MSCSMessageManager**, so that it can be accessed across all pages, as shown in the following code:

```
    set Application("MSCSMessageManager") = MSCSMessageManager
```

Understanding the Plan Pipeline

In this section, you will learn about the stages and components of a Plan pipeline.

This section contains the following topics:

◆ Stages in the Plan Pipeline

◆ Components in the Plan Pipeline

Stages in the Plan Pipeline

The Plan pipeline consists of 14 stages, shown in the illustration on the next page. These stages are made up of components that verify the integrity of the **OrderForm**. For example, if the items list in an **OrderForm** does not contain any item, then the RequiredProdInfo component in the Product Info stage fails.

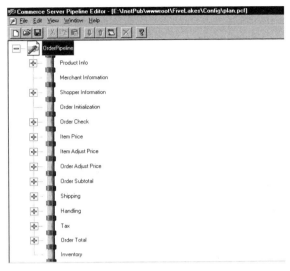

The following table lists and describes each stage of the Plan pipeline.

Stage	Description
Product Info	Contains components that retrieve product information about the items from the site database.
Merchant Information	Can contain custom components to retrieve merchant data and write the data to the **OrderForm**.
Shopper Information	Adds information about the shopper to the **OrderForm**.
Order Initialization	Sets initial order information on the **OrderForm** and verifies that the **OrderForm** contains an Order ID.
Order Check	Verifies that the order can be processed.
Item Price	Ensures that the _iadjust_regularprice for each item contains the most current price information.
Item Adjust Price	Ensures that the _iadjust_currentprice for each item contains the current price adjusted for sales or promotions.
Order Adjust Price	Contains components that set the adjusted price of each item.

table continued on next page

Stage	Description
Order Subtotal	Calculates the subtotal for an order.
Shipping	Calculates the total shipping charge for the order.
Handling	Calculates the total handling charge for the order.
Tax	Computes the sales tax for each item on the order and the sum of the tax for the entire order.
Order Total	Sums the subtotal, tax, shipping, and handling values.
Inventory	Verifies that every item ordered is in stock.

Components in the Plan Pipeline

Each stage in the Plan pipeline consists of zero or more components, and each of these components is run in sequence. A component is a COM object that performs some operation on an OrderForm. These are shown in the following illustration.

You can configure the Plan pipeline by inserting, deleting, and modifying the stages and their components to suit the needs of your site. The following table lists and describes the components in the various stages of the Plan pipeline used in the Five Lakes Publishing sample site.

Stage	Component	Description
Product Info	QueryProdInfo	Executes a database query based on the SKUs in the OrderForm's item list and puts the returned data in the items collection. If data is not found for an SKU, the item is marked for deletion.
Product Info	RequiredProdInfo	Deletes any item that is marked for deletion.
Shopper Information	DefaultShopperInfo	Initializes entries in the **OrderForm** to contain values about the shopper.
Order Initialization	RequiredOrderInit	Initializes values in the **OrderForm** prior to processing the order.
Order Check	RequiredOrderCheck	Ensures that there is at least one item in the **OrderForm**.
Item Price	DefaultItemPrice	Initializes _iadjust_regularprice for each item in the items list to store the most current item price.
Item Price	RequiredItemPrice	Ensures that _iadjust_regularprice is set for each item in the items list.

table continued on next page

Stage	Component	Description
Item Adjust Price	SaleAdjust	Determines whether an item is on sale and sets the _iadjust_currentprice name/value pair to the current price of the item, adjusted for sales or promotions.
Item Adjust Price	RequiredItemAdjustPrice	Verifies that the _iadjust_currentprice name/value pair is set.
Order Adjust Price	DbOrderPromoADO	Queries the database to determine the promotion amount for an item.
Order Adjust Price	RequiredOrderAdjustPrice	Ensures that the _oadjust_adjustedprice member of every item, containing total cost of an item, is set.
Order Subtotal	DefaultOrderSubtotal	Calculates the subtotal for an order and stores the result in order._oadjust_subtotal.
Order Subtotal	RequiredOrderSubtotal	Ensures that order._oadjust_subtotal is not NULL.

For more information about the other stages of the Plan pipeline, see Chapter 6, "Checking Out," on page 95.

Review

The review questions cover some of the key concepts taught in the chapter.

1. How can you run the Pipeline Editor in expert mode?

2. What are the advantages of running the Pipeline Editor in expert mode?

3. Which stage of the Plan pipeline calculates the subtotal, tax, shipping, and handling values for an order?

4. Which two collections store the error strings describing the error conditions detected by the OPP while processing elements of the OrderForm?

Review Answers

1. To run the Pipeline Editor in expert mode, invoke PipeEditor.exe from the command prompt as follows:

    ```
    PipeEditor.exe /e
    ```

2. Running the Pipeline Editor in expert mode allows you to create a custom pipeline without using a pre-configured template file. You can insert, move, and delete pipeline stages including their components, as well as view the required components that are not displayed in the standard mode.

3. The Order Total stage calculates the subtotal, tax, shipping, and handling values for an order.

4. The collections _Basket_Errors and _Purchase_Errors store the error strings describing the error conditions detected by the OPP.

Chapter 6:
Checking Out

Objectives

After completing this chapter, you will be able to:

◆ Explain the components in the Plan pipeline that compute tax, shipping and handling charges, and the total cost of an order.

◆ Customize the shipping page to allow shoppers from all countries to shop at the site.

◆ Add a Scriptor component to compute tax.

Capturing Shopper Information

A site must accept a shopper's address and payment information to complete the purchase.

This section includes the following topics:

◆ Understanding Checkout
◆ Practice: Customizing the Shipping Page

Understanding Checkout

The illustration on the following page shows how the site validates and saves the shopper's ship-to address information in the OrderForm object.

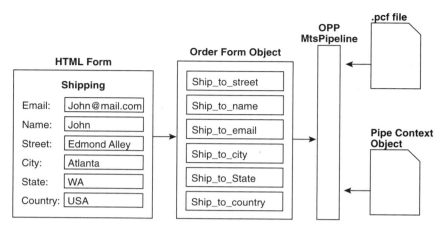

When a shopper is ready to complete the purchase of the selected items, a Commerce Server site:

◆ Accepts the shopper's ship-to address information.

◆ Stores the shopper information in the **OrderForm** object.

◆ Executes the Plan pipeline to validate shopper information and compute the total cost of the order.

Accepting Ship-to Address Information

Once a shopper confirms purchase on the shopping cart page, the shopper is redirected to the shipping page (shipping.asp). Here, the shopper enters the ship-to address information in an HTML form or by using Microsoft Wallet. Wallet provides shoppers an easy and secure way to store address and payment information.

For more information on Wallet, see Chapter 7, "Completing the Purchase Process," on page 113.

Storing Information in the OrderForm Object

The script in shipping.asp posts the shopper information to xt_orderform_prepare.asp, which validates the shopper's ship-to address information and stores this information in the **OrderForm** object.

Executing the Plan Pipeline

Finally, the Plan pipeline is executed to:

◆ Validate the shopper's ship-to address information.

◆ Compute shipping, handling, and tax charges for the order and store it in the **OrderForm** object.

◆ Compute the total cost of the order and store it in the **OrderForm** object.

Practice: Customizing the Shipping Page

In this practice, you will modify the shipping page to allow shoppers from other countries to shop at your site.

Caution The activities in this practice are a prerequisite for successful completion of Lab 6.

▶ **Define a query in global.asa**

1. In Microsoft Visual InterDev 6.0, open the FiveLakes project.

2. Double-click global.asa in the Project Explorer window.

3. In the **InitQueryMap** function, add a query to retrieve a list of country names from the FiveLakes_country table as follows:

```
set MSCSQueryMap.country = _
AddQuery("select country from FiveLakes_country")
```

4. On the **File** menu, click **Save global.asa,** and then click **Close.**

▶ **Display the list of country names on the shipping page**

1. Double-click shipping.asp in the Project Explorer window.

2. In shipping.asp, delete the following line of code to allow any country to be accepted:

```
<INPUT TYPE="HIDDEN" NAME="ship_to_country" VALUE="USA">
```

3. Next, scroll to the code that reads as follows:

```
        VALUE="<% = _
        mscsPage.HTMLEncode(mscsOrderForm.ship_to_zip) %>">
         
    </TD>
    </TR>
```

4. Below this code, add code to create an HTML select element that displays a list of country names from the FiveLakes_country table as follows:

```
    <TR>
        <TD ALIGN="RIGHT">
          <B> Country: </B>
        </TD>

        <% sqlText = MSCSQueryMap.country.SQLCommand
        cmdTemp.CommandText = sqlText
        set rscountry=Server.CreateObject("ADODB.Recordset")
        rscountry.Open cmdTemp, , adOpenForwardOnly, _
        adLockReadOnly  %>

        <TD ALIGN="LEFT">
          <select name="Ship_to_country" size="1">

          <% While not rscountry.EOF %>
            <%= mscsPage.Option(rscountry("country").value, _
            mscsOrderForm.ship_to_country)%>
            <%= rscountry("country").value %>

            <% rscountry.MoveNext
          Wend %>

          </select VALUE="<%= _
          mscsPage.HTMLEncode(mscsOrderForm.ship_to_country) _
          %>">
        </TD>
    </TR>
```

5. On the **File** menu, click **Save shipping.asp**, and then click **Close**.

▶ **Modify the Plan pipeline**

1. Start Microsoft Internet Explorer and type the URL **http://localhost/FiveLakes/ manager** in the address bar of Internet Explorer.

2. On the Site Manager page, select **plan.pcf** from the drop-down list box in the **System** section and click **Edit Pipeline**.

3. On the Editing file:/FiveLakes/config/plan.pcf page, scroll to Stage 5: Order Check and click **Edit** in the Validate Ship-To [Scriptor: Internal] component.

4. In the **MSCSExecute** function within the **Script** text box, delete the following line of code that allows shoppers from only one country to shop at the site:

```
if orderform.ship_to_country <> "USA" then call _
errors.Add(msg_mgr.GetMessage("val_shipcountrymustbe")): _
result = 2
```

5. Click **Update** to save the script changes.

6. Click **Save** to save the plan.pcf file.

▶ **View the country list on the shipping page**

1. Start Microsoft Internet Explorer and type the URL **http://localhost/FiveLakes** in the address bar of Internet Explorer.

2. Shop at the site for at least one product and click **Purchase** on the Shopping Basket page.

3. On the Shipping page, click **Click here if you have problems with the Wallet.**

4. Notice the drop-down list box on the shipping page that displays the list of countries.

Computing Order Value

This section contains the following topics:

◆ Computing Shipping and Handling Charges

◆ Computing Tax

◆ Computing Order Total

Computing Shipping and Handling Charges

Shipping and handling charges are computed when the Plan pipeline executes the components in the following stages:

◆ The Shipping Stage

◆ The Handling Stage

The Shipping Stage

The Shipping stage in the Plan pipeline:

◆ Computes the shipping cost for the order.

◆ Stores the computed value in the _shipping_total name/value pair in the **OrderForm** object.

Commerce Server provides a number of pipeline components to compute the shipping cost.

The following table lists and describes some of the components of the shipping stage.

Component	Description
DefaultShipping	Sets _shipping_total to zero.
FixedShipping	Sets _shipping_total to a fixed amount.
TableShippingADO	Sets _shipping_total to a value returned by a specified query.
RequiredShipping	Checks the order form to ensure that _shipping_total has been set.

Shipping Options

Multiple components can be inserted to allow for different shipping costs depending upon the shipping method used. The Site Builder Wizard provides two shipping methods: Overnight and second Day. The wizard includes two instances of the FixedShipping component in the shipping stage. One instance will set the _shipping_total name/value pair to a cost specified for the Overnight shipping method, and the other instance will set it to a cost specified for the second Day shipping method. If you do not want to charge shipping on an order, you can include only the DefaultShipping component, which sets _shipping_total to zero.

The Handling Stage

The handling stage in the Plan pipeline:

◆ Computes the total handling cost of an order.

◆ Stores the computed value in the _handling_total name/value pair in the **OrderForm** object.

The following table lists and describes some of the components provided by Commerce Server to compute handling charges.

Component	Description
DefaultHandling	Sets the _handling_total name/value pair to zero.
FixedHandling	Sets the _handling_total name/value pair to a fixed amount.
TableHandlingADO	Computes the value for the _handling_total name/value pair based on the results of a query.
RequiredHandling	Checks the order form to ensure that the _handling_total name/value pair has been set.

Handling Options

The Site Builder Wizard provides an option to specify the handling charges for an order. The wizard includes a FixedHandling component that applies the specified handling charges to the order. If you do not want to charge handling on an order, you can include only the DefaultHandling component that sets _handling_total to zero.

Computing Tax

The Plan pipeline executes the components in the Tax stage to compute tax and store the results in the OrderForm object.

The Tax Stage

The Tax stage in the Plan pipeline:

◆ Computes tax for every item in the order.

◆ Computes the total tax for the order.

◆ Sets the _tax_total and _tax_included name/value pairs for every item in the items list of the **OrderForm** object.

◆ Sets the _tax_total and _tax_included name/value pairs for the complete order in the **OrderForm** object.

The following table lists and describes some of the components provided by Commerce Server to compute tax.

Component	Description
DefaultTax	Sets the OrderForm's _tax_total and _tax_included values to zero.
SimpleCanadaTax	Applies a specified tax for Canada, including GST (Goods and Services tax) and PST (Provincial Sales tax).
SimpleJapanTax	Applies a specified tax for the Japanese model.
SimpleUSTax	Applies a specified tax to any order from a given state.
RequiredTax	Checks if the OrderForm object's _tax_total and _tax_included values are set.

Computing Tax on Individual Items

The Site Builder Wizard allows you to specify a tax rate to be applied for the country you have selected on the Commerce Site Builder Wizard: Locale page. Multiple tax components can be inserted in the pipeline, each one applying a tax rate for a specific country. The country name is specified as a parameter in the tax component. For a tax component to execute, the value in the **OrderForm** object's ship_to_country name/value pair must be set to the country specified within the component.

Even though the component name may include the country name, you need to specify the country name as a parameter because the name of the component only indicates the model for computing tax and not the country to which it applies. For example, the SimpleCanadaTax component can be used for another country whose tax model is similar to Canada.

Every component in the tax stage must check the values in the _tax_total and _tax_included name/value pairs before execution. If these values are already set, the component must return without doing anything. If the values are not set, the component must attempt to compute the tax, and if it is successful, set the values in the two name/value pairs. If you are writing a custom tax-processing component, you must ensure that your component writes to _tax_total and _tax_included name/value pairs.

Computing Order Total

The Plan pipeline executes the components in the Order Total stage to compute the total cost of an order and store it in the **OrderForm** object.

The Order Total stage

The Order Total stage in the Plan pipeline:

◆ Sums the subtotal (less any discount), shipping, handling, and tax charges.

◆ Sets the total value of the order in the **OrderForm** object.

In other words, this stage reads and sums the values in _oadjust_subtotal, _shipping_total, _tax_total, and _handling_total name/value pairs and writes the sum in the _total_total name/value pair in the **OrderForm** object.

The following table lists and describes the components provided by Commerce Server to store the order total in the order form.

Component	Description
DefaultTotal	Writes the total cost of the order in the _total_total name/value pair.
RequiredTotal	Performs a _VERIFY_WITH check on the **OrderForm** object.

Once the Plan pipeline is executed completely, the script in payment.asp reads the updated **OrderForm** values and displays the complete order along with the shipping, handling, and tax charges on the Final Purchase Approval page.

Adding a Scriptor Component

This section contains the following topics:

◆ Understanding the Scripting Component

◆ Adding a Scriptor Component to Compute Tax

Understanding the Scriptor Component

The Site Manager page enables you to add and configure a Scriptor component.

A Scriptor component is a custom component that can be inserted in any stage of a pipeline. The code in a Scriptor component can be written by using either the Microsoft Visual Basic Scripting Edition or Microsoft JScript scripting language.

A Scriptor component allows you to:

◆ Access and modify the **OrderForm** object.

◆ Access the pipe context information.

◆ Execute a pipeline.

The script run by a Scriptor component can be stored internally as part of the .pcf file, or externally in a separate file that is called by the component when it runs.

▶ **To add a Scriptor component**

1. Start Microsoft Internet Explorer and type the URL **http://localhost/ <Sitename>/manager** in the address bar of Internet Explorer.

2. On the Site Manager page, under the **System** section, select the .pcf file to which you want to add the Scriptor component, and then click **Edit Pipeline**.

3. Scroll to the stage to which you want to add the Scriptor component and click **Insert component**.

4. Select **Scriptor** from the list of available components.

Once you have added a Scriptor component to a pipeline, you need to configure the component to specify:

◆ The scripting language to write the code.

◆ The location of the script that indicates whether the script will be stored internally in the .pcf file or externally in a file.

◆ The parameters that will be passed to the script.

▶ **To configure a Scriptor component**

1. Add a Scriptor component to the pipeline.
2. Scroll to the stage to which you added the Scriptor component and click the **Edit** link that appears under the component.
3. Select a scripting language from the **Scripting Engine** drop-down list box.
4. Select the Source as **Internal** or **External**.
5. If the Source is Internal, type the code in the **Script** box. If the Source is External, type the path and filename that contains the script in the **filename** box.
6. Type the parameters in the **Config** box, in the form name=value.
7. Click **Update** to save the values in the .pcf file.

Adding a Scriptor Component to Compute Tax

The Site Builder Wizard requires a locale value for your site. The wizard uses this locale value to configure your site to compute tax and display time and currency in the proper locale format. For example, if you select English (United States) as the locale for your site, the tax charges for an order will be computed based on the tax rates applicable in the United States.

Computing Tax Based on the Shopper's Location

If you want your site to cater to shoppers from other countries, you can create a Scriptor component that performs processing based on a shopper's country. For example, you can include a Scriptor component in the Tax stage that computes tax based on the country name stored in the **OrderForm** object's ship_to_country name/value pair. The tax component must ensure that it sets the _tax_total and _tax_included name/value pairs in the **OrderForm** object.

Understanding the Scriptor Component

When you configure a Scriptor component by using the Site Manager page, select the Scripting engine as **VBScript** and select the source as **Internal**. Three functions are inserted in the Script text box: **MSCSOpen**, **MSCSExecute**, and **MSCSClose**. These functions are called the entry points of a Scriptor component.

◆ The **MSCSOpen** function

This function is executed immediately when the Scriptor component is run. It receives as a parameter the configuration dictionary information such as the script text and the script name.

◆ The **MSCSExecute** function

This function is executed immediately after the **MSCSOpen** function and receives the following parameters:

- The configuration dictionary information such as the script text and the script name.
- The OrderForm dictionary.
- The pipe context dictionary.
- The flags that you pass to the pipeline object.

◆ The **MSCSClose** function

This function is executed after the **MSCSExecute** function has returned.

You can write your own task-specific code within these functions. The Five Lakes Publishing sample site contains an Internal Scriptor component called Tax Calculator in the Tax stage of the Plan pipeline. The following script in the Tax Calculator component computes the tax for each item in the **OrderForm** object's items list and for the complete order:

```
function MSCSExecute(config, orderform, context, flags)
item_tax_rate = orderform.tax_rate
set itemlist = orderform.items
for each item in itemlist
  item.[_tax_total] = (item.list_price*item_tax_rate)/100
  item.[_tax_included] = 0
  orderform.[_tax_total] = item.[_tax_total] +
orderform.[_tax_total]
next
MSCSExecute = 1     'set function return value to 1 for _
                   'success
end function
```

Lab 6: Adding a Scriptor Component

Objectives

After completing this lab, you will be able to modify the Plan pipeline to incorporate shoppers from other countries.

Before You Begin

Prerequisites

This lab assumes that you have successfully completed the following:

- Lab 2: Creating a New Commerce Server Site
- Lab 3: Customizing Product Catalog Pages
- Lab 4: Implementing Upsell
- Practice: Customizing the Shipping Page

Before you begin this lab, you must meet the following prerequisites:

- Familiarity with Microsoft Internet Explorer
- Basic knowledge of ASP scripting

Estimated time to complete this lab: 20 minutes

Exercise 1: Creating a Component to Compute Tax

In this exercise, you will add an Internal Scriptor component to compute tax for several countries.

 Caution To successfully complete this lab, you must have completed the practice Customizing the Shipping Page in the chapter.

▶ **Define a query in global.asa**

1. In Microsoft Visual InterDev 6.0, open the FiveLakes project and then open global.asa.

2. In the **InitQueryMap** function, add a query to retrieve the tax rate for a specific country as follows:

```
set MSCSQueryMap.country_tax = AddQuery("select country, _
tax_rate from FiveLakes_country where country = :1 or _
code = :2")
```

3. On the **File** menu, click **Save global.asa,** and then click **Close.**

▶ **Store the tax rate in the OrderForm object**

1. Edit the xt_orderform_prepare.asp file.

2. Before the end function statement of the **OrderFormPrepareArgs** function, add the following code to retrieve the tax rate for the selected country from the country table and to store the tax rate in the **OrderForm** object:

```
REM Retrieve tax_rate and code from FiveLakes_country table

quoted_country = "'" & Replace(ship_to_country,"'","''") _
& "'"      REM - add quotes

    sqlText = MSCSQueryMap.country_tax.SQLCommand
    sqlText = Replace(sqlText, ":1", quoted_country)
    sqlText = Replace(sqlText, ":2", quoted_country)
    cmdTemp.CommandText = sqlText
    Set rscountry_tax = _
        Server.CreateObject("ADODB.Recordset")
    rscountry_tax.Open cmdTemp, , adOpenForwardOnly, _
        adLockReadOnly
    if not rscountry_tax.EOF then
        orderform.ship_to_country=rscountry_tax("country")
        orderForm.tax_rate = rscountry_tax("tax_rate")
    end if
```

3. On the **File** menu, click **Save xt_orderform_prepare.asp,** and then click **Close.**

▶ **Add a Scriptor component to the Plan pipeline**

1. Start Microsoft Internet Explorer and type the URL address **http://localhost/ FiveLakes/manager.**

2. On the Site Manager page, select **plan.pcf** from the drop-down list box in the System section, and click **Edit Pipeline.**

Note Alternatively, you can edit the pipeline using the Win32 Pipeline Editor.

3. On the Editing file:/FiveLakes/config/plan.pcf page, scroll to **Stage 12: Tax** and click **Insert component** below the **SimpleUSTax** component.

4. Select **Scriptor** to add a Scriptor component to the pipeline.

▶ **Configure the Scriptor component**

1. On the Editing file:/FiveLakes/config/plan.pcf page, scroll to **Stage 12: Tax** and click the **Edit** link that appears under the Scriptor component.

2. Replace the current label in the **label** text box with **Tax Calculator**.

3. Select **VBScript** from the **Scripting Engine** drop-down list box.

4. Select the Source as **Internal**.

5. Type the following script to compute tax in the **MSCSExecute** function in the **Script** text box. The script must set the _tax_total and _tax_included name/value pairs for every item in the OrderForm and for the entire order.

```
function MSCSExecute(config, orderform, context, flags)
    if orderform.ship_to_country <> "USA" then
        item_tax_rate=0
        item_tax_rate = orderform.tax_rate
        set itemlist = orderform.items
        orderform.[_tax_total]=0
        orderform.[_tax_included]=0
        for each item in itemlist
            item.[_tax_total]= _
            (item.list_price*item_tax_rate)/100
            item.[_tax_included] = 0
            orderform.[_tax_total] = item.[_tax_total] + _
                orderform.[_tax_total]
        next
    end if
    MSCSExecute = 1  'set function return value to 1 _
                    'for success
end function
```

Note Tax for USA is computed by the SimpleUSTax component inserted by the wizard.

6. Click **Update** to save the configuration parameters.

7. Click **Save** to save the plan.pcf file.

▶ **View Tax charges**

1. Start Microsoft Internet Explorer and type the URL address **http://localhost/ FiveLakes**.

2. Shop at the site for at least one product and click **Purchase** on the Shopping Basket page.

3. On the Shipping page, click **Click here if you have problems with the Wallet**.

 Note The reason you are using the form is to select a country from the country list that you added on the shipping page in the earlier practice.

4. Select a method of shipping from the **Shipping Method** drop-down list box.

5. Type the values in the Shipping Address fields, including the ship-to country, and then click **Total**.

6. Notice the tax charges on the Final Purchase Approval page.

Review

The review questions cover some of the key concepts taught in the chapter.

1. How is the total tax for an order computed?

2. What are the charges included in the total order value?

3. Explain the need to configure a Scriptor component.

4. What can you do with a Scriptor component?

Review Answers

1. The components in the Tax stage apply a tax rate specified for the shopper's country to every item in the order and write the total tax to the OrderForm object.

2. The total order value includes the order subtotal, tax, shipping, and handling charges computed by the stages in the Plan pipeline.

3. Once you have added a Scriptor component to a pipeline, you need to configure the component to specify the scripting language to write the code, the location of the script, and the parameters that will be passed to the script.

4. A Scriptor component allows you to access and modify the OrderForm.

Chapter 7:
Completing the Purchase Process

Objectives

After completing this chapter, you will be able to:

- Capture payment information in an HTML form or by using Microsoft Wallet.
- Generate simple order numbers.
- Track the status of an order.
- Explain how business transactions are secured by using Hypertext Transfer Protocol Secure (HTTPS) and Digital Certificates.

Understanding Purchase

This section includes the following topics:

- Overview of the Purchase Process
- Capture Payment Information

Overview of the Purchase Process

The Purchase pipeline is executed to verify credit card information that the shopper has provided.

Once a shopper provides a ship-to address for the purchase, the checkout process enables the shopper to provide payment details such as:

- Credit card number
- Name on the card

◆ Expiration date

◆ Bill-to address

These details can be typed into an HTML form or by using Microsoft Wallet. When the shopper confirms the purchase, the purchase pipeline is executed to verify credit card information that the shopper has provided. If the information is valid, the pipeline saves the order, then generates and displays a receipt.

Capture Payment Information

There are two ways to capture payment information from users:

Using HTML Forms

HTML forms are created by using HTML tags in .asp files. The payment.asp file contains the HTML code for accepting the shopper's credit card information and bill-to address and posts this information to xt_orderform_purchase.asp.

The xt_orderform_purchase.asp file validates the shopper information and then executes the Purchase OPP as a transacted pipeline. You will learn more about a transacted pipeline later in this chapter.

Using Microsoft Wallet

Microsoft Wallet provides shoppers an easy and secure way to store payment and address information on the shopper's computer. Microsoft Wallet consists of The Payment Selector and the Address Selector, which are available as plug-ins for Netscape Navigator, and as ActiveX controls for Microsoft Internet Explorer.

The Payment Selector and the Address Selector provide an interface that an online shopper can use to securely store payment and address information, and supply that information to vendors. The Payment Selector includes support for major credit card types such as VISA, MasterCard, American Express, Discover, and JCB.

If the Wallet controls are implemented, shoppers need not type their name, address, and other information into HTML forms every time they shop, as they usually would, because data can be stored in Wallet controls for reuse.

When a site is created by using Commerce Server's Site Builder Wizard, the scripting necessary for the Wallet controls is automatically built into the site.

Executing the Purchase OPP

This section contains the following topics:

- Overview of the Purchase OPP
- Stages of the Purchase OPP

Overview of the Purchase OPP

The Purchase OPP is used in the payment stage of the shopping process.

The Purchase pipeline is executed after an order form has successfully passed through the Plan pipeline and the shopper has confirmed the purchase.

The Purchase pipeline:

- Verifies the shopper's payment details.
- Accepts the final purchase of an order form.
- Writes the order to the site database.

The configuration of a Purchase pipeline is saved in purchase.pcf.

As stated previously, a Purchase pipeline is a transacted pipeline. A transacted pipeline consists of components that are designed and configured to support Microsoft Transaction Server (MTS) transactions. A MTS transaction is a unit of work that is performed as an atomic operation. The Commerce Server OPP supports MTS transactions through the **MtsTxPipeline** object. The **MtsTxPipeline** object executes a Purchase pipeline as shown in the following code:

```
Set pipeline = _
Server.CreateObject("Commerce.MtsTxPipeline")
Call pipeline.LoadPipe("<path and filename of the _
.pcf file>")
pipeline.Execute(1, orderForm, pipeContext, 0)
```

For the creation and execution of a pipeline, see i_util.asp in Appendix A.

Stages of the Purchase OPP

The Purchase pipeline consists of three stages.

Purchase Check Stage

The Purchase Check stage is used to verify a shopper's bill-to address and credit card information. The following table describes the components stored in Purchase.pcf created by the Site Builder Wizard.

Component	Description
Validate Bill_to	Verifies that each Bill_to field on the order form contains data.
Validate CC Info	Verifies that each credit card field on the order form contains data and that the site supports the credit card type.
Validate CCNumber	Verifies that the credit card date has not expired and that the number is properly formed.

The script in the Validate Bill_to and Validate CC Info components can be customized to perform additional validation on bill-to address and credit card fields.

Payment Stage

The Payment stage is used to approve credit card payments. The DefaultPayment component of this stage sets an initial value in the _payment_auth_code name/value pair. The RequiredPayment component ensures that _payment_auth_code is not NULL.

Accept Stage

The Accept stage handles the completed order, including initiating order tracking, generating the purchase order, and saving the order. The following table describes some of the components related to this stage.

Component	Description
SaveReceipt	Saves all fields on the order form that have a corresponding column name in the database table.
SQLItemADO	Runs the SQL command for each item in the order, passing the specified order form fields as parameters to the SQL command.
SQLOrderADO	Runs the SQL command once for each order passing the specified order parameters to the SQL command.

Tracking an Order

This section contains the following topics:

◆ How to Generate a Simple Order Number

◆ How to Track an Order

◆ Practice: Generating a Simple Order Number

How to Generate a Simple Order Number

As mentioned in Chapter 5, the order number, or the order ID, uniquely identifies an order. It is assigned during a shopper's initial order activity and is used to track the order through completion. The order number is a 26-character Globally Unique Identifier (GUID) generated by Commerce Server. Because the length of the GUID makes it difficult to remember, most merchants prefer to use a shorter order number for the convenience of their shoppers. The following procedure uses the Five Lakes Publishing sample site as an example to generate order numbers in the format

```
<current month><current year><n>
```

where n is the running sequence number.

The following illustration shows how a simple order number is generated.

▶ To create a short order number

1. Create a table named <Sitename>_orderid with an attribute named NewOrderID of type char(26).

2. Insert a row in the <Sitename>_orderid table to store the starting order number for the site.

3. In the **OrderFormPurchase** function of xt_orderform_purchase.asp file:

   a. Retrieve the NewOrderID value from the <Sitename>_orderid table into a variable named New_oid. The order number stored in New_oid will be used for the current shopping session.

   b. Extract the sequence number from New_oid and increment it by 1.

   c. Prefix the incremented sequence number with the current month and current year to get the order number to be used for the subsequent shopping session.

   d. Replace NewOrderID value in the <Sitename>_orderid table with the newly created order number.

   e. Replace the default order id in the **OrderForm** object with the order number in New_oid.

How to Track an Order

On successful completion of a purchase transaction, Commerce Server generates a purchase confirmation. The purchase confirmation, displayed in the form of an HTML page, contains the order number that can be used by a shopper to check the status of an order.

A shopper may be interested in viewing receipt details or shipping details. For example, in the Five Lakes Publishing sample site, a shopper can return to the site to view the shipping status of an order.

Retrieve Order Details from Database

The following code retrieves order details from the <Sitename>_receipt table and sets the shipping status of an order:

```
<%   cmdTemp.CommandText = _
Replace(MSCSQueryMap.orderid.SQLCommand,":1", _
Request("order_track_id"))
Set rsorderid = Server.CreateObject("ADODB.Recordset")
rsorderid.Open cmdTemp, , adOpenForwardOnly, _
adLockReadOnly
if not rsorderid.EOF then
    if (now() - rsorderid("date_entered"))>2 then
        ship_status="Shipped"
    else
        ship_status="Not Shipped"
    end if
```

Practice: Generating a Simple Order Number

In this practice, you will replace the complex GUID order number generated by Commerce Server with a short order number. Your site database contains a table named FiveLakes_orderid to store the order number.

Caution The activities in this practice are a prerequisite for successful completion of Lab 7.

▶ **Insert a row in the FiveLakes_orderid table**

1. On the **Start** menu, point to **Programs, Microsoft SQL Server 7.0,** and then click **Query Analyzer.**

2. In the **Connect to SQL Server** dialog box, select the **Use SQL Server authentication** option button, type **sa** in the **Login Name** text box, leave the **Password** text box blank, and then click **OK.**

Note You do not need to select the Server name because it is selected by default.

3. In the **New query** dialog box, select the **FiveLakes** database from the **DB** drop-down list box.

4. Type the following SQL statement into the Query window to store the initial order number in the format *mmyyyyn*, where *mm* is the current month, *yyyy* is the current year, and *n* is a running sequence number starting with 1.

```
update FiveLakes_orderid set NewOrderID="mmyyyy1"
```

For example, if the current month is May 1999, the initial order number would be created using the following SQL statement:

```
update FiveLakes_orderid set NewOrderID="0519991"
```

5. Press F5 to execute the query.

   The result should show "1 row(s) affected".

6. Close the Query Analyzer.

▶ **Modify the xt_orderform_purchase.asp file to generate a simple order number**

1. In Microsoft Visual InterDev 6.0, open the FiveLakes project and then double-click xt_orderform_purchase.asp in the Project Explorer window.

2. In the **OrderFormPurchase** function, below the line **OrderFormPurchase = null**, add the following code to create a short order number:

```
Set rsOrderID = Server.CreateObject("ADODB.Recordset")

REM Extract Order ID value from the table
cmdTemp.CommandText = "select NewOrderID from _
FiveLakes_orderid"
set rsOrderID = cmdTemp.Execute
New_oid=rsOrderID("NewOrderID")

temp_val=Int(Mid(New_oid,7)) + Int("1")
if len(month(now())) = 2 then
    next_order_id = month(now()) & year(now()) & _
    CStr(temp_val)
else
    next_order_id = "0" & month(now()) & year(now()) & _
    CStr(temp_val)
end if

cmdTemp.CommandText="update FiveLakes_orderid set _
    NewOrderID = :1"
next_order_id = "'" & next_order_id & "'"
cmdTemp.CommandText=Replace(cmdTemp.CommandText,":1", _
    next_order_id)
set rsOrderID = cmdTemp.Execute
```

3. Scroll to the following line, which initializes an order form object.

```
Set MSCSOrderForm = _
UtilGetOrderForm(MSCSOrderFormStorage,created)
```

4. On the next line, add code to replace the default order_id in the order form object with the short order number retrieved from the database as follows:

```
mscsOrderForm.order_id = New_oid
```

5. On the **File** menu, click **Save xt_orderform_purchase.asp**, and then click **Close**.

▶ **Display the country on the payment page**

> **Note** If you have completed the practice and the lab in Chapter 6, "Checking Out," you will need to modify the payment page to accept the shopper's bill-to-country and store it in the **OrderForm** object.

1. Edit the payment.asp file.

2. Locate the following code:

```
VALUE="<%= _
mscsPage.HTMLEncode(mscsOrderForm.bill_to_zip) _
%>"> 
</TD>
</TR>
```

3. On the next line, add the following code to display the bill-to-country, which is the country selected by the shopper on the shipping page:

```
<TR>
    <TD ALIGN="RIGHT">
        <B>Country:</B>
    </TD>
    <% sqlText = MSCSQueryMap.country.SQLCommand
    cmdTemp.CommandText = sqlText
    Set rscountry = Server.CreateObject("ADODB.Recordset")
    rscountry.Open cmdTemp, , adOpenForwardOnly, _
    adLockReadOnly %>

    <td align="left">
        <select name="bill_to_country" size="1">

        <%While not rscountry.EOF %>
            <%= _
            mscsPage.Option(rscountry("country").value, _
            mscsOrderForm.bill_to_country)%> <%= _
            rscountry("country").value %>
            <% rscountry.MoveNext
        Wend %>
        </select VALUE="<%= _
        mscsPage.HTMLEncode(mscsOrderForm.bill_to_country) _
        %>"> 
    </td>
</TR>
```

4. On the **File** menu, click **Save payment.asp,** and then click **Close.**

▶ **View the short order number on the site**

1. Start Microsoft Internet Explorer and type **http://localhost/FiveLakes** in the address bar of Internet Explorer.

2. Shop for a product on the site.

3. On the Purchase Confirmation page, notice the short order number.

Securing Business Transactions

This section contains the following topics:

◆ Introducing HTTPS

◆ Introducing Digital Certificates

Introducing HTTPS

Shoppers using a Commerce Server site need assurance that passwords and credit card numbers are protected from unauthorized access. A shopper must get a secure connection to an ASP that processes confidential information. When a shopper submits credit card information by using a form, Secure Sockets Layer (SSL) should secure the ASP file that receives the form's post data. SSL is a method of data encryption used to secure transactions between a client (the shopper's browser) and Commerce Server. To receive a page that is secured by SSL, the browser must send a request by using HTTPS protocol as follows:

```
https://example.microsoft.com/
```

To generate a URL by using HTTPS, you can use the **page.SURL** method. By default, HTTPS is disabled in the site that you create by using the Site Foundation Wizard and can be enabled by setting the Site.Disable HTTPS value to zero (0). The following code, when invoked from ASP, enables HTTPS:

```
MSCSSite.Disable HTTPS = 0
```

Assuming that HTTPS is enabled by setting Site.Disable HTTPS value to zero, the following code will generate the URL https://localhost/<Sitename>/purchase.asp:

```
<FORM METHOD = "POST" _
ACTION="<%=mscsPage.SURL("xt_orderform_purchase.asp") %>"
```

Introducing Digital Certificates

For a shopper to get a secure connection to a Web site, the server hosting the site should have a digital certificate.

Digital certificates are electronic documents that authenticate users and entities on a network and are issued by a Certificate Authority. Along with the digital certificate, the Certificate Authority also issues public and private keys.

For authentication, Commerce Server sends the digital certificate to the client. If messages are to be sent to the client, the messages are encrypted by using a private key and the public key is sent along with the digital certificate. Once the client receives the message, the client uses the sender's public key to decrypt the message.

To see the animation "Using Digital Certificates," see the accompanying CD-ROM.

Lab 7: Tracking Order Status

Objectives

After completing this lab, you will be able to:

◆ Retrieve order details from your site database.

◆ Display shipping status and order details for a specific order number.

Before You Begin

Prerequisites

This lab assumes that you have successfully completed all the labs in the previous chapters and the practice in Chapter 7.

To complete this lab, you must have the following prerequisites:

◆ Familiarity with Microsoft Internet Explorer and Microsoft Visual InterDev 6.0

◆ Basic knowledge of HTML and ASP scripting

Estimated time to complete this lab: 30 minutes

Exercise 1: Determining Order Status

In this exercise, you will create two .asp files to add order-tracking functionality to your site. The ordertrack.asp file will track an order number from a shopper. The order_status.asp file will accept the shipping status for a given order number and redirect to receipt.asp, which displays the order.

Caution The startup code for this lab does not contain the changes made to the xt_order_form.asp page during the practice. To successfully complete this lab, you must have completed the Generating a Simple Order Number practice first.

▶ **Define a query in global.asa**

1. In Microsoft Visual InterDev 6.0, open the FiveLakes project and then open global.asa.

2. In the **InitQueryMap** function, add a query to retrieve the order details for a specific order number as follows:

```
Set MSCSQueryMap.orderid = AddQuery _
("SELECT * FROM FiveLakes_receipt _
  WHERE order_id = ':1'")
```

3. On the **File** menu, click **Save global.asa**, and then click **Close**.

▶ **Create two new .asp files in the site directory**

◆ In Microsoft Visual InterDev 6.0, create two new .asp files and save them as ordertrack.asp and order_status.asp, respectively in your project folder.

▶ **Add code to accept an order number and post it to order_status.asp**

1. Open the ordertrack.asp file.

2. On the first line, modify the code to specify the Locale ID as **1033** and session state as **false** as follows:

```
<%@ LANGUAGE=vbscript enablesessionstate=false LCID=1033 %>
```

3. On the next line, include the i_shop.asp file that contains definitions for a **Page** object, shopper ID, and ADO connection and command object:

```
<!--#INCLUDE FILE="i_shop.asp" -->
```

4. On the next line, include i_header.asp, which displays the logo and navigation bar:

```
<!--#INCLUDE FILE="i_header.asp" -->
```

5. Between the Body tags, create an HTML form element to:

    a. Accept an order number in a text input element.

b. Post the order number to the order_status.asp file as follows:

```
<form name="order_status" method="post" _
action="order_status.asp">

<Table width = "100%">
<tr>
   <td width = "20%">
   Order Number:
   </td>

   <td>
   <Input type="text" name="order_track_id" size="10" _
   maxlength="100">
   </td>
</tr>
<tr>
   <td colspan="2">
    
   </td>
</tr>
<tr>
   <td width="20%">
   <input type="submit" value ="Go">
   </td>
   <td>
   <input type="reset" value ="Reset">
   </td>
</tr>
</table>

</form>
```

6. On the **File** menu, click **Save ordertrack.asp**, and the click **Close**.

▶ **Determine the shipping status**

1. Open the order_status.asp file.

2. On the first line, modify the code to specify the Locale ID as **1033** and session state as **false** as follows:

```
<%@ LANGUAGE=vbscript enablesessionstate=false _
LCID=1033 %>
```

3. On the next line, add the following code to allow execution of response.redirect and response.write statements:

```
<% Response.buffer = true %>
```

4. On the next line, include i_shop.asp and i_header.asp as follows:

```
<!-#INCLUDE FILE="i_shop.asp" ->
<!-#INCLUDE FILE="i_header.asp" ->
```

5. Between the Body tags, add the following code to search for an order number and determine the shipping status. The shipping status is set to true if the current date is two days after the order date.

```
<%
cmdTemp.CommandText = _
Replace(MSCSQueryMap.orderid.SQLCommand,":1", _
Request("order_track_id"))
Set rsorderid = Server.CreateObject("ADODB.Recordset")
rsorderid.Open cmdTemp, , adOpenForwardOnly, adLockReadOnly
if not rsorderid.EOF then
    if (now() - rsorderid("date_entered"))>2 then
        ship_status="Yes"
    else
        ship_status="No"
    end if
end if
%>
```

6. On the next line, add the following code to build and redirect a URL to receipt.asp:

```
<%
strurl = "receipt.asp?order_id=" & _
Request("order_track_id") & "&ship_status=" & _
ship_status
Response.Redirect strurl
%>
```

7. On the **File** menu, click **Save order_status.asp,** and then click **Close.**

For the complete code of ordertrack.asp and order_status.asp created in the Five Lakes Publishing sample site, see Appendix A.

Exercise 2: Displaying Shipping Status

In this exercise, you will modify the receipt.asp file to display the shipping status of the specified order number.

▶ **Display the shipping status**

1. Edit the receipt.asp file.

> **Note** Be sure not to open receipts.asp.

2. Locate the line **< % REM divider: %>** and add the following code to display the shipping status for an order after it:

```
<TR>
    <%
    ship_status = Request("ship_status")
    if trim(ship_status) = "Yes" then
        shipping_message = "The order has been shipped"
    else
        shipping_message = "The order has not yet been shipped"
    end if

    %>

    <TH BGCOLOR="#000000">
    <FONT COLOR="#FFFFFF">Shipping Status:</FONT>
    </TH>
    <TD>
        <B><%=Shipping_Message%></B>
    </TD>
</TR>
```

3. On the **File** menu, click **Save receipt.asp**, and then click **Close**.

▶ **Add a link in the Home page to the Track Your Order page**

1. Edit the default.asp file.

2. Add the following code before the INCLUDE FILE="i_footer.asp" statement:

```
<p>
You can see your order status on the <A HREF="<%= _
pageURL("ordertrack.asp") %>">Track Your Order Page</A>
```

▶ **View the order status**

1. Start Microsoft Internet Explorer and type **http://localhost/FiveLakes** in the address bar of Internet Explorer.

2. On the site Home page, click the **Track Your Order Page** link.

3. Type the order number you received in your earlier purchase in the **Order Number** text box, and then click **Go**.

Notice the order details and shipping status is displayed on the page.

Review

The review questions cover some of the key concepts taught in the chapter.

1. What is the advantage of using Microsoft Wallet over HTML forms?

2. What is the advantage of a simple order tracking number?

3. What is needed to get a secure connection to a Web Site?

4. What is HTTPS?

Review Answers

1. With the Wallet controls implemented, shoppers need not type their name, address, and other information every time they shop, as with HTML forms, because data can be stored in Wallet controls for reuse.

2. The default order number is a 26-character GUID generated by Commerce Server, which is difficult for shoppers to remember. A simple order number makes order tracking easier for the shopper.

3. To get a secure connection, the server hosting the Web Site should have a server certificate, also referred to as a digital certificate.

4. HTTPS is a protocol that provides access to a Web page secured by SSL.

Chapter 8:
Tracking Shopper Information

Objectives

After completing this chapter, you will be able to:

◆ Store and retrieve shopper information by using cookies.

◆ Store and retrieve shopper information by using a registration table.

Using Cookies to Track Shoppers

This section includes the following topics:

◆ Why Track Shoppers?

◆ Setting a Cookie

◆ Retrieving Shopper Information from a Cookie

◆ Practice: Using Cookies to Track Shoppers

Why Track Shoppers?

On a shopper's first visit to a site, the site can capture and save shopper information or in other words, register the shopper. Registering a shopper provides the following benefits:

◆ The site can display a customized catalog based on the previous orders placed by a shopper.

◆ The site can notify a shopper of the latest products in the site by sending e-mail.

◆ The shopper need not type address and payment information on each visit to the site.

Commerce Server supports registration of shoppers to keep track of returning shoppers. The Site Builder Wizard supports three models of shopper registration:

◆ None

◆ On Entry

◆ On Ordering

Shoppers can be registered when they enter a site or when they add items to the shopping cart. When a shopper registers, the shopper information is saved in a database table.

On each new visit to a site that requires registration, the shopper signs in and the shopper's information is retrieved from the database and associated with a new shopper_ID for the shopping session.

Setting a Cookie

As mentioned in Chapter 4, a cookie is a file that is created on a shopper's computer. It is stored under the shopper's login profile on the hard disk.

Information can be read from a cookie only if the cookie is set. Using the **Response.Cookies** method of ASP, you can set values in a cookie as follows:

```
EM—Writing shopper information into the cookie
<% Response.Cookies("<Cookiename>")("name")= _
mscsOrderForm.ship_to_name %>
<% Response.Cookies("<Cookiename>")("street")= _
mscsOrderForm.ship_to_street %>
```

Information stored in a cookie is lost when the shoppers quit their Web browser. This sort of cookie is referred to as a session cookie. To retain cookie information through multiple shopping sessions, you must set the **Expires** property of the cookie to a future date as follows:

```
REM-To set the Expires property of the cookie
<% Response.Cookies("<Cookiename>").Expires=#<Month> <DD> _
<YYYY># %>
```

> **Note** In an .asp file, the **Response** and **Request** methods of the cookies collection must be executed prior to executing any HTML code.

Retrieving Shopper Information from a Cookie

Using the **Request.Cookies** method of ASP, you can retrieve and display shopper information stored in a cookie as follows:

```
<% mscsOrderForm.ship_to_name= _
Request.Cookies("<Cookiename>")("name") %>
<% mscsOrderForm.ship_to_street= _
Request.Cookies("<Cookiename>")("street") %>
```

These details can now be modified and written back into the cookie by using the **Response.Cookies** method.

Practice: Using Cookies to Track Shoppers

In this practice, you will retrieve and store shopper information by using a cookie.

▶ Configure a site to use URLs instead of cookies

1. In Microsoft Visual InterDev 6.0, open the FiveLakes project, and then open global.asa.
2. Locate the following line of code:

```
call MSCSShopperManager.InitManager(vRoot,"cookieurl")
```

3. Change this code to:

```
call MSCSShopperManager.InitManager(vRoot,"url")
```

4. Locate the following line of code:

```
Set Application("MSCSShopperManager")= MSCSShopperManager
```

5. On the next line, add the following code to initialize an Application MSCSSIDUrlKey variable. This provides a name to be used for the query string variable to be appended to the URL.

```
Application("MSCSSIDUrlKey") = "mscssid"
```

6. Save and close global.asa.

7. Open the i_shop.asp file.

8. Locate and delete the following code in i_shop.asp:

```
call Response.Redirect(pageURL("default.asp"))
```

9. Save and close i_shop.asp.

▶ **Store shopper information in a cookie**

1. Edit the payment.asp file.

2. Before the <html> tag, insert the following code to set the expiration date of the cookie to a future date:

```
<% Response.Cookies("<Cookiename>").Expires=#<Month> _
<DD>, <YYYY># %>
```

Note <Cookiename> should be changed to some useful string without the brackets. Also, the month should be a text string. Finally, the day and year information should be numerals, all set at some time in the future.

3. On the next line, add code to store the shopper information in the cookie as follows:

```
<%Response.Cookies("<Cookiename>")("name")= _
mscsOrderForm.ship_to_name %>
<%Response.Cookies("<Cookiename>")("street")= _
mscsOrderForm.ship_to_street %>
<%Response.Cookies("<Cookiename>")("city")= _
mscsOrderForm.ship_to_city %>
<%Response.Cookies("<Cookiename>")("state")= _
mscsOrderForm.ship_to_state %>
<%Response.Cookies("<Cookiename>")("country")= _
mscsOrderForm.ship_to_country %>
<%Response.Cookies("<Cookiename>")("zip")= _
mscsOrderForm.ship_to_zip %>
<%Response.Cookies("<Cookiename>")("phone")= _
mscsOrderForm.ship_to_phone %>
```

4. On the **File** menu, click **Save payment.asp,** and then click **Close.**

▶ **Retrieve shopper information from a cookie**

1. In the Project Explorer window, double-click **shipping.asp.**

2. Insert the following code before the <html> tag in shipping.asp to retrieve shopper information from the cookie and store it in the OrderForm:

```
<% mscsOrderForm.ship_to_name= _
Request.Cookies("<Cookiename>")("name") %>
<% mscsOrderForm.ship_to_street= _
Request.Cookies("<Cookiename>")("street") %>
<% mscsOrderForm.ship_to_city= _
Request.Cookies("<Cookiename>")("city") %>
<% mscsOrderForm.ship_to_state= _
Request.Cookies("<Cookiename>")("state") %>
<% mscsOrderForm.ship_to_country= _
Request.Cookies("<Cookiename>")("country") %>
<% mscsOrderForm.ship_to_zip= _
Request.Cookies("<Cookiename>")("zip") %>
<% mscsOrderForm.ship_to_phone= _
Request.Cookies("<Cookiename>")("phone") %>
```

3. On the **File** menu, click **Save shipping.asp,** and then click **Close.**

▶ **View shopper information retrieved from a cookie**

1. Start Microsoft Internet Explorer and type in the URL address **http://localhost/ FiveLakes**.

2. Shop at the site and on the Shipping page, click **Click here if you have problems with the wallet** to view the HTML form.

3. Type your shipping information in the HTML form as a new shopper and click **Total**. The script in payment.asp will save the shipping details in a cookie.

4. On the Final Purchase Approval page, type in the credit card information and click **Purchase** to complete the purchase.

5. Return to the site and view your shipping information on the shipping page. The script in shipping.asp has successfully retrieved your shipping details from the cookie.

Using Registration Table to Track Shoppers

This section contains the following topics:

◆ Creating a Shopper Table
◆ Retrieving Shopper Information
◆ Modifying the Purchase Pipeline

Creating a Shopper Table

Storing shopper information in a table is more secure than storing it in a cookie because a cookie can be accidentally deleted from the shopper's computer. Also, a database table is preferred over a cookie because the shopper's Web browser may not always support cookies.

Saving Shopper Information in a Table

Commerce Server creates a <Sitename>_shopper table on the site database for the sites that require shopper registration. The <Sitename>_shopper table contains name, street, city, state, zip, country, phone, e-mail, and shopper_ID attributes.

On the sites that are created with the registration option set to **None** in the Site Builder Wizard, such as the Five Lakes Publishing sample site, you can add the shopper registration functionality at a later stage.

Adding Shopper Registration Information to a Site

To include the shopper registration functionality in your site, you need to add the following elements:

◆ A table in the site database to store shopper information.

◆ A query description in global.asa to retrieve shopper information.

◆ A component in the Purchase pipeline to update shopper information in the site database for returning shoppers.

◆ A component in the Purchase pipeline to insert shopper information in the site database for new shoppers.

▶ **To create a shopper table in the site database**

1. On the **Start** menu, point to **Programs, Microsoft SQL Server 7.0,** and then click **Query Analyzer.**

2. Log on to the SQL Server.

3. Execute the query to create a table as follows:

```
create table <Sitename>_shopper
(shopper_ID varchar(64) constraint Prime_Key PRIMARY KEY,
name varchar(30),
city varchar(20),
state varchar(20),
zip varchar(10),
country varchar(30),
phone varchar(20),
email varchar(30))
```

Retrieving Shopper Information

Shopper information can be captured and retrieved from the <Sitename>_shopper table when:

◆ A shopper enters the site.

◆ A shopper types in shipping details.

In the Five Lakes Publishing sample site, the script in shipping.asp accepts shopper information for a new shopper and displays shopper information for a returning shopper.

▶ **To retrieve returning shopper's information from the site database**

1. Add a query in global.asa to retrieve shopper information from the <Sitename>_shopper table as follows:

```
Set MSCSQueryMap.email_search = AddQuery(" _
SELECT * FROM <Sitename>_shopper _
WHERE email = ':1'")
```

2. In Microsoft Visual InterDev 6.0, modify the script in shipping.asp to:

   a. Accept the returning shopper's e-mail address by using HTML tags.

   b. Execute the query to retrieve shopper information from the <Sitename>_shopper table as follows:

```
cmdTemp.CommandText = _
"SELECT * FROM FiveLakes_shopper _
 WHERE email = '" & email & "'"

Set rsShopperFindSpec = _
Server.CreateObject("ADODB.Recordset")
rsShopperFindSpec.Open cmdTemp, , adOpenStatic, _
adLockReadOnly
```

3. Store the shopper information in the **OrderForm** object as follows:

```
REM—If the email exists in the table
if not rsShopperFindSpec.EOF  then
mscsOrderForm.ship_to_email = rsShopperFindSpec("email")
```

4. Display the **OrderForm** values by using HTML tags.

   For the complete code of shipping.asp created in the Five Lakes Publishing sample site, refer to Appendix A.

Modifying the Purchase Pipeline

Once a shopper confirms a purchase, the shopper information is posted to the xt_orderform_purchase.asp file where the Purchase pipeline is executed and the shopper's information is committed to the site database.

Two SQLOrderADO components are required to insert and update shopper information in the site database for the new and returning shoppers, respectively.

Because the Purchase pipeline is a transacted pipeline that requires either all or none of the components to be executed, the two SQLOrderADO components cannot be added to the same pipeline. The reason is that, at any point in time, either an update operation for a returning shopper or an insert operation for a new shopper should occur.

Inserting Information to the Site Database

The Five Lakes Publishing sample site contains two Purchase pipelines, each having a SQLOrderADO component. The SQLOrderADO component in the first pipeline inserts shopper information in the <Sitename>_shopper table for a new shopper as follows:

```
insert into_
<Sitename>_shopper(email,name,street,city,state,country, _
zip,phone) values (?,?,?,?,?,?,?,?)
```

with the following parameter list:

```
order.ship_to_email    order.ship_to_name
order.ship_to_street   order.ship_to_city
order.ship_to_state    order.ship_to_country
order.ship_to_zip      order.ship_to_phone
```

The following illustration shows editing in the PurchaseInsert.pcf file.

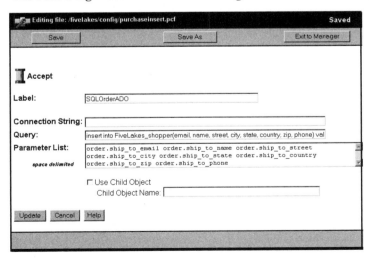

Updating Information to the Site Database

The SQLOrderADO component in the second pipeline updates shopper information in the <Sitename>_shopper table for a returning shopper as follows:

```
update <Sitename>_shopper set name=?, _
street=?,city=?,state=?,country=?,zip=?,phone=? where email=?
```

with the following parameter list:

```
order.ship_to_name      order.ship_to_street
order.ship_to_city      order.ship_to_state
order.ship_to_country   order.ship_to_zip
order.ship_to_phone     order.ship_to_email
```

The following illustration shows editing in the PurchaseUpdate.pcf file.

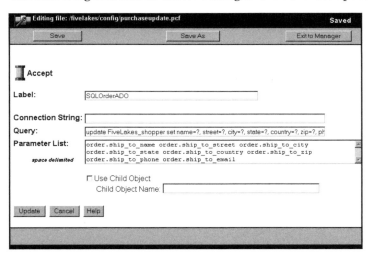

The script in xt_orderform_purchase.asp is then modified to execute the appropriate pipeline.

```
REM—Execute the query in global.asa to determine whether the
shopper is a new shopper or a returning shopper.
cmdTemp.CommandText = _
Replace(MSCSQueryMap.email_search.SQLCommand,":1", _
Replace(mscsOrderForm.ship_to_email, "'", "''"))
Set rsEmail = Server.CreateObject("ADODB.Recordset")
rsEmail.Open cmdTemp, , adOpenKeyset, adLockReadOnly
```

code continued on next page

code continued from previous page

```
REM—If the shopper is a returning shopper
if not rsEmail.EOF  then
    errorLevel = UtilRunTxPipe("purchaseupdate.pcf", _
    mscsOrderForm, mscsPipeContext)
    else
    REM —If the shopper is a new shopper
    errorLevel = UtilRunTxPipe("purchaseinsert.pcf", _
    mscsOrderForm, mscsPipeContext)
end if
```

Note UtilRunTxPipe is a function in i_util.asp that contains the code to execute the pipeline. The i_util.asp file is included in xt_orderform_purchase.asp.

Lab 8: Tracking Shoppers Using Registration Table

Objectives

After completing this lab, you will be able to:

◆ Retrieve and update shopper information for a returning shopper.

◆ Insert shopper information for a new shopper in the table.

◆ View shopper information retrieved from a table.

Before You Begin

Prerequisites

This lab assumes that you have successfully created a site using the Site Builder Wizard and added departments and products to your site.

Before you begin this lab, you must have the following prerequisites:

◆ Familiarity with Microsoft Internet Explorer and Microsoft Visual InterDev 6.0

◆ Knowledge of HTML and ASP scripting

Estimated time to complete this lab: 45 minutes

Exercise 1: Modifying Shipping Page to Identify a Returning Shopper

In this exercise, you will modify the shipping page to track a returning shopper and display the shopper information.

▶ **Configure a site to use URLs instead of cookies**

1. In Microsoft Visual InterDev 6.0, open the FiveLakes project, and then open global.asa.

2. Locate the following line of code:

```
call MSCSShopperManager.InitManager(vRoot,"cookieurl")
```

3. Change this code to:

```
call MSCSShopperManager.InitManager(vRoot,"url")
```

4. Locate the following line of code:

```
Set Application("MSCSShopperManager")= MSCSShopperManager
```

5. On the next line, add the following code to initialize an Application MSCSSIDUrlKey variable. This provides a name to be used for the query string variable to be appended to the URL.

```
Application("MSCSSIDUrlKey") = "mscssid"
```

6. Edit the i_shop.asp file.

7. Locate and delete the following code in i_shop.asp:

```
call Response.Redirect(pageURL("default.asp"))
```

▶ **Add a query to the QueryMap in global.asa**

1. Edit the global.asa file.

2. In the **InitQueryMap** function, add a query to retrieve information for a specific shopper as follows:

```
Set MSCSQueryMap.email_search = AddQuery("SELECT * _
    FROM FiveLakes_shopper WHERE email = ':1'")
```

3. On the **File** menu, click **Save global.asa,** and then click **Close.**

▶ **Add a field to accept e-mail address from a shopper**

1. Edit the shipping.asp file.

> **Note** If you have completed the practice in Chapter 8, delete the code in shipping.asp for retrieving shopper information from a cookie.

2. Scroll to the following code:

```
    <FONT SIZE ="+1"> <STRONG>Shipping Address
    </STRONG></FONT>
</TD>
</TR>
```

3. On the next line, add the following code to accept an e-mail address from a shopper:

```
<TR>
    <TD ALIGN="RIGHT">
    <B>E-Mail:</B>
    </TD>

    <TD colspan="3">
    <INPUT TYPE="text" NAME="ship_to_email"_
    SIZE="40,1" VALUE="<%= _
    mscsPage.HTMLEncode(mscsOrderForm.ship_to_email) _
    %>"> 
    </TD>

</TR>
```

▶ **Add the code to display returning shopper information in the HTML form**

1. In the shipping.asp file, locate the following lines:

```
    If the total is satisfactory, then you'll be able to
    complete the purchase.
</TD>
</TR>
</TABLE>
```

2. On the next line, add the following code to retrieve the value stored in the URL key return_shopper:

```
<%return_shopper = request.QueryString("return_shopper")
```

3. On the next line, add the following code to retrieve an e-mail address from the text element:

```
email = Request.Form("search_email")%>
```

4. On the next line, add the following code to retrieve and display shopper information from the shopper table:

```
<%if return_shopper = "yes" and (len(trim(email)))<> 0 then
cmdTemp.CommandText = "SELECT * FROM FiveLakes_shopper _
WHERE email = '" & email & "'"

Set rsShopperFindSpec = _
Server.CreateObject("ADODB.Recordset")
rsShopperFindSpec.Open cmdTemp, , adOpenStatic, _
adLockReadOnly

if not rsShopperFindSpec.EOF then
    mscsOrderForm.shopper_id= mscsShopperID
    mscsOrderForm.ship_to_email=rsShopperFindSpec("email")
    mscsOrderForm.ship_to_name=rsShopperFindSpec("name")
    mscsOrderForm.ship_to_street=rsShopperFindSpec("street")
    mscsOrderForm.ship_to_city=rsShopperFindSpec("city")
    mscsOrderForm.ship_to_state=rsShopperFindSpec("state")
    mscsOrderForm.ship_to_country=rsShopperFindSpec("country")
    mscsOrderForm.ship_to_zip=rsShopperFindSpec("zip")
    mscsOrderForm.ship_to_phone=rsShopperFindSpec("phone")
end if

end if
%>
```

5. On the next line, add the following code to accept the e-mail address for a returning shopper and post the data to shipping.asp:

```
<FORM NAME = "SEARCH_EMAIL" METHOD="POST" ACTION = _
"<%= pageURL("shipping.asp")& _
"&return_shopper=yes&use_form=1" %>">

<TABLE BORDER="0" COLS="4" WIDTH="550">
<TR>
    <TD WIDTH="80"></TD>
    <TD ALIGN="CENTER" COLSPAN="3">
        <FONT SIZE="+1"><STRONG>Returning _
        Shoppers</STRONG></FONT>
    </TD>
</TR>
<TR>
    <TD ALIGN="RIGHT">
        <B>E-Mail:</B>
    </TD>
    <TD COLSPAN="3">
        <INPUT TYPE="text" NAME="search_email" SIZE="54,1">
    </TD>
</TR>

<TR>
    <TD ALIGN="RIGHT">
        <INPUT TYPE = "SUBMIT" VALUE = "Submit">
    </TD>
    <TD COLSPAN="3">
     
    </TD>
</TR>
</TABLE>
</FORM>
```

6. On the **File** menu, click **Save shipping.asp**, and then click **Close**.

Exercise 2: Modifying the Purchase Pipeline to Store Shopper Information

In this exercise, you will update and insert shopper information into the table by modifying the Purchase pipeline.

▶ **Create and modify the Purchase pipeline to update and insert shopper information into the table**

1. In the Windows NT Explorer window, open the config subfolder under the FiveLakes folder.

2. Make a copy of purchase.pcf and name it purchaseinsert.pcf.

3. Rename purchase.pcf as purchaseupdate.pcf.

4. Start Microsoft Internet Explorer and type in the URL address http://localhost/ FiveLakes/Manager.

5. On the Site Manager page, under **System,** select **purchaseupdate.pcf** from the drop-down list box, and then click **Edit Pipeline.**

Note Alternatively, you can edit the pipeline using the Win32 Pipeline Editor.

6. Scroll to **Stage3: Accept** and click the first **Insert component** link that appears within the stage.

7. On the Editing file: /FiveLakes/config/purchaseupdate.pcf page, click **SQLOrderADO.**

8. Scroll to **Stage3: Accept** and click the **Edit** link that appears under SQLOrderADO.

9. Add the following query in the **Query** text box to update shopper information in the FiveLakes_shopper table:

```
update FiveLakes_shopper set _
    name=?, street=?,city=?,state=?,country=?, _
    zip=?,phone=? where email=?
```

10. Add the following parameter list in the **Parameter** text box:

    ```
    order.ship_to_name        order.ship_to_street
    order.ship_to_city        order.ship_to_state
    order.ship_to_country     order.ship_to_zip
    order.ship_to_phone       order.ship_to_email
    ```

11. Click **Update,** and then click **Save** to save the changes made to the pipeline.

12. Click **Exit to Manager** to return to the Site Manager page.

13. On the Site Manager page, under System, select **purchaseinsert.pcf** from the list box, and then click **Edit Pipeline.**

14. Scroll to **Stage3: Accept** and click the first **Insert component** link that appears within the stage.

15. On the Editing file: /FiveLakes/config/purchaseinsert.pcf page, click **SQLOrderADO.**

16. Scroll to **Stage3: Accept** and click the **Edit** link that appears under SQLOrderADO.

17. Add the following query in the **Query** text box to insert shopper information in the FiveLakes_shopper table:

    ```
    insert into _
    FiveLakes_shopper(email,name,street,city,state, _
    country,zip,phone) values (?,?,?,?,?,?,?,?)
    ```

18. Add the following parameter list in the **Parameter** text box:

    ```
    order.ship_to_email       order.ship_to_name
    order.ship_to_street      order.ship_to_city
    order.ship_to_state       order.ship_to_country
    order.ship_to_zip         order.ship_to_phone
    ```

19. Click **Update,** and then click **Save** to save the changes made to the pipeline.

20. Click **Exit to Manager** to return to the Site Manager page.

▶ **Modify xt_orderform_prepare.asp to save the shopper's e-mail address**

1. In Microsoft Visual InterDev 6.0, open the FiveLakes project and then open xt_orderform_prepare.asp.

2. Locate the following lines of code:

```
orderForm.bill_to_phone = orderForm.ship_to_phone
    end if
```

3. On the next line, add the following code to store the e-mail address in the **OrderForm** object:

```
ship_to_email = mscsPage.RequestString("ship_to_email", _
null, 1, 100)
if IsNull(ship_to_email) then
    errorList.Add("Ship to email must be a string between _
    1 and 100 characters")
else
    orderForm.ship_to_email = ship_to_email
    orderForm.bill_to_email = orderForm.ship_to_email
end if
```

4. On the **File** menu, click **Save xt_orderform_prepare.asp**, and then click **Close**.

▶ **Modify xt_orderform_purchase.asp to execute the appropriate Purchase pipeline**

1. Edit xt_orderform_purchase.asp.

2. Locate the line **REM Run the transacted pipe** and delete the following code after it:

```
errorLevel=UtilRunTxPipe("purchase.pcf", _
mscsOrderForm,mscsPipeContext)
```

3. Add the following code to execute the appropriate pipeline after determining whether the shopper is new or a returning shopper:

```
cmdTemp.CommandText =
Replace(MSCSQueryMap.email_search.SQLCommand,":1", _
Replace(mscsOrderForm.ship_to_email, "'", "''"))
    Set rsEmail = Server.CreateObject("ADODB.Recordset")
    rsEmail.Open cmdTemp, , adOpenKeyset, adLockReadOnly
    if not rsEmail.EOF  then
errorLevel = UtilRunTxPipe("purchaseupdate.pcf", _
mscsOrderForm, mscsPipeContext)
    else
errorLevel = UtilRunTxPipe("purchaseinsert.pcf", _
mscsOrderForm, mscsPipeContext)
    end if
```

4. On the **File** menu, click **Save xt_orderform_purchase.asp**, and then click **Close**.

▶ **Register at the site**

1. Start Microsoft Internet Explorer and type in the URL **http://localhost/ FiveLakes** in the address bar of Internet Explorer.

2. Shop at the site and, on the Shipping page, click **Click here if you have problems with the wallet** to view the HTML form.

3. Type information in the HTML form as a new shopper and click **Total**.

4. Complete the shopping process.

▶ **View and modify information for a returning shopper**

1. Start Microsoft Internet Explorer and type in the URL **http://localhost/ FiveLakes** in the address bar of Internet Explorer.

2. Shop at the site and, on the Shipping page, click **Click here if you have problems with the wallet** to view the HTML form.

3. Enter an e-mail address in the text box provided for a returning shopper and click **Submit**.

4. View the shopper information for the returning shopper.

5. Modify the shopper address.

6. Complete the shopping process.

7. Return to the site to view the modified shopper information.

Note Making the above changes alters the behavior of the upsell code in product_alt.asp.

▶ **To restore the upsell functionality**

1. Open product_alt.asp.

2. Locate the following line of code:

```
<FORM METHOD=POST ACTION="<%= _
pageSURL("xt_orderform_edititem.asp") _
%>index=<%=index%>">
```

3. Add an ampersand (&) after %> and before index as follows:

```
<FORM METHOD=POST ACTION="<%= _
pageSURL("xt_orderform_edititem.asp") %> & _
index=<%=index%>">
```

Review

The review questions cover some of the key concepts taught in the chapter.

1. What is the advantage of registering shoppers on your site?

2. What are the three models of shopper registration supported by the Site Builder Wizard?

3. Which method do you use to set a cookie?

4. Explain the advantage of using a database table, instead of a cookie, to store shopper information.

Review Answers

1. If a registration table or cookies are implemented, shoppers need not type their name, address, and other information every time they shop. Shopper information is stored in a registration table or cookie and can be retrieved when the shopper returns.

2. None, On Ordering, and On Entry are the three models of shopper registration supported by the Site Builder Wizard.

3. The Response.Cookies method is used to set a cookie.

4. A database table is stored on the server and is therefore more secure than a cookie, which is stored on the client computer and can be accidentally deleted. Also, a shopper's Web browser may not always support cookies.

Chapter 9:
Introducing Business-to-Business Commerce

Objectives

After completing this chapter, you will be able to:

◆ Explain business-to-business commerce.

◆ Implement business partner functionality in your site.

Business-to-Business Commerce

This section includes the following topics:

◆ Overview of Business-to-Business Commerce

◆ A Business-to-Business Scenario

Overview of Business-to-Business Commerce

Business-to-business commerce includes online wholesaling, in which businesses sell goods and services to other businesses over the Web. Enabling businesses to exchange information electronically is critical to the success of a business-to-business commerce site. The Commerce Interchange Pipeline (CIP) enables businesses of all sizes to exchange information electronically.

You can use the CIP to securely transmit business data objects between business partners. A business data object is defined as a data container for business information such as:

◆ Purchase orders

◆ Purchase order receipts

- ◆ Sale notices
- ◆ Invoices
- ◆ Billing records

Creating a Commerce Interchange Pipeline

A CIP is created in the same way that an OPP is created.

A business-to-business scenario often involves two CIPs running on separate servers. One pipeline packages information and transmits it over the network and the second pipeline reads the information from the network.

Commerce Server is a platform that facilitates the development of Web-based commerce sites for business-to-business transactions.

A Business-to-Business Scenario

The implementation of the business-to-business commerce on the Five Lakes Publishing sample site is as follows:

Five Lakes Publishing advertises its Web site through other popular sites. The incentive for the owners of other Web sites to advertise the Five Lakes Publishing site is a commission on every sale referred through their sites. These Web-site owners are called business partners, or ePartners. Every ePartner is given a unique ID. In addition, every order has an ePartner ID associated with it. This enables Five Lakes Publishing to compute commissions for its trading partners.

Business Partner Functionality

This section contains the following topics:

- ◆ Storing ePartner Information
- ◆ Verifying an ePartner
- ◆ Associating ePartner ID with an Order
- ◆ Displaying Orders Received through ePartners

Storing ePartner Information

To implement business partner functionality, the sample site includes the following elements:

◆ A table in the site database to store ePartner information.

◆ An epartner_ID attribute in the receipt table to associate every order with an ePartner.

◆ A query description in global.asa to retrieve ePartner information.

◆ An .asp file to retrieve epartner_ID from the URL and verify its existence in the ePartner table.

◆ An .asp file to display orders received through ePartners.

Five Lakes Publishing maintains a table with the following attributes to store information about its ePartners:

◆ epartner_ID

◆ name

◆ site_address

Verifying an ePartner

When a shopper enters the Five Lakes Publishing sample site from an ePartner's site, the ePartner ID is passed through the URL into the sample site. This ePartner must have a valid entry in the FiveLakes_epartner table. In other words, the ePartner information must exist in the ePartner table of the sample site or the referring site will not be credited.

In the Five Lakes Publishing sample site, the script in i_epartner.asp retrieves the epartner_ID from the URL and checks for the existence of a business partner in the FiveLakes_epartner table. The i_epartner.asp file is included in every page a shopper might visit.

In the sample site:

◆ The global.asa file contains a query to retrieve ePartner information from the FiveLakes_epartner table as follows:

```
Set MSCSQueryMap.epartner = AddQuery(" _
    SELECT epartner_ID _
    FROM FiveLakes_epartner _
    WHERE epartner_id = ':1'")
```

◆ The i_epartner.asp file contains a script to verify the existence of an ePartner as follows:

```
epartner_id=0
epartner_id=Request.QueryString("epartner_id")
if epartner_id=0 then
    epartner_id=1
else
    cmdTemp.CommandText =_
    Replace(MSCSQueryMap.epartner.SQLCommand,":1", _
    epartner_id)
    Set rsepartner = _
    Server.CreateObject("ADODB.Recordset")
    rsepartner.Open cmdTemp, , adOpenForwardOnly, _
    adLockReadOnly
    if rsepartner.EOF then
        epartner_id=1
    end if
end if %>
```

Associating ePartner ID with an Order

Every order is stored along with the ePartner ID in the FiveLakes_receipt table. This helps the site to compute the commission for an ePartner based on the number of orders and the total order value.

Orders that are not received through an ePartner are assigned the epartner_ID value of 1 in the FiveLakes_receipt table.

In the Five Lakes Publishing sample site:

◆ The FiveLakes_receipt table contains an attribute epartner_ID.

◆ The xt_orderform_prepare.asp file contains a script to store the epartner_ID in the OrderForm object as follows:

```
orderform.epartner_id=request.QueryString("epartner_id")
```

◆ The SaveReceipt component in the Accept stage of the Purchase pipeline stores the OrderForm values in the FiveLakes_receipt table.

Displaying Orders Received through ePartners

The Five Lakes Publishing sample site enables site operators and site administrators to view orders received through ePartners. The site contains an **Orders by ePartner** report that can be viewed from the Site Manager page. This report displays the following information for every order in the FiveLakes_receipt table:

◆ ePartner ID

◆ Order ID

◆ Order Date

◆ Number of items

◆ Order total

In the sample site, the order_epartner.asp file contains the script to retrieve and display order information from the FiveLakes_receipt table.

For the complete code of order_epartner.asp, see Appendix A.

Lab 9: Implementing Business Partner Functionality (Optional)

Objectives

After completing this lab, you will be able to:

- ◆ Create a database table to store the ePartner information.
- ◆ Create an .asp file to validate the ePartner ID passed in the URL.
- ◆ Create an .asp file to display orders received through ePartners.

Before You Begin

Prerequisites

Before you begin this lab, you must have the following prerequisites:

- ◆ Familiarity with Microsoft Internet Explorer and Microsoft Visual InterDev 6.0.
- ◆ Knowledge of HTML and ASP programming.

Estimated time to complete this lab: 45 minutes

Exercise 1: Adding ePartner Information to the Table

In this exercise, you will store ePartner information in the epartner table.

> **Note** The epartner table already exists.

▶ **Insert ePartner information in FiveLakes_epartner table**

1. Add the following query to insert a row for your site by using SQL Server Query Analyzer:

```
insert into FiveLakes_epartner (epartner_id, _
name, site_address) values ("1", "FiveLakes", _
"http://localhost/FiveLakes")
```

2. Repeat step 1 to insert a row for an ePartner:

```
insert into FiveLakes_epartner (epartner_id, name, _
site_address) values ("2", "Hanson Brothers", _
"http://HansonBrothers.com")
```

Exercise 2: Verifying an ePartner

In this exercise, you will create an .asp file to retrieve ePartner ID from the URL and query the FiveLakes_epartner table to check the existence of the ePartner.

▶ **Define a query in global.asa**

1. In Microsoft Visual InterDev 6.0, open the FiveLakes project, and then open global.asa.

2. In the **InitQueryMap** function, add a query to retrieve information for a specific business partner as follows:

```
set MSCSQueryMap.epartner = AddQuery _
("SELECT epartner_id, name, site_address _
 FROM FiveLakes_epartner _
 WHERE ePartner_id = ':1'")
```

3. On the **File** menu, click **Save global.asa**, and then click **Close**.

▶ **Create a new .asp file in the site directory**

1. In the Project Explorer-localhost/FiveLakes window, right-click **localhost/ FiveLakes**.

2. On the **localhost/FiveLakes** submenu option, point to **Add**, click **Active Server Page**, and then click **Open**.

3. Delete all the code from the new .asp file that is generated automatically by Visual InterDev.

4. Double-click **ASP Page1.asp** in the Project Explorer window. Then, on the **File** menu, click **Save ASP Page1.asp As** to save the file as i_ePartner.asp.

▶ **Verify existence of the ePartner in the site database**

1. Double-click i_ePartner.asp in the Project Explorer window.

2. Select and delete all of the content of i_ePartner.asp that Visual InterDev added.

3. On the first line, add the following code to retrieve epartner_id from the URL:

```
<%
epartner_id=0
epartner_id=request.QueryString("epartner_id")
```

4. Next, add the following code to verify the existence of the ePartner in FiveLakes epartner table:

```
if epartner_id=0 then
epartner_id=1

else
    cmdTemp.CommandText=Replace _
    (MSCSQueryMap.epartner.SQLCommand,":1", epartner_id)
    set rsepartner = Server.CreateObject("ADODB.Recordset")
    rsepartner.Open cmdTemp, , adOpenForwardOnly, _
    adLockReadOnly
    if rsepartner.EOF then
        epartner_id=1
    end if
end if %>
```

5. On the **File** menu, click **Save i_ePartner.asp**, and then click **Close**.

▶ **Store ePartner ID in the URL**

1. Include the i_ePartner.asp in every page through which a shopper can enter the site as follows:

```
<!-#INCLUDE FILE="i_ePartner.asp" ->
```

This line should be added after the `<!-#INCLUDE FILE="i_shop.asp" ->` statement.

2. Modify the code in every .asp file that generates a URL to include ePartner ID in the given form:

```
epartner_id = <ePartner ID>
```

> **Note** This is an advanced lab. This step requires advanced programming skills.

For example, in the product.asp file, the code to generate the URL using the **pageSURL** function will be:

```
<form METHOD="POST" ACTION="<%= _
pageSURL("xt_orderform_additem.asp")& "&epartner_id=" _
&epartner_id %>">
```

In the default.asp file, the code to generate the URL using the **baseURL** function will be:

```
<LI><A HREF="<%= baseURL("dept.asp") & _
mscsPage.URLShopperArgs("dept_id", _
dept_idField.value, "epartner_id", _
epartner_id) %>"><%= dept_nameField.value %></A>
```

3. Open the i_selector.asp file.

4. In the MSWltLastChanceText(strDownlevelURL) function, modify the code to pass the epartner_id in the URL as follows:

```
function MSWltLastChanceText(strDownlevelURL)
if fMSWltUplevelBrowser And (fMSWltAddressSelector Or _
   fMSWltPaymentSelector) then
   MSWltLastChanceText = "<A HREF=""" & _
   MSWltDownlevelURL(strDownlevelURL) & _
   "&epartner_id="&epartner_id & _
   """>Click here if you have problems with the _
   Wallet</A> "
end if
end function
```

5. Save and close the .asp files.

Exercise 3: Associating ePartner ID with an Order

In this exercise, you will modify xt_orderform_prepare.asp to store ePartner ID in the **OrderForm** object.

▶ **Modify xt_orderform_prepare.asp to store ePartner ID in the OrderForm object**

1. Edit the xt_orderform_prepare.asp file.

2. In the **OrderFormPrepareArgs** function, on the first line, add code to retrieve epartner_id from the URL and store it in the **OrderForm** object as follows:

```
orderform.epartner_id=request.QueryString("epartner_id")
```

Exercise 4: Displaying Orders Received through ePartners

In this exercise, you will create an .asp file to retrieve and display orders received through ePartners.

▶ **Create a new .asp file in the site directory**

1. In the Project Explorer-localhost/FiveLakes window, right-click **localhost/ FiveLakes**.

2. On the **localhost/FiveLakes** submenu option, point to **Add**, click **Active Server Page**, and then click **Open**.

3. Double-click **ASP Page1.asp** in the Project Explorer window. Then, on the **File** menu, click **Save ASP Page1.asp As** to save the file as order_ePartner.asp in the Manager folder.

▶ **Add code to retrieve and display order information from the FiveLakes_receipt table**

1. Double-click **order_ePartner.asp** in the Project Explorer window.

2. On the first line, modify the code to specify the Locale ID as **1033** and session state as **false** as follows:

```
<%@ LANGUAGE=vbscript enablesessionstate=false LCID=1033 %>
```

3. On the next line, include the manager.asp file that contains definitions of the ADO connection and command object, and functions for reading the manager dictionary.

```
<!-#INCLUDE FILE="include/Manager.asp" ->
```

4. On the next line, add code to assign a title for the report as follows:

```
<% pageTitle = "Orders By ePartner" %>
```

5. Within the Head tags, add code to display the report title and include mgmt_define.asp as follows:

```
<head>
    <title> <% = pageTitle %> </title>

    <!-#INCLUDE FILE="include/mgmt_define.asp" ->
</head>
```

6. After the <body> tag, add code to include mgmt_header.asp as follows:

```
<!-#INCLUDE FILE="include/mgmt_header.asp" ->
```

7. Next, add the following code to create and initialize a **DBStorage** object:

```
<% set  mscsReceiptStorage= _
    Server.CreateObject("Commerce.DBStorage")
On Error Resume Next

call mscsReceiptStorage.InitStorage _
    (mscsManagerSite.DefaultConnectionString _
    "FiveLakes_receipt", "order_id", _
    "Commerce.OrderForm", "marshalled_receipt", _
    "date_entered")
if Err.Number <> 0 then
    Set errorList = _
    Server.CreateObject("Commerce.SimpleList")
    errorList.Add "The table could not be found or the _
    database connection failed."
%>
    <!-#INCLUDE FILE="include/error.asp" ->
    <!-#INCLUDE FILE="include/mgmt_footer.asp" ->
<%
    Response.end
else
    mscsReceiptStorage.Mapping.Value("_total_total") = _
    "total"
end if
%>
```

8. Next, add the following code to retrieve order information from the **DBStorage** object and create HTML table elements to display ePartner ID, order ID, order date, shopper ID, number of items, and order value:

```
<%  function ShowRow()
on error resume next
set receipt = mscsReceiptStorage.GetData(null, _
CStr(rsList("order_id")))
on error goto 0
if IsEmpty(receipt) then
    nitems = 0
else
    set items = receipt.items
    nitems = items.Count
end if %>

<td ALIGN="CENTER"> <% = RowCount %> </td>
<td ALIGN="CENTER"> <% = rsList("epartner_id").value %>  </td>
<td ALIGN="LEFT"> <a HREF="<% = listElemTemplate & "?" _
    & mscsPage.URLArgs("order_id", _
    rsList("order_id").value) %>"> <% = _
    rsList("order_id").value %></a>
</td>
<td VALIGN="TOP" ALIGN="LEFT"> <% = _
    MSCSDataFunctions.Date(rsList("date_entered") _
    .value) %>
</td>

<td VALIGN="TOP" ALIGN="CENTER"> <% = nitems %> </td>
<td VALIGN="TOP" ALIGN="RIGHT"> <% = _
MSCSDataFunctions.Money(rsList("total").value) _
    %> </td>
<%  end function %>
```

9. Next, add the following code to store the format for displaying column headings in a variable:

```
<%
listElemTemplate = "order_view.asp"
listColumns = "<TH ALIGN=""LEFT""> # </TH>" & vbCr & _
    "<TH ALIGN=""LEFT""> ePartner ID </TH>" & vbCr & _
    "<TH ALIGN=""LEFT""> Order ID </TH>" & vbCr & _
    "<TH ALIGN=""LEFT""> Date </TH>" & vbCr & _
    "<TH ALIGN=""LEFT""> # Items </TH>" & vbCr & _
    "<TH ALIGN=""LEFT""> Total </TH>" & vbCr
listNoRows = "<I>No orders in table</I>"
%>
```

10. Next, add the following code to define the SQL query to retrieve order information from the receipt table. The list.asp file contains the code to create and open a recordset with the specified query.

```
<%
cmdTemp.CommandText = "SELECT order_id,epartner_id, _
shopper_id, date_entered, total, status _
FROM Fivelakes_receipt ORDER BY epartner_id"
%>
<!--#INCLUDE FILE="include/list.asp" -->

<!--#INCLUDE FILE="include/mgmt_footer.asp" -->
```

11. On the **File** menu, click **Save order_ePartner.asp,** and then click **Close.**

▶ **Modify order.asp to include a link to order_ePartner.asp**

1. Edit the order.asp file.

2. Scroll to the line **REM body:** and add the following code after it:

```
<Li> <a HREF="order_ePartner.asp"> Orders by ePartner </a>
```

3. On the **File** menu, click **Save order.asp,** and then click **Close.**

▶ **Connect to the site with an ePartner ID**

1. Start Microsoft Internet Explorer and type **http://localhost/FiveLakes/ default.asp?epartner_id=2** in the address bar of Internet Explorer.

2. Shop at the site for at least one product and complete the shopping process.

▶ **View the orders received through ePartners**

1. Start Microsoft Internet Explorer and type **http://localhost/FiveLakes/Manager** in the address bar of Internet Explorer.

2. On the Site Manager page, click **Orders**.

3. On the Order Manager page, click **Orders by ePartner** to view the order received through the ePartner.

4. For the complete code of i_ePartner.asp and order_ePartner.asp files created in the Five Lakes Publishing sample site, see Appendix A.

Review

The review questions cover some of the key concepts taught in the chapter.

1. What is business-to-business commerce?

2. What is Commerce Interchange Pipeline?

3. How can you view the orders received through ePartners?

Review Answers

1. Business-to-business commerce includes online wholesaling, in which businesses sell goods and services to other businesses on the Web.

2. Commerce Interchange Pipeline is used to securely transmit business data objects between business partners.

3. The orders received through ePartners can be viewed from the Site Manager page.

Appendix A:
Lab and Practice Solution Files

This appendix contains printed versions of all the files that students work with during the course, as well as number of other important files in the sample site.

These files are presented just as the Commerce Server wizards created them, without making changes to enhance readability.

All of these files were taken from the Solution folder for Chapter 9.

Table of Contents

basket.asp

```
<%@ LANGUAGE=vbscript enablesessionstate=false LCID=1033 %>

<% Response.ExpiresAbsolute=DateAdd("yyyy", -10, Date) %>

<!--#INCLUDE FILE="i_shop.asp" -->
<!--#INCLUDE FILE="i_ePartner.asp" -->
<!--#INCLUDE FILE="i_util.asp" -->

<%
REM Run the basic plan
Set mscsOrderForm = UtilRunPlan()

Set orderFormItems = mscsOrderForm.Items
nOrderFormItems = orderFormItems.Count

Set mscsBasketErrors = mscsOrderForm.[_Basket_Errors]
nBasketErrors = mscsBasketErrors.Count
%>


<HTML>

<HEAD>
    <TITLE><%= displayName %>: Basket</TITLE>
    <META HTTP-EQUIV="Content-Type" CONTENT="text/html;
charset=ISO-8859-1">
</HEAD>

<BODY
    BGCOLOR="#FFFFFF"
    TEXT=   "#000000"
    LINK=   "#FF0000"
    VLINK=  "#FF0000"
    ALINK=  "#FF0000"
>

<!-#INCLUDE FILE="i_header.asp" ->

<H1>Shopping Basket</H1>

<% if Request("error").Count <> 0 then %>
<TABLE WIDTH="500">
```

code continued on next page

code continued from previous page

```
    <TR><TD><FONT COLOR="#FF0000"><STRONG>Quantity must be a number
less than 1000.</STRONG></FONT></TD></TR>
</TABLE>
<P>
 
<P>
<% end if %>
<% if nOrderFormItems = 0 then %>

    <BLOCKQUOTE>
        <STRONG>Your basket is empty.</STRONG>
    </BLOCKQUOTE>

<% else %>
    <% if nBasketErrors > 0 then %>
    <TABLE WIDTH="500">
        <% for iError = 0 to nBasketErrors - 1 %>
        <TR><TD><FONT COLOR="#FF0000"><STRONG><%=
mscsPage.HTMLEncode(mscsBasketErrors(iError))
%></STRONG></FONT></TD></TR>
        <% next %>
    </TABLE>
    <P>
     
    <P>
    <% end if %>

    <% if nOrderFormItems > 1 then %>
        You have <%= nOrderFormItems %> items in your shopping
basket:
    <% else %>
        You have <%= nOrderFormItems %> item in your shopping
basket:
    <% end if %>

    <P>
    To change an item's quantity, edit the number and press "Update
Basket".
    <P>

    <TABLE>
        <TR>
        <FORM METHOD="POST" ACTION="<%=
pageSURL("shipping.asp")& "&epartner_id=" &
epartner_id %>">
```

code continued on next page

code continued from previous page

```
        <TD>

        <INPUT TYPE="Image"
                VALUE="Purchase"
                SRC="<%= "/" & siteRoot
%>/manager/MSCS_Images/buttons/btnpurchase1.gif"
                WIDTH="116"
                HEIGHT="25"
                BORDER="0"
                ALT="Purchase">

        </TD>
        </FORM>

        <FORM METHOD="POST" ACTION="<%=
pageSURL("xt_orderform_clearitems.asp")& "&epartner_id=" &
epartner_id %>">
        <TD>

        <INPUT TYPE="Image"
                VALUE="Clear Order"
                SRC="<%= "/" & siteRoot
%>/manager/MSCS_Images/buttons/btnempty1.gif"
                WIDTH="116"
                HEIGHT="25"
                BORDER="0"
                ALT="Clear Basket">

        </TD>
        </FORM>

        <FORM METHOD="POST" ACTION="<%=
pageSURL("xt_orderform_editquantities.asp")& "&epartner_id=" &
epartner_id %>">
        <TD>
        <INPUT TYPE="Image"
                VALUE="Update Order"
                SRC="<%= "/" & siteRoot
%>/manager/MSCS_Images/buttons/btnupdatebskt1.gif"
                WIDTH="116"
                HEIGHT="25"
                BORDER="0"
                ALT="Update Basket">

        </TD>
```

code continued on next page

code continued from previous page

```
            </TR>
        </TABLE>

        <TABLE
            BORDER=      "0"
            CELLPADDING="2"
            CELLSPACING="2"
        >
            <TR>
                <TH BGCOLOR="#000000" ALIGN=LEFT>
                    <FONT COLOR="#FFFFFF">Label</FONT>
                </TH>
                <TH BGCOLOR="#000000" ALIGN=LEFT>
                    <FONT COLOR="#FFFFFF">Name</FONT>
                </TH>

                <TH BGCOLOR="#000000" ALIGN=CENTER>
                    <FONT COLOR="#FFFFFF">Unit Price</FONT>
                </TH>
                <TH BGCOLOR="#000000" ALIGN=CENTER>
                    <FONT COLOR="#FFFFFF">Today's Price</FONT>
                </TH>
                <TH BGCOLOR="#000000" ALIGN=LEFT>
                    <FONT COLOR="#FFFFFF">Qty</FONT>
                </TH>

                <TH BGCOLOR="#000000" ALIGN=CENTER>
                    <FONT COLOR="#FFFFFF">Extra Disc.</FONT>
                </TH>

                <TH BGCOLOR="#000000" ALIGN=CENTER>
                    <FONT COLOR="#FFFFFF">Total Price</FONT>
                </TH>
                <TH></TH>
            </TR>
            <% for iLineItem = 0 to nOrderFormItems - 1 %>
                <% set lineItem = orderFormItems(iLineItem) %>
                <TR>
                    <TD VALIGN="TOP">
                        <%= mscsPage.HTMLEncode(lineItem.sku) %>
                    </TD>
                    <TD VALIGN="TOP">
                        <%=
mscsPage.HTMLEncode(lineItem.[_product_name]) %>
                    </TD>
```

code continued on next page

code continued from previous page

```
                        <TD VALIGN="TOP" ALIGN="RIGHT">
                            <%=
MSCSDataFunctions.Money(lineItem.[_product_list_price]) %>
                        </TD>
                        <TD VALIGN="TOP" ALIGN="RIGHT">
                            <% =
MSCSDataFunctions.Money(lineItem.[_iadjust_currentprice]) %>
                        </TD>
                         <TD VALIGN="TOP">
                            <INPUT TYPE="Text"
                                    NAME="<%=
mscsPage.HTMLEncode("qty_" & iLineItem) %>"
                                    SIZE=3,1
                                    VALUE="<%= lineItem.quantity %>">
                        </TD>

                        <TD WIDTH="60" VALIGN="TOP" ALIGN="RIGHT">
                            <% =
MSCSDataFunctions.Money(lineItem.[_oadjust_discount]) %>
                        </TD>

                        <TD VALIGN="TOP" ALIGN="RIGHT">
                            <%=
MSCSDataFunctions.Money(lineItem.[_oadjust_adjustedprice]) %>
                        </TD>
                        <TD VALIGN="TOP">
                            <A HREF="<%=
baseSURL("xt_orderform_delitem.asp") & "&epartner_id=" &
epartner_id & "&" & mscsPage.URLShopperArgs("index",
iLineItem) %>">
                                <IMG SRC="<%= "/" & siteRoot
%>/manager/MSCS_Images/buttons/btnremove1.gif" BORDER="0"
ALT="Delete item">
                            </A>
                        </TD>
                    </TR>


        <%REM -- Create Recordset, execute Query

cmdTemp.CommandText=Replace(MSCSQueryMap.related_products_upsell.
SQLCommand,":1",Replace(lineitem.sku,"'","''"))
        set rsUpsell=Server.CreateObject("ADODB.Recordset")
        rsUpsell.Open cmdTemp, , adOpenKeyset,
adLockReadOnly
```

code continued on next page

code continued from previous page

```
            if rsUpsell.recordcount >0 then
                while not rsUpsell.EOF
                    set checkitem=mscsOrderForm.items
                    inbasket=0
                    for each row_checkitem in checkitem
                        if
row_checkitem.sku=rsUpsell("Upsell_sku").value  then
                            inbasket=1
                        end if
                    next

                    if Cbool(inbasket=0) then %>
                    <tr>
                        <td colspan="1">  </td>
                        <td colspan="5">
                    <a
HREF="<%=mscsPage.URL("product_alt.asp","sku",rsUpsell("Upsell_sku").
value,"index",ilineitem,"quantity",lineItem.quantity,"dept_id",lineItem.
[_product_dept_id])%>"><font face="Arial" size="2"COLOR="#FF0000">
***<%=rsUpsell("description")%>***</font></a>
                        </td>
                    </tr>


                    <%end if
                    rsUpsell.MoveNext
                Wend
            end if %>

        <% next %>

        <% REM show subtotal:  %>
        <TR>



                <TH BGCOLOR="#000000" COLSPAN="6" ALIGN="RIGHT">
                    <FONT COLOR="#FFFFFF">Subtotal:</FONT>
                </TH>
                <TD ALIGN="RIGHT"> <%=
MSCSDataFunctions.Money(mscsOrderForm.[_oadjust_subtotal]) %>
</TD>
            </TR>
        </FORM>
        </TABLE>
```

code continued on next page

code continued from previous page

```
<% end if %>

<P>

<!-#INCLUDE FILE="i_footer.asp" ->

</BODY>

</HTML>
```

confirmed.asp

```
<%@ LANGUAGE=vbscript enablesessionstate=false LCID=1033 %>

<!--#INCLUDE FILE="i_shop.asp" -->
<!--#INCLUDE FILE="i_ePartner.asp" -->
<!--#INCLUDE FILE="i_ePartner.asp" -->
<HTML>

<HEAD>
    <TITLE><%= displayName %>: Purchase Confirmation</TITLE>
    <META HTTP-EQUIV="Content-Type" CONTENT="text/html;
charset=ISO-8859-1">
</HEAD>

<BODY
    BGCOLOR="#FFFFFF"
    TEXT=   "#000000"
    LINK=   "#FF0000"
    VLINK=  "#FF0000"
    ALINK=  "#FF0000"
>

<!--#INCLUDE FILE="i_header.asp" -->

<H1>Purchase Confirmation</H1>

<P>
Your order number is
<% order_id = mscsPage.HTMLEncode(Request("order_id")) %>

    <A HREF="<% = baseURL("receipt.asp") &
mscsPage.URLShopperArgs("order_id",
```

code continued on next page

code continued from previous page

```
Request("order_id"),"epartner_id=", epartner_id) %>">
<STRONG><% = order_id %></STRONG></A>.



Please record it for referencing your order.

<P>
Thank you for your shopping at <%= displayName %>.

<P>
If you want to continue shopping, simply return to the <A
HREF="<%= pageURL("default.asp") & "&epartner_id=" &
epartner_id %>">lobby</A>.

<!-#INCLUDE FILE="i_footer.asp" ->

</BODY>

</HTML>
```

Default.asp

```
<%@ LANGUAGE=vbscript enablesessionstate=false LCID=1033 %>

<!--#INCLUDE FILE="i_shop.asp" -->
<!--#INCLUDE FILE="i_ePartner.asp" -->
<HTML>

<HEAD>
    <TITLE><%= displayName %>: Lobby</TITLE>
    <META HTTP-EQUIV="Content-Type" CONTENT="text/html;
charset=ISO-8859-1">
</HEAD>

<BODY
    BGCOLOR="#FFFFFF"
    TEXT=    "#000000"
    LINK=    "#FF0000"
    VLINK=   "#FF0000"
    ALINK=   "#FF0000"
>
```

code continued on next page

code continued from previous page

```asp
<!--#INCLUDE FILE="i_header.asp" -->

<H1><%= displayName %></H1>

<P>
Welcome to our shop. We have a broad range of products you can
choose from.

<%

sqlText = MSCSQueryMap.depts.SQLCommand

Set rsDepts = MSCS.Execute (sqlText, nDepts, adCmdText)

if rsDepts.EOF then
    %>
    <P>
    There are currently no departments available.
<% else %>
    <P>
    Select a department below:

    <UL>
    <%
      set dept_idField = rsDepts("dept_id")
      set dept_nameField = rsDepts("dept_name")
    do while Not rsDepts.EOF
        %>
        <LI><A HREF="<%= baseURL("dept.asp") &
mscsPage.URLShopperArgs("dept_id", dept_idField.value,
"epartner_id", epartner_id )%>"><%= dept_nameField.value
%></A>
        <% rsDepts.MoveNext
    loop
    rsDepts.Close
    MSCS.Close

    %>
    </UL>
<% end if %>


<BR>
```

code continued on next page

code.continued from previous page

```
You can see your order history on the <A HREF="<%=
pageURL("receipts.asp") & "&epartner_id="
&epartner_id%>">Order History Page</A>.
<p>
You can see your order status on the <A
HREF="<%=pageURL("ordertrack.asp") & "&epartner_id="
&epartner_id%>">Track Your Order Page</A>

<!-#INCLUDE FILE="i_footer.asp" ->

</BODY>

</HTML>
```

dept.asp

```
<%@ LANGUAGE=vbscript enablesessionstate=false LCID=1033 %>

<!--#INCLUDE FILE="i_shop.asp" -->
<!--#INCLUDE FILE="i_ePartner.asp" -->
<%
dept_id = mscsPage.RequestNumber("dept_id","0")
sqlText = Replace(MSCSQueryMap.dept_by_id.SQLCommand,":1",
dept_id)
Set rsDept = MSCS.Execute (sqlText, nDepts, adCmdText)

if rsDept.EOF then
    dept_exists = false
    dept_name = "Unknown Department"
else
    dept_exists = true

    REM - get fields:
    dept_name = rsDept("dept_name").value
    dept_description = rsDept("dept_description").value

    REM - Log department for UA
    Response.AppendToLog "&" &
mscsPage.URLArgs("MSS.Request.Category Name", dept_name)
end if
rsDept.Close
%>
```

code continued on next page

code continued from previous page

```
<HTML>

<HEAD>
    <TITLE><%= displayName %>: Department: '<%=
mscsPage.HTMLEncode(dept_name) %>'</TITLE>
    <META HTTP-EQUIV="Content-Type" CONTENT="text/html;
charset=ISO-8859-1">
</HEAD>

<BODY
    BGCOLOR="#FFFFFF"
    TEXT=    "#000000"
    LINK=    "#FF0000"
    VLINK=   "#FF0000"
    ALINK=   "#FF0000"
>
<%

    if dept_exists then
        cmdTemp.CommandText =
Replace(MSCSQueryMap.products_by_dept.SQLCommand,":1",dept_id)
        Set rsProducts =
Server.CreateObject("ADODB.Recordset")
        rsProducts.Open cmdTemp, , adOpenStatic,
adLockReadOnly

        if rsProducts.EOF then
            products_exist = false
        else
            products_exist = true
        end if
    end if

%>

<!--#INCLUDE FILE="i_header.asp" -->

<%
    if not dept_exists then %>
        <P>The department you requested is currently not available.
    <% else %>
        <H1><%= mscsPage.HTMLEncode(dept_name) %></H1>

        <P>
        <%= mscsPage.HTMLEncode(dept_description) %>
```

code continued on next page

code continued from previous page

```
        <P>

    <% if products_exist then %>
        Select a product from the list below:

        <UL>
            <%
              set skuField = rsProducts("sku")
              set nameField = rsProducts("name")
              do while Not rsProducts.EOF
              %>
            <LI><A HREF="<%= baseURL("product.asp") &
mscsPage.URLShopperArgs("dept_id" , dept_id, "sku",
skuField.value)& "&epartner_id=" & epartner_id %>"><%=
mscsPage.HTMLEncode(nameField.value) %></A>
              <% rsProducts.MoveNext
            loop
              rsProducts.Close
            %>
        </UL>
    <% else %>
        <FONT SIZE="2">No products at this time.</FONT>
    <% end if %>

<% end if %>

<!--#INCLUDE FILE="i_footer.asp" -->

</BODY>

</HTML>
```

find.asp

```
<%@ LANGUAGE=vbscript enablesessionstate=false LCID=1033 %>

<!--#INCLUDE FILE="i_shop.asp" -->
<!--#INCLUDE FILE="i_ePartner.asp" -->
<HTML>

<HEAD>
    <TITLE><%= displayName %>: Find</TITLE>
```

code continued on next page

code continued from previous page

```
      <META HTTP-EQUIV="Content-Type" CONTENT="text/html;
charset=ISO-8859-1">
</HEAD>

<BODY
    BGCOLOR="#FFFFFF"
    TEXT=    "#000000"
    LINK=    "#FF0000"
    VLINK=   "#FF0000"
    ALINK=   "#FF0000"
>

<!--#INCLUDE FILE="i_header.asp" -->

<H1>Find</H1>

<P>
<FORM NAME="find_spec" METHOD="POST" ACTION="<%=
pageURL("find.asp")& "&epartner_id=" &epartner_id %>">
    Find:
    <%
    search_by = trim(mscsPage.RequestString("sselect"))
    strFindSpec = mscsPage.RequestString("find_spec")
    %>
    <td width="125%" colspan="2"><select name="sselect"
size="1" tabindex="20">
       <%= mscsPage.Option("Keyword", search_by) %>Keyword
       <%= mscsPage.Option("Category", search_by) %>Category
      </select></td>
    <INPUT TYPE="TEXT" NAME="find_spec" SIZE="32"
MAXLENGTH="200" VALUE="<%= mscsPage.HTMLEncode(strFindSpec)
%>">
    <INPUT TYPE="SUBMIT" VALUE="Find">
</FORM>


<%
if Request("find_spec").Count = 0 then
    hasFindSpec = false
    strFindSpec = ""
    nProductsFindSpec = 0
else
    hasFindSpec = true
    strFindSpec = mscsPage.RequestString("find_spec")
```

code continued on next page

code continued from previous page

```
      REM - escape wildcard characters and quote: ', _, %
      if IsNull(strFindSpec) then
          strFindSpec = ""
          nProductsFindSpec = 0
      else
          safeFindSpec =
Replace(Replace(Replace(strFindSpec,"'","''"),"_","[_]"),"%",
"[%]")

          if search_by = "Keyword" then
            sqlText=MSCSQueryMap.find_by_keyword.SQLCommand
          elseif search_by = "Category" then
              sqlText=MSCSQueryMap.find_by_category.SQLCommand

          end if
          sqlText=Replace(sqlText,":1",safeFindSpec)
          cmdTemp.CommandText = sqlText

          Set rsProductsFindSpec =
Server.CreateObject("ADODB.Recordset")
          rsProductsFindSpec.Open cmdTemp, , adOpenStatic,
adLockReadOnly
          nProductsFindSpec = 0
          Do While Not rsProductsFindSpec.EOF
              nProductsFindSpec = nProductsFindSpec + 1
              rsProductsFindSpec.MoveNext
          Loop
          if Not rsProductsFindSpec.BOF then
rsProductsFindSpec.MoveFirst
      end if
end if

if hasFindSpec then %>
    <P>
    <% if strFindSpec = "" then %>
        You must enter a find string before clicking Find.
    <% elseif nProductsFindSpec = 0 then %>
        There are no products that contain "<%= strFindSpec %>".
    <% else %>
        <%if nProductsFindSpec = 1 then %>
            There is 1 product that contains "<%= strFindSpec %>":
        <% else %>
            There are <%= nProductsFindSpec %> products that
contain "<%= strFindSpec %>":
        <% end if %>
```

code continued on next page

code continued from previous page

```
<P>
<TABLE>

<%
set skuField = rsProductsFindSpec("sku")
set dept_idField = rsProductsFindSpec("dept_id")
set nameField = rsProductsFindSpec("name")
set list_priceField = rsProductsFindSpec("list_price")
do while Not rsProductsFindSpec.EOF
    %>
    <TR>
        <TD>
            <A HREF="<%= baseURL("product.asp") &
mscsPage.URLShopperArgs("sku", skuField.value, "dept_id",
dept_idField.value,"epartner_id=" epartner_id) %>">
                <%= mscsPage.HTMLEncode(skuField.value) %>
            </A>
        </TD>
        <TD>
            <A HREF="<%= baseURL("product.asp") &
mscsPage.URLShopperArgs("sku", skuField.value, "dept_id",
dept_idField.value,"epartner_id=" epartner_id) %>">
                <%= mscsPage.HTMLEncode(nameField.value) %>
            </A>
        </TD>
        <TD>
            <%=
MSCSDataFunctions.Money(list_priceField.value) %>
        </TD>
    </TR>
    <%
    rsProductsFindSpec.MoveNext
loop
%>
</TABLE>
<% end if %>
<% end if %>

<!--#INCLUDE FILE="i_footer.asp" -->

</BODY>

</HTML>
```

global.asa

```
<OBJECT RUNAT=Server SCOPE=Application ID=MSCSSite
PROGID="Commerce.Dictionary"></OBJECT>
<OBJECT RUNAT=Server SCOPE=Application ID=MSCSQueryMap
PROGID="Commerce.Dictionary"></OBJECT>
<OBJECT RUNAT=Server SCOPE=Application ID=MSCSCache
PROGID="Commerce.Dictionary"></OBJECT>
<OBJECT RUNAT=Server SCOPE=Application ID=MSCSMessageManager
PROGID="Commerce.MessageManager"></OBJECT>
<OBJECT RUNAT=Server SCOPE=Application ID=MSCSDataFunctions
PROGID="Commerce.DataFunctions"></OBJECT>
<OBJECT RUNAT=Server SCOPE=Application ID=MSCSShopperManager
PROGID="Commerce.StandardSManager"></OBJECT>

<SCRIPT LANGUAGE=VBScript RUNAT=Server>
    Sub Application_OnStart
        vRoot = "FiveLakes"

        Dim MSCSSite
        Dim MSCSQueryMap
        Dim MSCSMessageManager
        Dim MSCSDataFunctions
        Dim MSCSShopperManager

        REM - Read Store Dictionary
        Set MSCSSite = ReadSiteDict(vroot)

        REM - Create a Query Map and add all queries:
        set MSCSQueryMap = InitQueryMap()

        REM - Initialize Message Manager (for use in
pipeline) and add all messages:
        set MSCSMessageManager = InitMessageManager()

        REM - Initialize Shopper Manager for managing
shopperId values
        set MSCSShopperManager = InitShopperManager

        REM - Initialize Data Functions with locale:
        set MSCSDataFunctions = InitDataFunctions

    Set Application("MSCSSite")              = MSCSSite
    Set Application("MSCSQueryMap")          = MSCSQueryMap
    Set Application("MSCSMessageManager")    = MSCSMessageManager
```

code continued on next page

code continued from previous page

```
   Set Application("MSCSDataFunctions")     = MSCSDataFunctions
   Set Application("MSCSShopperManager")    = MSCSShopperManager
   Application("MSCSSIDUrlKey") = "mscssid"

  End Sub

  Function InitShopperManager
       call MSCSShopperManager.InitManager(vRoot, "url")
       set InitShopperManager = MSCSShopperManager
  End Function

  Function InitDataFunctions
       MSCSDataFunctions.locale = 1033
       set InitDataFunctions = MSCSDataFunctions
  End Function

  Function ReadSiteDict(vRoot)
       REM - Read Store Dictionary
       Set fileDocument =
Server.CreateObject("Commerce.FileDocument")
       vRootDir = Server.MapPath("/" & vRoot)
       Call fileDocument.ReadDictionaryFromFile(vRootDir &
"\config\site.csc", "IISProperties", MSCSSite)
       Set fileDocument = Nothing

       set ReadSiteDict = MSCSSite
  End Function

  Function InitQueryMap
       REM - Create Query Map Dictionary
       Set MSCSQueryMap.related_products_upsell =
AddQuery("Select sku, Upsell_sku, description from
FiveLakes_promo_upsell where sku=':1'")
       Set MSCSQueryMap.depts = AddQuery("SELECT dept_id,
dept_name, dept_description FROM fivelakes_dept")
       Set MSCSQueryMap.dept_by_id = AddQuery("SELECT dept_id,
dept_name, dept_description FROM fivelakes_dept WHERE
dept_id = :1")
       Set MSCSQueryMap.products_by_dept = AddQuery("SELECT
prod.sku, prod.name FROM fivelakes_product prod,
fivelakes_dept_prod dept WHERE dept.sku = prod.sku and
dept.dept_id = :1")
       Set MSCSQueryMap.price_promo_system = AddQuery("SELECT
promo_name, date_start, date_end, shopper_all, shopper_column,
shopper_op, shopper_value, cond_all, cond_column, cond_op,
```

code continued on next page

code continued from previous page

```
cond_value, cond_basis, cond_min, award_all, award_column,
award_op, award_value, award_max, disjoint_cond_award,
disc_type, disc_value FROM fivelakes_promo_price WHERE active
<> 0 ORDER BY promo_rank")
        Set MSCSQueryMap.related_products = AddQuery("SELECT
prod.sku, prod.name FROM fivelakes_promo_cross promo_cross,
fivelakes_product prod WHERE promo_cross.sku = :1 and
promo_cross.rel_sku = prod.sku")
        Set MSCSQueryMap.related_products_with_dept =
AddQuery("SELECT prod.sku, prod.name, deptprod.dept_id FROM
fivelakes_promo_cross promo_cross, fivelakes_product prod,
fivelakes_dept_prod deptprod WHERE promo_cross.sku = :1 and
prod.sku = deptprod.sku and promo_cross.rel_sku = prod.sku")
        Set MSCSQueryMap.receipts_for_shopper =
AddQuery("SELECT shopper_id, order_id, date_entered, total,
status, marshalled_receipt FROM fivelakes_receipt WHERE
shopper_id = :1 ORDER BY date_entered")
        Set MSCSQueryMap.product_by_sku = AddQuery("SELECT pf.sku,
pf.name, pf.description, pf.list_price, pf.sale_price,
pf.sale_start, pf.sale_end, pf.image_file, pf.image_width,
pf.image_height, pf.author, pf.edition,
pf.publisher,dept.dept_id, dept.dept_name FROM
Fivelakes_product pf, Fivelakes_dept_prod deptprod,
Fivelakes_dept dept WHERE pf.sku = :1 and pf.sku =
deptprod.sku and dept.dept_id = deptprod.dept_id and
dept.dept_id = :2")
        Set MSCSQueryMap.product_info = AddQuery("SELECT
pf.sku, pf.name, pf.list_price, pf.sale_price, pf.sale_start,
pf.sale_end, dept.dept_id FROM fivelakes_product pf,
fivelakes_dept_prod deptprod, fivelakes_dept dept WHERE pf.sku
= ? and pf.sku = deptprod.sku and dept.dept_id =
deptprod.dept_id and dept.dept_id = ?")
        Set MSCSQueryMap.find_by_keyword = AddQuery("select
p.sku, p.name, p.list_price, dp.dept_id from FiveLakes_product
p, FiveLakes_dept_prod dp where p.name like '%:1%' and p.sku =
dp.sku order by p.name")
        Set MSCSQueryMap.find_by_category = AddQuery("select
p.sku, p.name, p.category, p.list_price, dp.dept_id from
FiveLakes_product p, FiveLakes_dept_prod dp where p.category =
':1' and p.sku = dp.sku order by p.name")
        set MSCSQueryMap.country = AddQuery("select country
from FiveLakes_country")
        set MSCSQueryMap.country_tax = AddQuery("select
country, tax_rate from FiveLakes_country where country = :1 or
code = :2")
```

code continued on next page

code continued from previous page

```
        Set MSCSQueryMap.orderid = AddQuery("SELECT * FROM
FiveLakes_receipt WHERE order_id = ':1'")
        Set MSCSQueryMap.email_search = AddQuery("SELECT * FROM
FiveLakes_shopper WHERE email = ':1'")
        Set MSCSQueryMap.epartner = AddQuery("SELECT
epartner_id, name, site_address FROM FiveLakes_ePartner where
ePartner_id = ':1'")
        set InitQueryMap = MSCSQueryMap
    End Function

    Function AddQuery(SQLCommand)
        REM - sets defaults that can be overridden per query
on the page

        REM - ADO command types
        adCmdText        = 1
        adCmdTable       = 2
        adCmdStoredProc  = 4
        adCmdUnknown     = 8

        REM - ADO cursor types
        adOpenForwardOnly = 0 '# (Default)
        adOpenKeyset      = 1
        adOpenDynamic     = 2
        adOpenStatic      = 3

        REM - ADO lock types
        adLockReadOnly        = 1
        adLockPessimistic     = 2
        adLockOptimistic      = 3
        adLockBatchOptimistic = 4

        Set query = Server.CreateObject("Commerce.Dictionary")

        query.SQLCommand    = SQLCommand
        query.Timeout       = 0
        query.CommandType   = adCmdText
        query.MaxRows       = 0
        query.CursorType    = adOpenStatic
        query.CursorSize    = 0

        Set AddQuery = query
    End Function
```

code continued on next page

code continued from previous page

```
Function InitMessageManager
        call MSCSMessageManager.AddLanguage("USA", 1033)
        MSCSMessageManager.defaultLanguage = "USA"
        call MSCSMessageManager.AddMessage("pur_out_of_stock",
"At least one item is out of stock.")
        call MSCSMessageManager.AddMessage("pur_badsku",
"Please note that one or more items were removed from your basket
because the product is no longer sold.")
        call MSCSMessageManager.AddMessage("pur_badplacedprice",
"Please note that prices of products in your basket have been
updated.")
        call MSCSMessageManager.AddMessage("pur_noitems",
"An order must have at least one item.")
        call MSCSMessageManager.AddMessage("pur_badshipping",
"Unable to complete order: cannot compute shipping cost.")
        call MSCSMessageManager.AddMessage("pur_badtax",
"Unable to complete order: cannot compute tax.")
        call MSCSMessageManager.AddMessage("pur_badhandling",
"Unable to complete order: cannot compute handling cost.")
        call MSCSMessageManager.AddMessage("pur_badverify",
"Changes to the data require your review. Please review and
resubmit.")
        call MSCSMessageManager.AddMessage("pur_badpayment",
"There was a problem authorizing your credit. Please verify your
payment information or use a different card.")
        call MSCSMessageManager.AddMessage("pur_badcc",
"The credit-card number you provided is not valid. Please verify
your payment information or use a different card.")
        call MSCSMessageManager.AddMessage("val_noshipmethod",
"No Shipping Method was specified")
        call MSCSMessageManager.AddMessage("val_shiponeof",
"Shipping Method Type must be one of: ")
        call MSCSMessageManager.AddMessage("val_noshipname",
"No Ship-to Name was specified")
        call MSCSMessageManager.AddMessage("val_noshipstreet",
"No Ship-to Street was specified")
        call MSCSMessageManager.AddMessage("val_noshipcity",
"No Ship-to City was specified")
        call MSCSMessageManager.AddMessage("val_noshipstate",
"No Ship-to State was specified")
        call MSCSMessageManager.AddMessage("val_noshipzip",
"No Ship-to ZIP Code was specified")
        call MSCSMessageManager.AddMessage("val_noshipprovince",
"No Ship-to Province was specified")
```

code continued on next page

code continued from previous page

```
        call MSCSMessageManager.AddMessage("val_noshippostal_code",
"No Ship-to Postal Code was specified")
        call MSCSMessageManager.AddMessage("val_noshipaddress1",
"No Ship-to Address 1 was specified")
        call MSCSMessageManager.AddMessage("val_noshipaddress2",
"No Ship-to Address 2 was specified")
        call MSCSMessageManager.AddMessage("val_noshipcountry",
"No Ship-to Country was specified")
        call MSCSMessageManager.AddMessage("val_shipcountrymustbe",
"The Ship-to Country must be United States.")
        call MSCSMessageManager.AddMessage("val_nobillname",
"No Bill-to Name was specified")
        call MSCSMessageManager.AddMessage("val_nobillstreet",
"No Bill-to Street was specified")
        call MSCSMessageManager.AddMessage("val_nobillcity",
"No Bill-to City was specified")
        call MSCSMessageManager.AddMessage("val_nobillstate",
"No Bill-to State was specified")
        call MSCSMessageManager.AddMessage("val_nobillzip",
"No Bill-to ZIP Code was specified")
        call MSCSMessageManager.AddMessage("val_nobillprovince",
"No Bill-to Province was specified")
        call MSCSMessageManager.AddMessage("val_nobillpostal_code",
"No Bill-to Postal Code was specified")
        call MSCSMessageManager.AddMessage("val_nobilladdress1",
"No Bill-to Address 1 was specified")
        call MSCSMessageManager.AddMessage("val_nobilladdress2",
"No Bill-to Address 2 was specified")
        call MSCSMessageManager.AddMessage("val_nobillcountry",
"No Bill-to Country was specified")
        call MSCSMessageManager.AddMessage("val_noccname",
"No Credit-card Name was specified")
        call MSCSMessageManager.AddMessage("val_nocctype",
"No Credit-card Type was specified")
        call MSCSMessageManager.AddMessage("val_cctypeoneof",
"Credit-card Type must be one of: ")
        call MSCSMessageManager.AddMessage("val_noccnumber",
"No Credit-card Number was specified")
        call MSCSMessageManager.AddMessage("val_invalidccdate",
"Credit card expiration date must contain a valid month (1-12) and
year (1997-2003)")

        set InitMessageManager = MSCSMessageManager
    End Function
</SCRIPT>
```

i_epartner.asp

```
<% REM Check for E-partner
epartner_id=0
epartner_id=request.QueryString("epartner_id")
if epartner_id=0 then
  epartner_id=1
else
  cmdTemp.CommandText =
Replace(MSCSQueryMap.epartner.SQLCommand,":1", epartner_id)
  Set rsepartner = Server.CreateObject("ADODB.Recordset")
  rsepartner.Open cmdTemp, , adOpenForwardOnly, adLockReadOnly
    if rsepartner.EOF then
  epartner_id=1
  end if
end if
%>
```

i_error.asp

```
<HTML>
<HEAD>
    <TITLE>Error</TITLE>
    <META HTTP-EQUIV="Content-Type" CONTENT="text/html;
charset=ISO-8859-1">
</HEAD>

<BODY
    BGCOLOR="#FFFFFF"
    TEXT=    "#000000"
    LINK=    "#FF0000"
    VLINK=   "#FF0000"
    ALINK=   "#FF0000"
>

<BLOCKQUOTE>
We are sorry, but we are unable to process your request:
<BR>
<UL>
    <FONT COLOR=""#FF0000"">
    <%
    for each errorStr in errorList
        %><LI><%= errorStr %></LI>
```

code continued on next page

code continued from previous page

```
        <%
    next
    %>
    </FONT>
</UL>
Please go back and correct the error and try again.
</BLOCKQUOTE>

</BODY>
</HTML>
```

i_footer.asp

```
<!-- Web Site Created with Microsoft Site Server Commerce Edition
3.0 Site Builder Wizard -->
```

i_header.asp

```
<% if IsEmpty(flag_navbar) then %>
<TABLE BORDER="0" CELLPADDING="0" CELLSPACING="0" ALIGN="LEFT">
<TD VALIGN="TOP">
    <TR> <TD ALIGN="RIGHT" VALIGN="TOP">
        <A HREF="<%= pageURL("about.asp") %>"><IMG SRC=
"<%= "/" & siteRoot %>/manager/MSCS_Images/navbar/btnabout.gif"
WIDTH="53" HEIGHT="41" BORDER="0" ALT="About" ALIGN="TOP"></A>
    </TD><TD WIDTH="8" ROWSPAN="5"> </TD></TR>

    <TR> <TD ALIGN="RIGHT" VALIGN="TOP">
        <A HREF="<%= pageURL("default.asp") %>"><IMG SRC="<%=
"/" & siteRoot %>/manager/MSCS_Images/navbar/btnmenu.gif"
WIDTH="53" HEIGHT="41" BORDER="0" ALT="Lobby" ALIGN="TOP"></A>
    </TD></TR>

    <TR> <TD ALIGN="RIGHT" VALIGN="TOP">
        <A HREF="<%= pageURL("find.asp") %>"><IMG SRC="<%=
"/" & siteRoot %>/manager/MSCS_Images/navbar/btnfind.gif"
WIDTH="53" HEIGHT="41" BORDER="0" ALT="Find" ALIGN="TOP"></A>
    </TD></TR>

    <TR> <TD ALIGN="RIGHT" VALIGN="TOP">
```

code continued on next page

code continued from previous page

```
        <A HREF="<%= pageSURL("basket.asp") %>"><IMG SRC="<%=
"/" & siteRoot %>/manager/MSCS_Images/navbar/btnbskt.gif"
WIDTH="53" HEIGHT="41" BORDER="0" ALT="Basket" ALIGN="TOP"></A>

    </TD></TR>

    <TR> <TD ALIGN="RIGHT" VALIGN="TOP">

        <A HREF="<%= pageSURL("shipping.asp") %>"><IMG SRC="<%=
"/" & siteRoot %>/manager/MSCS_Images/navbar/btnpay.gif"
WIDTH="53" HEIGHT="41" BORDER="0" ALT="Pay" ALIGN="TOP"></A>

    </TD></TR>
    <TR><TD   COLSPAN="2" HEIGHT="200"> </TD></TR>
</TABLE>
<% end if %>
```

i_mswallet.asp

```
<%
    REM -- For intranets not connected to the internet,
override default
    REM    download location here.  For example:
    '  If LCase(CStr(Request("HTTP_UA_CPU"))) <> "alpha" Then
    '       strMSWltIEDwnldLoc  = "/" & siteRoot &
"/manager/MSCS_Images/controls/MSWallet.cab"
    '  Else
    '       strMSWltIEDwnldLoc  = "/" & siteRoot &
"/manager/MSCS_Images/controls/MSWltAlp.cab"
    '  End If
    '  strMSWltNavDwnldLoc = "/" & siteRoot &
"/manager/MSCS_Images/controls"

    REM - Set wallet control accept credit card types.
    strMSWltAcceptedTypes =
"visa:clear;mastercard:clear;amex:clear;"

    REM -- use_form set to 1 as a Request parameter will force
the downlevel page
%>
<!--#INCLUDE FILE="i_selector.asp" -->
```

i_selector.asp

```
<%  ' File Version 2,1,0,1378

    ' Variables set before including this file.
    '
    ' One of the following two variables should be set before
including this file:
    '    fMSWltAddressSelector    Set to "True" when the
AddressSelector appears on the
    '                             page.
    '    fMSWltPaymentSelector    Set to "True" when the
PaymentSelector appears on the
    '                             page.
    '
    ' The following variables may be optionally set before
including this file:
    '    strMSWltIEDwnldLoc       When not connected to the Internet,
set to the
    '                             location of the mswallet.cab, the
wallet download
    '                             package for IE.
    '    strMSWltNavDwnldLoc      When not connected to the
Internet, set to the
    '                             location of the HTM page
containing download
    '                             instructions (plginst.htm in
the SDK).
    '    strMSWltDwnldVer         Allows overriding the
downloaded version of Microsoft
    '                             Wallet.  Overriding the
version number should not be
    '                             necessary, so don't use this
unless you understand
    '                             what you're doing.
    '    fMSWltShowErrorDialogs   For debugging, set this to
"True" to show error
    '                             dialogs in GetValue calls.

    ' Variables set as a side effect of using including this
file.  You can use
    ' these in your ASP code:
    '    fMSWltActiveXBrowser         True if the browser supports
ActiveX.
```

code continued on next page

code continued from previous page

```
        '   fMSWltLiveConnectBrowser          True if the browser DOES
NOT support ActiveX and
        '                                      DOES support LiveConnect.
This covers Nav3 and
        '                                      probably Nav4.
        '   fMSWltUplevelBrowser              True if either of
fMSWltActiveXBrowser or
        '                                      fMSWltLiveConnectBrowser
-- e.g,, it's a control
        '                                      case.

        ' Server Side VBScript APIs
        '
        '   MSWltIEAddrSelectorClassid
        '   MSWltIEPaySelectorClassid
        '       Returns the <OBJECT> CLASSID field.  Always use as
the CLASSID value.  The
        '       returned classid is different on an Alpha NT machine.
        '
        '   MSWltIECodebase()
        '       Returns the <OBJECT> CODEBASE field.  Always use
as the CODEBASE value.
        '
        '   MSWltNavDwnldURL(strInstructionsFileName)
        '       Returns the <EMBED> PLUGINSPAGE field.  Always use
as the PLUGINSPAGE
        '       value.  strInstructionsFileName specifies the name
of the instructions
        '       file name.  When using the default download
location, call
        '       MSWltNavDwnldURL with 'plginst.htm'.  When using
an Intranet download
        '       location, call MSWltNavDwnldURL with the name of
the plugin instructions
        '       file (e.g., plginst.htm in the SDK).
        '
        '   MSWltLastChanceText(strDownlevelURL)
        '       Returns HTML text to place in your page.  This
text puts a link reading
        '       "Click here if you have problems with the
Microsoft Wallet".  When this
        '       link is clicked, the user navigates to the
strDownlevelURL parameter,
        '       which in many cases will be the same page.  This
routine automatically
```

code continued on next page

code continued from previous page

```
'          appends "use_form=1" to strDownlevelURL to force
the downlevel version of
'          the page.
'          We recommend setting the font to size 1.
'
'     MSWltLoadDone(strDownlevelURL)
'          Must be called in the uplevel browser case
(fMSWltUplevelBrowser = True) on
'          the <BODY> OnLoad field. Pass in the downlevel
URL, as with
'          MSWltLastChanceText.  This is only used when the
user refuses the
'          Nav plugin on initial install or subsequent
upgrade.
'
'
'  Client Side JavaScript APIs.
'
'     MSWltLoadDone(strDownlevelURL)
'          Use the server-side version or strDownlevelURL
won't be set correctly.
'
'     MSWltPrepareForm(form, cParams, xlationArray)
'          Use this to update the fields in form with values
from the
'          AddressSelector and/or PaymentSelector.  cParams
is the count of
'          the total number of parameters passed, including
the cParams
'          parameter.  xlationArray is an optional set of
parameters used to
'          translate when form field names to not match field
names returned by
'          the selectors; see the documentation for examples.
'          Call this routine before posting the form.  This
routine will routine
'          true if is succeeds, so it can be placed in a
OnSubmit event handler,
'          but this is not recommended, because if any
JavaScript errors occur, the
'          post will happen anyway erroneously.
'          In IE3 when using multiple frames and JavaScript-based
navigation
'          between frames, using this routine causes
subsequent  JavaScript-based
```

code continued on next page

code continued from previous page

```
    '           navigation to fail by navigating to the wrong
location.  We recommend
    '           not using this routine in those cases.  This only
applies in the most
    '           complex multi-frame/JavaScript-based navigation
cases, like Adventure
    '           Works in CommerceServer v3.00.


    ' Prepare miscellaneous variables.
    fMSWltAddressSelector = CBool(fMSWltAddressSelector)
    fMSWltPaymentSelector = CBool(fMSWltPaymentSelector)
    fMSWltShowErrorDialogs = CBool(fMSWltShowErrorDialogs)

    ' Browser Detection.
    Set objBrowser = Server.CreateObject("MSWC.BrowserType")
    strCPU = LCase(CStr(Request("HTTP_UA_CPU")))    ' CPU is
necessary to differentiate between
                                                    ' alpha, x86
and other CPUs on NT.
                                                    ' only set for
IE, Nav doesn't set.
    If strCPU = "alpha" Then
        fMSWltAlphaIE = true
    Else
        fMSWltAlphaIE = false
    End If

    ' Note that use_form = 1 forces a downlevel page.
    If Request.QueryString("use_form") = 0 And
objBrowser.JavaScript = "True" And _
        (fMSWltAddressSelector Or fMSWltPaymentSelector) Then

        If objBrowser.ActiveXControls = "True" Then
            fMSWltActiveXBrowser = True
            fMSWltUplevelBrowser = True
        ElseIf objBrowser.Browser = "Netscape" And _
            ( objBrowser.Platform = "Win95" Or
objBrowser.Platform = "Win98" Or _
                ( (objBrowser.Platform = "WinNT" Or
objBrowser.Platform = "Win32") And _
                ((Len(strCPU) = 0) Or (strCPU = "x86")) ) ) And _
            ( (CInt(objBrowser.majorver) > 3) Or _
                ((CInt(objBrowser.majorver) = 3) And
(objBrowser.beta = "False")) _
```

code continued on next page

code continued from previous page

```
                ) Then

            fMSWltLiveConnectBrowser = True
            fMSWltUplevelBrowser = True
        Else
            fMSWltActiveXBrowser = False
            fMSWltLiveConnectBrowser = False
            fMSWltUplevelBrowser = False
        End If
    Else
        fMSWltActiveXBrowser = False
        fMSWltLiveConnectBrowser = False
        fMSWltUplevelBrowser = False
    End If


    ' Examine to see if the download version or location has
    ' been overridden.  These should be overridden only when the
    ' consumer is not connected to the Internet (i.e, intranet
scenario).
    ' When not overriden, the default locations and version on
    ' Microsoft.com will be used.

    ' Download version.
    If IsEmpty(strMSWltDwnldVer) Then
        strMSWltDwnldVer = "2,1,0,1378"
    Else
        strMSWltDwnldVer = CStr(strMSWltDwnldVer)
    End If


    ' IE Wallet version location.
    If IsEmpty(strMSWltIEDwnldLoc) Then
        If fMSWltAlphaIE Then
            strMSWltIEDwnldLoc = "mswltalp.cab"
        Else
            strMSWltIEDwnldLoc = "mswallet.cab"
        End If
    Else
        strMSWltIEDwnldLoc = CStr(strMSWltIEDwnldLoc)
    End If


    ' Navigator Wallet version location.
    If IsEmpty(strMSWltNavDwnldLoc) Then
        strMSWltNavDwnldLoc =
"http://www.microsoft.com/commerce/wallet/local/"
```

code continued on next page

code continued from previous page

```
Else
    strMSWltNavDwnldLoc = CStr(strMSWltNavDwnldLoc)
    ' add trailing blank if missing
    If Right(strMSWltNavDwnldLoc, 1) <> "/" Then
        strMSWltNavDwnldLoc = strMSWltNavDwnldLoc & "/"
    End If
End If

Function MSWltIEAddrSelectorClassid
    If fMSWltAlphaIE Then
        MSWltIEAddrSelectorClassid =
"clsid:B7FB4D5B-9FBE-11d0-8965-0000F822DEA9"
    Else
        MSWltIEAddrSelectorClassid =
"clsid:87D3CB63-BA2E-11cf-B9D6-00A0C9083362"
    End If
End Function

Function MSWltIEPaySelectorClassid
    If fMSWltAlphaIE Then
        MSWltIEPaySelectorClassid =
"clsid:B7FB4D5C-9FBE-11d0-8965-0000F822DEA9"
    Else
        MSWltIEPaySelectorClassid =
"clsid:87D3CB66-BA2E-11cf-B9D6-00A0C9083362"
    End If
End Function

Function MSWltIECodebase
    MSWltIECodebase = strMSWltIEDwnldLoc & "#Version=" &
strMSWltDwnldVer
End Function

Function MSWltNavDwnldURL(strInstructionsFileName)
    MSWltNavDwnldURL = strMSWltNavDwnldLoc &
CStr(strInstructionsFileName)
End Function

' Tack use_form=1 on to the end of a URL
Function MSWltDownlevelURL(strDownlevelURL)
    MSWltDownlevelURL = Trim(CStr(strDownlevelURL)) ' any
spaces lurking?  get rid of them
    nQmarkLoc = InStr(MSWltDownlevelURL, "?")
    If nQmarkLoc > 0 Then
        If nQmarkLoc = Len(MSWltDownlevelURL) Then
```

code continued on next page

code continued from previous page

```
                    MSWltDownlevelURL = MSWltDownlevelURL &
"use_form=1"
            Else
                    MSWltDownlevelURL = MSWltDownlevelURL &
"&use_form=1"
            End If
        Else
            MSWltDownlevelURL = MSWltDownlevelURL & "?use_form=1"
        End If
        MSWltDownlevelURL = MSWltDownlevelURL
    End Function

    Function MSWltLastChanceText(strDownlevelURL)
        If fMSWltUplevelBrowser And (fMSWltAddressSelector Or
fMSWltPaymentSelector) Then
            MSWltLastChanceText = " <A HREF=""" & _
MSWltDownlevelURL(strDownlevelURL)& "&epartner_id="
&epartner_id &_
            """" > Click here if you have problems with the Wallet</A> "
        End If
    End Function

    Function MSWltLoadDone(strDownlevelURL)
        ' Call JavaScript MSWltLoadDone routine with downlevel
URL
        MSWltLoadDone = "MSWltLoadDone('" &
MSWltDownlevelURL(strDownlevelURL) & "')"
    End Function
%>

<% ' JavaScript to insert to support the controls. %>
<% If fMSWltUplevelBrowser Then %>
<SCRIPT LANGUAGE="JavaScript">
<!--
    var fMSWltLoaded = false     <% ' Has onLoad initialization
been done? %>

    <% If fMSWltAddressSelector Then %>
        var objAddrSelector     <% ' Address selector from
both IE and Nav %>
    <% End If %>

    <% If fMSWltPaymentSelector Then %>
        var objPaySelector      <% ' Payment selector from
both IE and Nav %>
```

code continued on next page

code continued from previous page

```
<% End If %>

// JavaScript version.
 function MSWltLoadDone(strDownlevelURL)
 {
      <% If fMSWltLiveConnectBrowser Then %>
        <% ' Is the plugin around? %>

      if (
          <% If fMSWltAddressSelector Then %>
          (document.addrSelector == null)
            <% If fMSWltPaymentSelector Then %>
               ||
            <% End If %>
          <% End If %>
          <% If fMSWltPaymentSelector Then %>
             (document.paySelector == null)
          <% End If %>
          )
      {
            if (confirm("Click OK to install Microsoft
Wallet Plugins."))
                <% ' open instructions page in a new window %>
                window.open("<% =
MSWltNavDwnldURL("plginst.htm") %>")
            else
                location = strDownlevelURL
            return
      }

            <% ' Take care of naming differences between
objects and plugins. %>
            <% If fMSWltAddressSelector Then %>
               objAddrSelector = document.addrSelector
               fVersionOK = objAddrSelector.VersionCheck()
            <% End If %>

            <% If fMSWltAddressSelector And
fMSWltPaymentSelector Then %>
                if (fVersionOK)
                {
                    objPaySelector = document.paySelector
                    fVersionOK = objPaySelector.VersionCheck()
                }
            <% ElseIf fMSWltPaymentSelector Then %>
```

code continued on next page

code continued from previous page

```
                    objPaySelector = document.paySelector
                    fVersionOK = objPaySelector.VersionCheck()
              <% End If %>

              <% ' Check plugin version.  Version requested set
on <embed> tag. %>
              <% ' This version is checked against the version
resource in the DLL. %>
              if (!fVersionOK)
              {
                    if (confirm("Your Microsoft Wallet Plugins are out
of date and you need to upgrade.\nClick OK to view upgrade
directions."))
                          <% ' open instructions page in a new window %>
                          window.open("<% =
MSWltNavDwnldURL("plginst.htm") %>")
                    else
                          location = strDownlevelURL
                    return
              }
              fMSWltLoaded = true
        <% End If %>
    }

    function MSWltCheckLoaded()
    {
        if (!fMSWltLoaded)
        {
            <% If fMSWltActiveXBrowser Then %>

            if (
                <% If fMSWltAddressSelector Then %>
                    (!(!addrSelector))
                    <% If fMSWltPaymentSelector Then %>
                        &&
                    <% End If %>
                <% End If %>
                <% If fMSWltPaymentSelector Then %>
                    (!(!paySelector))
                <% End If %>
                )
            {
                <% If fMSWltAddressSelector Then %>
                    objAddrSelector = addrSelector
                <% End If %>
```

code continued on next page

code continued from previous page

```
                <% If fMSWltPaymentSelector Then %>
                    objPaySelector = paySelector
                <% End If %>
                fMSWltLoaded = true
            }
            else
        <% End If %>

                <% ' Navigator JavaScript does not take
kindly to pushing buttons before the page is done %>
                <% ' loading; hence the warning that a
reload and wait may be necessary. %>
                alert("Page not done loading yet.  Try
again when it's loaded.  Refresh the page if you're having
difficulty (then wait for it to load).")
        }
        return fMSWltLoaded
    }

    function doNothing() { <% ' Do nothing, supports object
creation with no contents. %> }

    function MSWltPrepareForm(form, cParams, xlationArray)
    {
        if (!MSWltCheckLoaded())
            return false

        <% If fMSWltPaymentSelector Then %>
            PI = objPaySelector.GetValues()              <% ' get
payment information (PI) %>
            errorStatus = objPaySelector.GetLastError()  <% '
did an error occur?        %>
            if (errorStatus < 0)
            {
                if (errorStatus != (-2147220991) &&
errorStatus != (-2147220990))   <% ' HRESULT 0x80040201,
WALLET_E_CANCEL, and HRESULT 0x80040202, WALLET_E_HANDLEDERROR %>
                    alert("Payment selection failed due to an
unknown problem.")
                return false
            }
        <% End If %>

        <% If fMSWltAddressSelector Then %>
```

code continued on next page

code continued from previous page

```
        shipTo = objAddrSelector.GetValues()              <% ' get
ship to address information %>

        errorStatus = objAddrSelector.GetLastError()   <% ' did
an error occur? %>
        if (errorStatus < 0)
        {
            if (errorStatus != (-2147220991) &&
errorStatus != (-2147220990))   <% ' HRESULT 0x80040201,
WALLET_E_CANCEL, and HRESULT 0x80040202, WALLET_E_HANDLEDERROR %>
                alert("Address selection failed due to an
unknown problem.")
            return false
        }
    <% End If %>

    elements = form.elements


    <% ' Build xlation table from xlationArray %>
    xlate = new doNothing()

    for (i = 2; i < cParams; i += 2)
    {
        value = MSWltPrepareForm.arguments[i+1]
        if (value.length > 0)
            xlate[MSWltPrepareForm.arguments[i]] = value
    }

    <% If fMSWltPaymentSelector Or fMSWltAddressSelector
Then %>
        for (i = 0; i < elements.length; i++)
        {
            if (form.elements[i].name.length > 0)
            {
                xlateValue = xlate[elements[i].name]
                if (xlateValue)
                    name = xlateValue
                else
                    name = elements[i].name

                <% If fMSWltPaymentSelector Then %>
                    <% ' Have to make the string at least
1 long to get around Nav issue %>
                    value = 'a' +
```

code continued on next page

code continued from previous page

```
objPaySelector.GetValue(PI, name, <% =
-CInt(fMSWltShowErrorDialogs) %>)
                        if (value.length > 1)
                            elements[i].value = value.substring(1)
                <% End If %>

                <% If fMSWltAddressSelector Then %>
                    <% ' Have to make the string at least
1 long to get around Nav issue %>
                    value = 'a' +
objAddrSelector.GetValue(shipTo, name, <% = -
CInt(fMSWltShowErrorDialogs) %>)
                        if (value.length > 1)
                            elements[i].value = value.substring(1)
                <% End If %>
            }
        }
    <% End If %>

        return true
    }
//-->
</SCRIPT>
<% End If %>
```

i_shop.asp

```
<%
function this_page(nowat)
    this_page = (
Right(Request.ServerVariables("SCRIPT_NAME"),len(nowat)) = nowat)
end function

REM - ADO command types
adCmdText       = 1
adCmdTable      = 2
adCmdStoredProc = 4
adCmdUnknown    = 8

REM - ADO cursor types
adOpenForwardOnly = 0 '# (Default)
adOpenKeyset      = 1
adOpenDynamic     = 2
```

code continued on next page

code continued from previous page

```
adOpenStatic        = 3

REM -- ADO lock types
adLockReadOnly        = 1
adLockPessimistic     = 2
adLockOptimistic      = 3
adLockBatchOptimistic = 4

REM -- Used to check ADO Supports for Oracle
adApproxPosition = 16384

REM -- If store is not open then redirect to closed URL
if MSCSSite.Status <> "Open" then
  response.redirect(MSCSSite.CloseRedirectURL)
end if

REM -- mscs = created on the page; MSCS = created in
global.asa
set mscsPage = Server.CreateObject("Commerce.Page")

REM -- Manually create shopper id
mscsShopperID = mscsPage.GetShopperId


REM -- Handle shopper
if IsNull(mscsShopperID) then
    mscsShopperID = mscsShopperManager.CreateShopperID()
    mscsPage.PutShopperID(mscsShopperID)

end if


REM ********************************************************
REM -- functions for faster page links

function pageURL(pageName)
    pageURL = rootURL & pageName & "?" & emptyArgs
end function

function pageSURL(pageName)
    pageSURL = rootSURL & pageName & "?" & emptyArgs
end function

function baseURL(pageName)
    REM -- you must put on your own shopperArgs
```

code continued on next page

code continued from previous page

```
      baseURL = rootURL & pageName & "?"
end function

function baseSURL(pageName)
    REM -- you must put on your own shopperArgs
    baseSURL = rootSURL & pageName & "?"
end function

displayName  = MSCSSite.DisplayName
siteRoot     = mscsPage.SiteRoot()
rootURL      = mscsPage.URLPrefix() & "/" & siteRoot & "/"
rootSURL     = mscsPage.SURLPrefix() & "/" & siteRoot & "/"
emptyArgs    = mscsPage.URLShopperArgs()

REM ***********************************************************

REM -- Create ADO Connection and Command Objects
Set MSCS = Server.CreateObject("ADODB.Connection")
MSCS.Open MSCSSite.DefaultConnectionString
Set cmdTemp = Server.CreateObject("ADODB.Command")
cmdTemp.CommandType = adCmdText
Set cmdTemp.ActiveConnection = MSCS
%>
```

i_util.asp

```
<%

function UtilGetOrderFormStorage()
    Set orderFormStorage =
Server.CreateObject("Commerce.DBStorage")
    Call
orderFormStorage.InitStorage(MSCSSite.DefaultConnectionString,
"fivelakes_basket", "shopper_id", "Commerce.OrderForm",
"marshalled_basket", "date_changed")

    Set UtilGetOrderFormStorage = orderFormStorage
end function

function UtilGetOrderForm(byRef orderFormStorage, byRef created)
    created = 0
    On Error Resume Next
    Set orderForm = orderFormStorage.GetData(null, mscsShopperID)
```

code continued on next page

code continued from previous page

```
    On Error Goto 0
    if IsEmpty(orderForm) then
        set orderForm = Server.CreateObject("Commerce.OrderForm")
        orderForm.shopper_id = mscsShopperID
        created = 1
    end if
    set UtilGetOrderForm = orderForm
end function

function UtilPutOrderForm(byRef orderFormStorage, byRef
orderForm, byRef created)
    if created = 0 then
        Call orderFormStorage.CommitData(NULL, orderForm)
    else

        Call orderFormStorage.InsertData(NULL, orderForm)

    end if
end function

function UtilGetReceiptStorage()
    REM Create a storage object for receipts
    Set receiptStorage = Server.CreateObject("Commerce.DBStorage")
    Call
receiptStorage.InitStorage(MSCSSite.DefaultConnectionString,
"fivelakes_receipt", "order_id", "Commerce.OrderForm" ,
"marshalled_receipt", "date_entered")
    receiptStorage.Mapping.Value("_total_total") = "total"

    Set UtilGetReceiptStorage = receiptStorage
end function

function UtilGetPipeContext()
    Set pipeContext = Server.CreateObject("Commerce.Dictionary")
    Set pipeContext("MessageManager")      = MSCSMessageManager
    Set pipeContext("DataFunctions")       = MSCSDataFunctions
    Set pipeContext("QueryMap")            = MSCSQueryMap
    Set pipeContext("ConnectionStringMap") =
MSCSSite.ConnectionStringMap
    pipeContext("SiteName")                = displayName
    pipeContext("DefaultConnectionString") =
MSCSSite.DefaultConnectionString
    pipeContext("Language")                = "USA"

    Set UtilGetPipeContext = pipeContext
```

code continued on next page

code continued from previous page

```
end function

function UtilRunPipe(file, orderForm, pipeContext)
    Set pipeline = Server.CreateObject("Commerce.MtsPipeline")

    Call
pipeline.LoadPipe(Request.ServerVariables("APPL_PHYSICAL_PATH") &
"config\" & file)

    REM Call
pipeline.SetLogFile(Request.ServerVariables("APPL_PHYSICAL_PATH") &
"config\pipeline.log")

    errorLevel = pipeline.Execute(1, orderForm, pipeContext, 0)

    UtilRunPipe = errorLevel
end function

function UtilRunTxPipe(file, orderForm, pipeContext)
    Set pipeline = Server.CreateObject("Commerce.MtsTxPipeline")

    Call
pipeline.LoadPipe(Request.ServerVariables("APPL_PHYSICAL_PATH") &
"config\" & file)

    REM Call
pipeline.SetLogFile(Request.ServerVariables("APPL_PHYSICAL_PATH") &
"config\txpipeline.log")

    errorLevel = pipeline.Execute(1, orderForm, pipeContext, 0)

    UtilRunTxPipe = errorLevel
end function

function UtilRunPlan()

    REM Create a storage object for the order forms
    Set mscsOrderFormStorage = UtilGetOrderFormStorage()

    REM Get the orderform
    Set mscsOrderForm = UtilGetOrderForm(mscsOrderFormStorage,
created)

    REM Get the basic pipe context
    Set mscsPipeContext = UtilGetPipeContext()
```

code continued on next page

code continued from previous page

```
     REM Create and run the pipe
     errorLevel = UtilRunPipe("plan.pcf", mscsOrderForm,
mscsPipeContext)

     REM Save the order form in case running the pipe made changes
to the order form
     if created then

          Call mscsOrderFormStorage.InsertData(null, mscsOrderForm)

     else
          Call mscsOrderFormStorage.CommitData(null, mscsOrderForm)
     end if

     Set UtilRunPlan = mscsOrderForm
end function
%>
```

order.asp

```
<%@ LANGUAGE=vbscript enablesessionstate=false LCID=1033 %>

<!--#INCLUDE FILE="include/Manager.asp" -->

<% REM    header: %>
<% pageTitle = "Order Manager" %>
<HTML>
<HEAD>
     <TITLE> <% = pageTitle %> </TITLE>
     <META HTTP-EQUIV="Content-Type" CONTENT="text/html;
charset=ISO-8859-1">
     <!--#INCLUDE FILE="include/mgmt_define.asp" -->
</HEAD>

<BODY TOPMARGIN="8" LEFTMARGIN="8" BGCOLOR="#FFFFFF" TEXT="#000000"
LINK="#FF0000" ALINK="#FF0000" VLINK="#FF0000">
<!--#INCLUDE FILE="include/mgmt_header.asp" -->

<% REM    body: %>
<UL>
     <LI> <A HREF="order_ePartner.asp"> Orders by ePartner </A>
     <LI> <A HREF="order_list.asp"> All Orders </A>
```

code continued on next page

code continued from previous page

```
        <LI> <A HREF="order_day.asp"> Orders by Month </A>
        <LI> <A HREF="order_month.asp"> Orders by Year </A>
        <LI> <A HREF="order_product.asp"> Orders by Product </A>

    </UL>

    <% REM    footer: %>
    <!--#INCLUDE FILE="include/mgmt_footer.asp" -->
```

order_ePartner.asp

```
    <%@ LANGUAGE=vbscript enablesessionstate=false LCID=1033 %>

    <!--#INCLUDE FILE="include/Manager.asp" -->

    <% pageTitle="Orders By ePartner" %>

    <HTML>
    <HEAD>
        <TITLE> <% = pageTitle %> </TITLE>
      <META NAME="Generator" CONTENT="Microsoft Visual Studio 6.0">
        <!--#INCLUDE FILE="include/mgmt_define.asp" -->
    </HEAD>

    <BODY>
      <!--#INCLUDE FILE="include/mgmt_header.asp" -->
      <%Set  mscsReceiptStorage =
    Server.CreateObject("Commerce.DBStorage")
      On Error Resume Next
      Call mscsReceiptStorage.InitStorage(mscsManagerSite.
    DefaultConnectionString, "Fivelakes_receipt", "order_id",
    "Commerce.OrderForm", "marshalled_receipt", "date_entered")

      if Err.Number <> 0 then
      Set errorList = Server.CreateObject("Commerce.SimpleList")
      errorList.Add "The table could not be found or the
    database connection failed."
      %>
      <!--#INCLUDE FILE="include/error.asp" -->
      <!--#INCLUDE FILE="include/mgmt_footer.asp" -->
          <%
        Response.end
      else
```

code continued on next page

code continued from previous page

```
mscsReceiptStorage.Mapping.Value("_total_total") = "total"
end if
%>

<% function ShowRow()
        on error resume next
        set receipt = mscsReceiptStorage.GetData(null,
CStr(rsList("order_id")))
        on error goto 0
        if IsEmpty(receipt) then
            nitems = 0
        else
            set items = receipt.items
            nitems = items.Count
        end if %>

        <td ALIGN="CENTER"> <% = RowCount %> </td>
        <td ALIGN="CENTER"> <% = rsList("epartner_id").value %>
</td>
        <td ALIGN="LEFT"> <a HREF="<% = listElemTemplate & "?"
& mscsPage.URLArgs("order_id", rsList("order_id").value) %>">
<% = rsList("order_id").value %></a> </td>
        <td VALIGN="TOP" ALIGN="LEFT"> <% =
MSCSDataFunctions.Date(rsList("date_entered").value) %> </td>
        <td VALIGN="TOP" ALIGN="CENTER"> <% = nitems %> </td>
        <td VALIGN="TOP" ALIGN="RIGHT"> <% =
MSCSDataFunctions.Money(rsList("total").value) %> </td>
  <% end function %>

<%
listElemTemplate = "order_view.asp"
listColumns = "<TH ALIGN=""LEFT""> # </TH>" & vbCr & _
        "<TH ALIGN=""LEFT""> ePartner ID </TH>" & vbCr & _
        "<TH ALIGN=""LEFT""> Order ID </TH>" & vbCr & _
        "<TH ALIGN=""LEFT""> Date </TH>" & vbCr & _
        "<TH ALIGN=""LEFT""> # Items </TH>" & vbCr & _
        "<TH ALIGN=""LEFT""> Total </TH>" & vbCr
listNoRows = "<I>No orders in table</I>"
%>

<% cmdTemp.CommandText = "SELECT order_id,epartner_id,
shopper_id, date_entered, total, status FROM Fivelakes_receipt
ORDER BY epartner_id" %>

<!--#INCLUDE FILE="include/list.asp" -->
```

code continued on next page

code continued from previous page

```
        <!--#INCLUDE FILE="include/mgmt_footer.asp" -->


        </BODY>
        </HTML>
```

order_status.asp

```
<%@ LANGUAGE=vbscript enablesessionstate=false LCID=1033 %>

<% Response.buffer = true %>
<!--#INCLUDE FILE="i_shop.asp" -->
<!--#INCLUDE FILE="i_ePartner.asp" -->
<!--#INCLUDE FILE="i_header.asp" -->

<HTML>

<HEAD>
  <META NAME="Generator" CONTENT="Microsoft Visual Studio 6.0">
</HEAD>

<BODY>
<%cmdTemp.CommandText =
Replace(MSCSQueryMap.orderid.SQLCommand,":1",
Request("order_track_id"))
  Set rsorderid = Server.CreateObject("ADODB.Recordset")
  rsorderid.Open cmdTemp, , adOpenForwardOnly, adLockReadOnly
  if not rsorderid.EOF then

                if (now() - rsorderid("date_entered"))>2 then
                    ship_status="Yes"
                    else
                        ship_status="No"
                    end if
        end if
%>


<%
strurl = "receipt.asp?order_id=" & Request("order_track_id") &
"&ship_status=" & ship_status
Response.Redirect strurl
%>
<P>  </p>
```

code continued on next page

code continued from previous page

```
</BODY>

</HTML>
```

ordertrack.asp

```asp
<%@ LANGUAGE=vbscript enablesessionstate=false LCID=1033 %>

<!--#INCLUDE FILE="i_shop.asp" -->
<!--#INCLUDE FILE="i_ePartner.asp" -->
<!--#INCLUDE FILE="i_header.asp" -->
<HTML>

<HEAD>
    <META NAME="Generator" CONTENT="Microsoft Visual Studio 6.0">
</HEAD>

<BODY>
<form name="order_status" method="post" action="order_status.asp">
<Table width="100%">
<tr>
  <td width="20%">
  Order Number:
  </td>

  <td>
  <Input type="text" name="order_track_id" size="10"
maxlength="100">
  </td>
</tr>
<tr>
  <Td colspan="2">
   
  </td>
</tr>
<tr>
  <td width="20%">
  <input type="submit" value="Go">
  </td>
  <td>
  <input type="reset" value="Reset">
  </td>
</tr>
```

code continued on next page

code continued from previous page

```
</table>
</form>


<P> </p>

</BODY>

</HTML>
```

payment.asp

```
<%@ LANGUAGE=vbscript enablesessionstate=false LCID=1033 %>

<% Response.ExpiresAbsolute=DateAdd("yyyy", -10, Date) %>

<!--#INCLUDE FILE="i_shop.asp" -->
<!--#INCLUDE FILE="i_ePartner.asp" -->
<!--#INCLUDE FILE="i_util.asp" -->



<%
REM Run the basic plan
Set mscsOrderForm = UtilRunPlan()

set mscsOrderItems = mscsOrderForm.Items
nOrderItems = mscsOrderItems.Count

set mscsBasketErrors = mscsOrderForm.[_Basket_Errors]
nBasketErrors = mscsBasketErrors.Count

set mscsPurchaseErrors = mscsOrderForm.[_Purchase_Errors]
nPurchaseErrors = mscsPurchaseErrors.Count

strDownlevelURL = pageSURL("payment.asp")& "&epartner_id="
&epartner_id %>

<HTML>

<HEAD>
    <TITLE><%= displayName %>: Payment</TITLE>
    <META HTTP-EQUIV="Content-Type" CONTENT="text/html;
```

code continued on next page

code continued from previous page

```
charset=ISO-8859-1">
    <% fMSWltPaymentSelector = True %>
    <!--#INCLUDE FILE="i_mswallet.asp" -->
    <% if fMSWltUplevelBrowser and CBool(nOrderItems > 0) then %>
        <SCRIPT LANGUAGE="Javascript">
        <!--
            function submitPayinfo()
            {
                if (MSWltPrepareForm(document.payinfo, 2)) {

                    document.payinfo.submit();
                }
            }
        //-->
        </SCRIPT>
    <% end if %>
</HEAD>

<BODY
    BGCOLOR="#FFFFFF"
    TEXT=    "#000000"
    LINK=    "#FF0000"
    VLINK=   "#FF0000"
    ALINK=   "#FF0000"
    <% if fMSWltUplevelBrowser and CBool(nOrderItems > 0) then
        %>onLoad="<% = MSWltLoadDone(strDownlevelURL) %>"<%
    end if %>
>



<!--#INCLUDE FILE="i_header.asp" -->

<H1>Final Purchase Approval</H1>

<% if nOrderItems = 0 then %>
    <BLOCKQUOTE>
        <STRONG>Your basket is empty.</STRONG>
    </BLOCKQUOTE>
<% else %>

<% if nBasketErrors > 0 then %>
<TABLE WIDTH="500">
    <% for iError = 0 to nBasketErrors - 1 %>
```

code continued on next page

code continued from previous page

```
      <TR><TD><FONT COLOR="#FF0000"><STRONG><%=
mscsPage.HTMLEncode(mscsBasketErrors(iError)) %></STRONG></FONT>
</TD></TR>
    <% next %>
</TABLE>
<P>
 
<P>
<% end if %>

<% if nPurchaseErrors > 0 then %>
<TABLE WIDTH="500">
    <% for iError = 0 to nPurchaseErrors - 1 %>
    <TR><TD><FONT COLOR="#FF0000"><STRONG><%=
mscsPage.HTMLEncode(mscsPurchaseErrors(iError)) %></STRONG></FONT>
</TD></TR>
    <% next %>
</TABLE>
<P>
Please go back to the basket page, correct the error, and try
again.
<P>
<% else %>

<% if Request("error").Count <> 0 then %>
    <% call mscsOrderFormStorage.CommitData(null, mscsOrderForm) %>
<TABLE WIDTH="500">
    <TR><TD>
        <FONT COLOR="#FF0000"><STRONG>
        Your purchase could not be completed.
        Please make sure you have provided all the requested
billing
        and payment information.
        </STRONG></FONT>
    </TD></TR>
</TABLE>
<P> 
<P>
<% end if %>

<TABLE WIDTH="500">
    <TR>
        <TD>
            Your purchase will cost <%=
MSCSDataFunctions.Money(mscsOrderForm.[_total_total]) %>.
```

code continued on next page

code continued from previous page

```
                Please enter your payment information and press the
"Purchase" button below.
        </TD>
    </TR>
</TABLE>

<P>

<TABLE BORDER="0"<% if Request("use_form") <> 1 then %>
ALIGN="LEFT"<% end if %>>
    <TR>
        <TD ALIGN="RIGHT" WIDTH="100">
            <B>Subtotal:</B>
        </TD>
        <TD ALIGN="RIGHT">
            <%=
MSCSDataFunctions.Money(mscsOrderForm.[_oadjust_subtotal]) %>
        </TD>
    </TR>


    <TR>
        <TD ALIGN="RIGHT">
            <B>Shipping:</B>
        </TD>
        <TD ALIGN="RIGHT">
            <%=
MSCSDataFunctions.Money(mscsOrderForm.[_shipping_total]) %>
        </TD>
    </TR>



    <TR>
        <TD ALIGN="RIGHT">
            <B>Handling:</B>
        </TD>
        <TD ALIGN="RIGHT">
            <%=
MSCSDataFunctions.Money(mscsOrderForm.[_handling_total]) %>
        </TD>
    </TR>



    <TR>
        <TD ALIGN="RIGHT">
            <B>Tax:</B>
```

code continued on next page

code continued from previous page

```
            </TD>
            <TD ALIGN="RIGHT">
                <%= MSCSDataFunctions.Money(mscsOrderForm.[_tax_total])
%>
            </TD>
        </TR>

        <TR>
            <TD ALIGN="RIGHT">
                <B>TOTAL:</B>
            </TD>
            <TD ALIGN="RIGHT">
                <%=
MSCSDataFunctions.Money(mscsOrderForm.[_total_total]) %>
            </TD>
        </TR>
        <% if fMSWltUplevelBrowser then %>
        <TR><TD   COLSPAN="2" HEIGHT="100"> </TD></TR>
        <% end if %>
</TABLE>
<P>
    <% if fMSWltUplevelBrowser then %>
        <FORM NAME="payinfo" METHOD="POST" ACTION="<%=
pageSURL("xt_orderform_purchase.asp")& "&epartner_id="
&epartner_id %>">
            <INPUT TYPE="HIDDEN" NAME="use_form" VALUE="0">
            <INPUT TYPE="HIDDEN" NAME="bill_to_name">

            <% = mscsPage.VerifyWith(mscsOrderForm,
"_total_total", "ship_to_zip", "_tax_total") %>
            <INPUT TYPE="HIDDEN" NAME="bill_to_street">
            <INPUT TYPE="HIDDEN" NAME="bill_to_city">
            <INPUT TYPE="HIDDEN" NAME="bill_to_state">
            <INPUT TYPE="HIDDEN" NAME="bill_to_zip">

            <INPUT TYPE="HIDDEN" NAME="bill_to_country">
            <INPUT TYPE="HIDDEN" NAME="bill_to_phone">
            <INPUT TYPE="HIDDEN" NAME="bill_to_email">
            <INPUT TYPE="HIDDEN" NAME="cc_name">
            <INPUT TYPE="HIDDEN" NAME="cc_type">
            <INPUT TYPE="HIDDEN" NAME="_cc_number">
            <INPUT TYPE="HIDDEN" NAME="_cc_expmonth">
            <INPUT TYPE="HIDDEN" NAME="_cc_expyear">
        </FORM>
```

code continued on next page

code continued from previous page

```
<TABLE >
<TR>
<TD VALIGN="TOP">
<% if fMSWltActiveXBrowser then %>
    <OBJECT
        ID="paySelector"
        CLASSID="<% = MSWltIEPaySelectorClassid() %>"
        CODEBASE="<%= MSWltIECodebase() %>"
        HEIGHT="123"
        WIDTH="154">
        <PARAM NAME="AcceptedTypes" VALUE="<%=
strMSWltAcceptedTypes %>">
        <PARAM NAME="Total" VALUE="<%=
MSCSDataFunctions.Money(mscsOrderForm.[_total_total]) %>">
    </OBJECT>

    <% elseif fMSWltLiveConnectBrowser then %>
    <EMBED
        NAME="paySelector"
       TYPE="application/x-mswallet"
        PLUGINSPAGE="<%=
MSWltNavDwnldURL("plginst.htm") %>"
        VERSION="<%= strMSWltDwnldVer %>"
        HEIGHT="123"
        WIDTH="154"
        ACCEPTEDTYPES="<%= strMSWltAcceptedTypes %>"
        TOTAL="<%=
MSCSDataFunctions.Money(mscsOrderForm.[_total_total]) %>"
        >
    <% end if %>
</TD>

<TD VALIGN="TOP">
<FORM>
    <INPUT TYPE="BUTTON"
           VALUE="Purchase"
           onClick="submitPayinfo()"
           SRC="<%= "/" & siteRoot
%>/manager/MSCS_Images/buttons/btnpurchase1.gif"
           WIDTH="116"
           HEIGHT="25"
           BORDER="0"
           ALT="Purchase">
</FORM>
</TD>
```

code continued on next page

code continued from previous page

```
                </TR>
                </TABLE>

                <P>
                 <%= MSWltLastChanceText(strDownlevelURL) %>

        <% else %>


<FORM METHOD=POST ACTION="<%=
pageSURL("xt_orderform_purchase.asp")& "&epartner_id="
&epartner_id %>">
        <INPUT TYPE="HIDDEN" NAME="use_form" VALUE="1">


        <% = mscsPage.VerifyWith(mscsOrderForm, "_total_total",
"ship_to_zip", "_tax_total") %>


        <INPUT TYPE="HIDDEN" NAME="bill_to_country" VALUE="USA">

        <TABLE>
            <TR>
                <TD></TD>
                <TD ALIGN="CENTER" COLSPAN="4">
                    <FONT SIZE="+1"><STRONG>Credit Card Information
</STRONG></FONT>
                </TD>
            </TR>
            <TR>
                <TD ALIGN="RIGHT">
                    <B>Name on card:</B>
                </TD>
                <TD COLSPAN="4">
                    <INPUT TYPE="text"
                            NAME="cc_name"
                            SIZE="70,1">
                </TD>
            </TR>
            <TR>
                <TD ALIGN="RIGHT">
                    <B>Card Number:</B>
                </TD>
                <TD COLSPAN="4">
                    <INPUT TYPE="text"
```

code continued on next page

code continued from previous page

```
                        NAME="_cc_number"
                        SIZE="70,1">
        </TD>
    </TR>
    <TR>
        <TD ALIGN="RIGHT">
            <B>Type:</B>
        </TD>
        <TD>
            <SELECT NAME="cc_type">
                <OPTION VALUE="Visa"> VISA
                <OPTION VALUE="MasterCard"> MasterCard
                <OPTION VALUE="AMEX"> American Express

            </SELECT>
        </TD>

        <TD ALIGN="RIGHT">
            <B>Expiration Date:</B>
        </TD>
        <TD>
            <% iMonth = Month(Date) %>
            <SELECT NAME="_cc_expmonth">
                <%= mscsPage.Option(1, iMonth) %> Jan
                <%= mscsPage.Option(2, iMonth) %> Feb
                <%= mscsPage.Option(3, iMonth) %> Mar
                <%= mscsPage.Option(4, iMonth) %> Apr
                <%= mscsPage.Option(5, iMonth) %> May
                <%= mscsPage.Option(6, iMonth) %> Jun
                <%= mscsPage.Option(7, iMonth) %> Jul
                <%= mscsPage.Option(8, iMonth) %> Aug
                <%= mscsPage.Option(9, iMonth) %> Sep
                <%= mscsPage.Option(10, iMonth) %> Oct
                <%= mscsPage.Option(11, iMonth) %> Nov
                <%= mscsPage.Option(12, iMonth) %> Dec
            </SELECT>
        </TD>
        <TD>
            <% iYear = Year(Date) %>
            <SELECT NAME="_cc_expyear">
                <%= mscsPage.Option(1997, iYear) %> 1997
                <%= mscsPage.Option(1998, iYear) %> 1998
                <%= mscsPage.Option(1999, iYear) %> 1999
                <%= mscsPage.Option(2000, iYear) %> 2000
                <%= mscsPage.Option(2001, iYear) %> 2001
```

code continued on next page

code continued from previous page

```
                    <%= mscsPage.Option(2002, iYear) %> 2002
                    <%= mscsPage.Option(2003, iYear) %> 2003
            </SELECT>
        </TD>
    </TR>

    <TR>
        <TD>
             
        </TD>
    </TR>

    <% REM bill-to:  %>
    <TR>
        <TD></TD>
        <TD ALIGN="CENTER" COLSPAN="3">
            <FONT SIZE="+1"><STRONG>Billing Address</STRONG>
</FONT>
        </TD>
    </TR>

    <TR>
        <TD ALIGN="RIGHT">
            <B>Name:</B>
        </TD>
        <TD COLSPAN="3">
            <INPUT TYPE="text"
                    NAME="bill_to_name"
                    SIZE="54,1"
                    VALUE="<%=
mscsPage.HTMLEncode(mscsOrderForm.bill_to_name) %>">
        </TD>
    </TR>


    <TR>
        <TD ALIGN="RIGHT">
            <B>Street:</B>
        </TD>
        <TD COLSPAN="3">
            <INPUT TYPE="text"
                    NAME="bill_to_street"
                    SIZE="54,1"
                    VALUE="<%=
mscsPage.HTMLEncode(mscsOrderForm.bill_to_street) %>">
```

code continued on next page

code continued from previous page

```
                    </TD>
                </TR>
                <TR>
                    <TD ALIGN="RIGHT">
                        <B>City:</B>
                    </TD>
                    <TD COLSPAN="3">
                        <INPUT TYPE="text"
                                NAME="bill_to_city"
                                SIZE="54,1"
                                VALUE="<%=
mscsPage.HTMLEncode(mscsOrderForm.bill_to_city) %>">
                    </TD>
                </TR>
                <TR>
                    <TD ALIGN="RIGHT">
                        <B>State:</B>
                    </TD>
                    <TD>
                        <INPUT TYPE="text"
                                NAME="bill_to_state"
                                SIZE="5,1"
                                VALUE="<%=
mscsPage.HTMLEncode(mscsOrderForm.bill_to_state) %>">  
                    </TD>
                    <TD ALIGN="RIGHT">
                        <B>ZIP Code:</B>
                    </TD>
                    <TD>
                        <INPUT TYPE="text"
                                NAME="bill_to_zip"
                                SIZE="10,1"
                                VALUE="<%=
mscsPage.HTMLEncode(mscsOrderForm.bill_to_zip) %>"> 
                    </TD>
                </TR>

            <TR>
    <TD ALIGN="RIGHT">
                    <B>Country:</B>
                </TD>
        <% sqlText = MSCSQueryMap.country.SQLCommand

        cmdTemp.CommandText = sqlText
        Set rscountry = Server.CreateObject("ADODB.Recordset")
```

code continued on next page

code continued from previous page

```
        rscountry.Open cmdTemp, , adOpenForwardOnly,
adLockReadOnly  %>

        <td align="left">
        <select name="bill_to_country" size="1">

            <%While not rscountry.EOF %>
             <%=
mscsPage.Option(rscountry("country").value,mscsOrderForm.bill_to_country)
%> <%= rscountry("country").value %>
            <% rscountry.MoveNext
        Wend %>
            </select VALUE="<%=
mscsPage.HTMLEncode(mscsOrderForm.bill_to_country) %>"> 
        </td>
        </TR>


    <TR>
        <TD ALIGN="RIGHT">
            <B>Phone:</B>
        </TD>
        <TD COLSPAN="3">
            <INPUT TYPE="text"
                    NAME="bill_to_phone"
                    SIZE="54,1"
                    VALUE="<%=
mscsPage.HTMLEncode(mscsOrderForm.bill_to_phone) %>">
        </TD>
    </TR>

    <TR>
        <TD>
             
        </TD>
    </TR>

    <TR>
        <TD></TD>
        <TD COLSPAN="4">
            <INPUT TYPE="Image"
                    VALUE="Purchase"
                    SRC="<%= "/" & siteRoot %>/manager/
MSCS_Images/buttons/btnpurchase1.gif"
                    WIDTH="116"
```

code continued on next page

code continued from previous page

```
                                HEIGHT="25"
                                BORDER="0"
                                ALT="Purchase">
                </TD>
            </TR>
            </TABLE>
    </FORM>
    <% end if ' uplevel %>
    <% end if %>
    <% end if %>

    <!--#INCLUDE FILE="i_footer.asp" -->

    </BODY>
    </HTML>
```

product.asp

```
<%@ LANGUAGE=vbscript enablesessionstate=false LCID=1033 %>

<!--#INCLUDE FILE="i_shop.asp" -->
<!--#INCLUDE FILE="i_ePartner.asp" -->
<%
    sku = mscsPage.RequestString("sku")
    quoted_sku = "'" & Replace(sku,"'","''") & "'"     REM --
add quotes


    REM -- retrieve product:
    sqlText = MSCSQueryMap.product_by_sku.SQLCommand
    sqlText = Replace(sqlText, ":1", quoted_sku)
    sqlText = Replace(sqlText, ":2", Request("dept_id"))
    cmdTemp.CommandText = sqlText
    Set rsProduct = Server.CreateObject("ADODB.Recordset")
    rsProduct.Open cmdTemp, , adOpenForwardOnly, adLockReadOnly

    if rsProduct.EOF then
        product_exists = false
    else
        product_exists = true
```

code continued on next page

code continued from previous page

```
          REM -- get fields from recordset
          author = rsProduct("author").value
          publisher = rsProduct("publisher").value
          edition = rsProduct("edition").value

          name = rsProduct("name").value
          description = rsProduct("description").value
          dept_name = rsProduct("dept_name").value
          list_price = rsProduct("list_price").value

          sale_price = rsProduct("sale_price").value
          sale_start = rsProduct("sale_start").value
          sale_end = rsProduct("sale_end").value

          image_file = rsProduct("image_file").value
          image_width = rsProduct("image_width").value
          image_height = rsProduct("image_height").value

          rsProduct.Close

          REM -- Log department and product for UA
          Response.AppendToLog "&" &
mscsPage.URLArgs("MSS.Request.Category Name", dept_name,
"MSS.Request.SKU", sku, "MSS.Request.Product Name", name)


           REM -- determine if product is on sale:
          today = Date
          on_sale = DateDiff("d", today, sale_start) <= 0 and
DateDiff("d", today, sale_end) > 0

      end if
%>


<HTML>

<HEAD>
     <TITLE><%= displayName %>: Product<% if product_exists
then %>: '<%= mscsPage.HTMLEncode(name) %>'<% end if %></TITLE>
     <META HTTP-EQUIV="Content-Type" CONTENT="text/html;
charset=ISO-8859-1">
</HEAD>
```

code continued on next page

code continued from previous page

```
<BODY
    BGCOLOR="#FFFFFF"
    TEXT=    "#000000"
    LINK=    "#FF0000"
    VLINK=   "#FF0000"
    ALINK=   "#FF0000"
>

<!--#INCLUDE FILE="i_header.asp" -->



<% if not product_exists then %>
    <P>The product you requested is currently not available.
<% else %>


<FORM METHOD=POST ACTION="<%=
pageSURL("xt_orderform_additem.asp")& "&epartner_id="
&epartner_id %>">

    <INPUT TYPE="HIDDEN" NAME="sku" VALUE="<%=
mscsPage.HTMLEncode(sku) %>">
    <INPUT TYPE="HIDDEN" NAME="dept_id" VALUE="<%=
Request("dept_id") %>">

<TABLE
    BORDER=       "0"
    CELLPADDING="2"
    CELLSPACING="2"
>
<TR>
    <TD>
        <P><FONT SIZE="6"><B><%= mscsPage.HTMLEncode(name)
%></B></FONT>


        <% if on_sale then %>
        <P><FONT SIZE="4"><B>ON SALE! <%=
MSCSDataFunctions.Money(sale_price) %></B></FONT>
        <P>Regular Price: <%=
MSCSDataFunctions.Money(list_price) %>
        <% else %>
        <P><FONT SIZE="4"><B>
<%= MSCSDataFunctions.Money(list_price) %></B></FONT>
```

code continued on next page

code continued from previous page

```
            <% end if %>

            <P><%= mscsPage.HTMLEncode(description) %>


        <P>
        <P><FONT SIZE="4"><B>Author</B></FONT>
        <P><%= mscsPage.HTMLEncode(author) %>
        <P><FONT SIZE="4"><B>Publisher</B></FONT>
        <P><%= mscsPage.HTMLEncode(publisher) %>
        <P><FONT SIZE="4"><B>Edition</B></FONT>
        <P><%= mscsPage.HTMLEncode(edition) %>
        <P>
        <P>


        <P>
        <INPUT TYPE="Image"
               SRC="<%= "/"
& siteRoot %>/manager/MSCS_Images/buttons/btnaddbskt1.gif"
               WIDTH="112"
               HEIGHT="24"
               BORDER="0"
               ALT="Add to Basket"
               ALIGN="MIDDLE">
    </TD>
    <TD>
         
    </TD>
    <TD VALIGN="TOP">
        <% if not IsNull(image_file) then %>
            <IMG SRC="<%= "/" & siteRoot %>/assets/product_images/
<%= mscsPage.HTMLEncode(image_file) %>"
                WIDTH="<% = image_width %>"
                HEIGHT="<% = image_height %>">
        <% else %>
            Image not available
        <% end if %>
    </TD>
</TR>
</TABLE>


</FORM>
```

code continued on next page

code continued from previous page

```
<% end if %>


<%
REM get related products (if any):
cmdTemp.CommandText = Replace("SELECT prod.sku, prod.name,
deptprod.dept_id FROM fivelakes_promo_cross promo_cross,
fivelakes_product prod, fivelakes_dept_prod deptprod WHERE
promo_cross.sku = :1 and prod.sku = deptprod.sku and
promo_cross.rel_sku = prod.sku", ":1", quoted_sku)
Set rsRelated = Server.CreateObject("ADODB.Recordset")
rsRelated.Open cmdTemp, , adOpenForwardOnly, adLockReadOnly

REM display up to 5 related products:
if Not rsRelated.EOF then
%>
    <BR>
    <B>See Also</B>
    <%
    nRelated = 0
    set skuField = rsRelated("sku")
    set nameField = rsRelated("name")
    set dept_idField = rsRelated("dept_id")
    do while Not (rsRelated.EOF Or nRelated >= 5)
        %><BR>
        <A HREF="<% = baseURL("product.asp") &
mscsPage.URLShopperArgs("sku", skuField.value, "dept_id",
dept_idField.value,"epartner_id=",epartner_id) %>"> <% =
mscsPage.HTMLEncode(nameField.value) %> </A>
        <%
        nRelated = nRelated + 1
        rsRelated.MoveNext
    loop %>
<% end if %>


<P>

<!--#INCLUDE FILE="i_footer.asp" -->

</BODY>

</HTML>
```

product_alt.asp

```
<%@ LANGUAGE=vbscript enablesessionstate=false LCID=1033 %>

<!--#INCLUDE FILE="i_shop.asp" -->
<!--#INCLUDE FILE="i_ePartner.asp" -->
<%
    sku = mscsPage.RequestString("sku")
    quoted_sku = "'" & Replace(sku,"'","''") & "'"      REM --
add quotes
    index=Request.QueryString("index")
    dept_id=mscsPage.RequestNumber("dept_id")

    REM - retrieve product:
    sqlText = MSCSQueryMap.product_by_sku.SQLCommand
    sqlText = Replace(sqlText, ":1", quoted_sku)
    sqlText = Replace(sqlText, ":2", Request("dept_id"))
    cmdTemp.CommandText = sqlText

    Set rsProduct = Server.CreateObject("ADODB.Recordset")
    rsProduct.Open cmdTemp, , adOpenForwardOnly, adLockReadOnly

    if rsProduct.EOF then
        product_exists = false
    else
        product_exists = true

        REM - get fields from recordset
        author = rsProduct("author").value
        publisher = rsProduct("publisher").value
        edition = rsProduct("edition").value

        name = rsProduct("name").value
        description = rsProduct("description").value
        dept_name = rsProduct("dept_name").value
        list_price = rsProduct("list_price").value

        sale_price = rsProduct("sale_price").value
        sale_start = rsProduct("sale_start").value
        sale_end = rsProduct("sale_end").value

        image_file = rsProduct("image_file").value
        image_width = rsProduct("image_width").value
        image_height = rsProduct("image_height").value
```

code continued on next page

code continued from previous page

```
            rsProduct.Close

            REM -- Log department and product for UA
            Response.AppendToLog "&" &
mscsPage.URLArgs("MSS.Request.Category Name", dept_name,
"MSS.Request.SKU", sku, "MSS.Request.Product Name", name)


            REM -- determine if product is on sale:
            today = Date
            on_sale = DateDiff("d", today, sale_start) <= 0 and
DateDiff("d", today, sale_end) > 0

        end if
%>


<HTML>

<HEAD>
    <TITLE><%= displayName %>: Product<% if product_exists
then %>: '<%= mscsPage.HTMLEncode(name) %>'<% end if %></TITLE>
    <META HTTP-EQUIV="Content-Type" CONTENT="text/html;
charset=ISO-8859-1">
</HEAD>

<BODY
    BGCOLOR="#FFFFFF"
    TEXT=   "#000000"
    LINK=   "#FF0000"
    VLINK=  "#FF0000"
    ALINK=  "#FF0000"
>

<!--#INCLUDE FILE="i_header.asp" -->



<% if not product_exists then %>
    <P>The product you requested is currently not available.
<% else %>


<FORM METHOD=POST ACTION="<%=
pageSURL("xt_orderform_edititem.asp")& "&epartner_id="
```

code continued on next page

code continued from previous page

```
&epartner_id %>index=<%=index%>">

    <INPUT TYPE="HIDDEN" NAME="sku" VALUE="<%=
mscsPage.HTMLEncode(sku) %>">
    <INPUT TYPE="HIDDEN" NAME="dept_id" VALUE="<%=
Request("dept_id") %>">

<TABLE
    BORDER=      "0"
    CELLPADDING="2"
    CELLSPACING="2"
>
<TR>
    <TD>
        <P><FONT SIZE="6"><B><%= mscsPage.HTMLEncode(name) %></B>
</FONT>


        <% if on_sale then %>
        <P><FONT SIZE="4"><B>ON SALE! <%=
MSCSDataFunctions.Money(sale_price) %></B></FONT>
        <P>Regular Price: <%=
MSCSDataFunctions.Money(list_price) %>
        <% else %>
        <P><FONT SIZE="4"><B><%=
MSCSDataFunctions.Money(list_price) %></B></FONT>
        <% end if %>

        <P><%= mscsPage.HTMLEncode(description) %>


        <P>
        <P><FONT SIZE="4"><B>Author</B></FONT>
        <P><%= mscsPage.HTMLEncode(author) %>
        <P><FONT SIZE="4"><B>Publisher</B></FONT>
        <P><%= mscsPage.HTMLEncode(publisher) %>
        <P><FONT SIZE="4"><B>Edition</B></FONT>
        <P><%= mscsPage.HTMLEncode(edition) %>
        <P>
        <P>


        <P>
        <INPUT TYPE="Image"
                SRC="<%= "/" & siteRoot
```

code continued on next page

code continued from previous page

```
%>/manager/MSCS_Images/buttons/btnaddbskt1.gif"
                    WIDTH="112"
                    HEIGHT="24"
                    BORDER="0"
                    ALT="Add to Basket"
                    ALIGN="MIDDLE">
    </TD>
    <TD>
         
    </TD>
    <TD VALIGN="TOP">
        <% if not IsNull(image_file) then %>
            <IMG SRC="<%= "/" & siteRoot
%>/assets/product_images/<%= mscsPage.HTMLEncode(image_file) %>"
                WIDTH="<% = image_width %>"
                HEIGHT="<% = image_height %>">
        <% else %>
            Image not available
        <% end if %>
    </TD>
</TR>
</TABLE>


</FORM>


<% end if %>


<%
REM get related products (if any):
cmdTemp.CommandText = Replace("SELECT prod.sku, prod.name,
deptprod.dept_id FROM fivelakes_promo_cross promo_cross,
fivelakes_product prod, fivelakes_dept_prod deptprod WHERE
promo_cross.sku = :1 and prod.sku = deptprod.sku and
promo_cross.rel_sku = prod.sku", ":1", quoted_sku)
Set rsRelated = Server.CreateObject("ADODB.Recordset")
rsRelated.Open cmdTemp, , adOpenForwardOnly, adLockReadOnly

REM display up to 5 related products:
if Not rsRelated.EOF then
%>
    <BR>
```

code continued on next page

code continued from previous page

```
      <B>See Also</B>
      <%
      nRelated = 0
      set skuField = rsRelated("sku")
      set nameField = rsRelated("name")
      set dept_idField = rsRelated("dept_id")
      do while Not (rsRelated.EOF Or nRelated >= 5)
          %><BR>
          <A HREF="<% = baseURL("product.asp") &
mscsPage.URLShopperArgs("sku", skuField.value, "dept_id",
dept_idField.value,"epartner_id=",epartner_id) %>"> <% =
mscsPage.HTMLEncode(nameField.value) %> </A>
          <%
          nRelated = nRelated + 1
          rsRelated.MoveNext
      loop %>
<% end if %>


<P>

<!--#INCLUDE FILE="i_footer.asp" -->

</BODY>

</HTML>
```

product_edit.asp

```
<%@ LANGUAGE=vbscript enablesessionstate=false LCID=1033 %>

<!--#INCLUDE FILE="include/Manager.asp" -->
<!-#INCLUDE FILE="xt_product_update.asp" ->


<SCRIPT>
<!--
dirty = false
//-->
</SCRIPT>

<% REM   header: %>
```

code continued on next page

code continued from previous page

```asp
<%
cmdTemp.CommandText = Replace("SELECT * FROM fivelakes_product
WHERE sku = ?", "?", "'" & Replace(Request("sku"),"'","''") &
"'")
Set rsProduct = Server.CreateObject("ADODB.Recordset")
rsProduct.Open cmdTemp, , adOpenStatic, adLockReadOnly

pageTitle = "Edit Product '" & rsProduct("name").value & "'"
%>
<HTML>
<HEAD>
    <TITLE> <% = pageTitle %> </TITLE>
    <META HTTP-EQUIV="Content-Type" CONTENT="text/html;
charset=ISO-8859-1">
    <!--#INCLUDE FILE="include/mgmt_define.asp" -->
</HEAD>

<BODY TOPMARGIN="8" LEFTMARGIN="8" BGCOLOR="#FFFFFF"
TEXT="#000000" LINK="#FF0000" ALINK="#FF0000" VLINK="#FF0000">
<!--#INCLUDE FILE="include/mgmt_header.asp" -->

<% REM    body: %>
<!--#INCLUDE FILE="include/error.asp" -->

<% if Not rsProduct.EOF then %>

<FORM METHOD="POST"
    ACTION="product_edit.asp">
    <INPUT TYPE="HIDDEN" NAME="Validate" VALUE="1">

<TABLE BORDER="0" CELLPADDING="0" CELLSPACING="0">
    <TR>
        <TD VALIGN="TOP">

            <TABLE CELLPADDING="5">
                <TR>
                    <% REM    label: %>
                    <TH ALIGN="LEFT" VALIGN="TOP">
                        Sku:
                    </TH>

                    <% REM    value: %>
                    <TD VALIGN="TOP">
                        <INPUT   TYPE="hidden"
                                 NAME="sku"
```

code continued on next page

code continued from previous page

```
                                        VALUE="<% =
mscsPage.HTMLEncode(rsProduct("sku").value) %>">
                          <STRONG><% = rsProduct("sku").value %></
STRONG>
                   </TD>
               </TR>

               <TR>
                   <% REM  label: %>
                   <TH ALIGN="LEFT" VALIGN="TOP">
                       Name:
                   </TH ALIGN="LEFT">

                   <% REM  value: %>
                   <TD VALIGN="TOP">
                          <INPUTTYPE="text" SIZE=32
NAME="name" VALUE = "<%=
mscsPage.HTMLEncode(rsProduct("name").value) %>"
onChange="dirty = true">
                   </TD>
               </TR>

               <TR>
                   <% REM  label: %>
                   <TH ALIGN="LEFT" VALIGN="TOP">
                       Description:
                   </TH ALIGN="LEFT">

                   <% REM  value: %>
                   <TD VALIGN="TOP">
                          <INPUTTYPE="text" SIZE=32
NAME="description" VALUE = "<%=
mscsPage.HTMLEncode(rsProduct("description").value) %>"
onChange="dirty = true">
                   </TD>
               </TR>

               <TR>
                   <% REM  label: %>
                   <TH ALIGN="LEFT" VALIGN="TOP">
                       List Price:
                   </TH ALIGN="LEFT">

                   <% REM  value: %>
                   <TD VALIGN="TOP">
```

code continued on next page

code continued from previous page

```
                                <INPUTTYPE="text"  SIZE=32
NAME="list_price" VALUE = "<% =
MSCSDataFunctions.Money(rsProduct("list_price").value) %>"
onChange="dirty = true">
                </TD>
            </TR>

            <TR>
                <% REM  label: %>
                <TD VALIGN="TOP">
                    Image File:
                </TD>

                <% REM  value: %>
                <TD VALIGN="TOP">
                    <INPUT TYPE="text" SIZE=32
NAME="image_file" VALUE="<% if Request("image_file").count > 0
then %><%= mscsPage.HTMLEncode(Request("image_file")) %><%
else %><%= mscsPage.HTMLEncode(rsProduct("image_file").value)
%><% end if %>" onChange="dirty = true">
<BR><FONT SIZE="-1">put filename above, place file in <BR>"<%=
Server.MapPath("/" & mscsPage.SiteRoot)
%>\assets\product_images"</FONT>
                </TD>
            </TR>

            <TR>
                <% REM  label: %>
                <TD VALIGN="TOP">
                    Image Width:
                </TD>

                <% REM  value: %>
                <TD VALIGN="TOP">
                    <INPUTTYPE="text"  SIZE=32
NAME="image_width" VALUE = "<%=
mscsPage.HTMLEncode(rsProduct("image_width").value) %>"
onChange="dirty = true">
                </TD>
            </TR>

            <TR>
                <% REM  label: %>
                <TD VALIGN="TOP">
                    Image Height:
```

code continued on next page

code continued from previous page

```
                              </TD>

                              <% REM  value: %>
                              <TD VALIGN="TOP">
                                      <INPUTTYPE="text"  SIZE=32
NAME="image_height" VALUE = "<%=
mscsPage.HTMLEncode(rsProduct("image_height").value) %>"
onChange="dirty = true">
                              </TD>
                      </TR>

                      <TR>
                              <% REM  label: %>
                              <TD VALIGN="TOP">
                                 Sale Price:
                              </TD>

                              <% REM  value: %>
                              <TD VALIGN="TOP">
                                      <INPUTTYPE="text"  SIZE=32
NAME="sale_price" VALUE = "<% =
MSCSDataFunctions.Money(rsProduct("sale_price").value) %>"
onChange="dirty = true">
                              </TD>
                      </TR>

                      <TR>
                              <% REM  label: %>
                              <TD VALIGN="TOP">
                                 Sale Start:
                              </TD>

                              <% REM  value: %>
                              <TD VALIGN="TOP">
                                      <INPUTTYPE="text"  SIZE=32
NAME="sale_start" VALUE = "<%=
mscsPage.HTMLEncode(rsProduct("sale_start").value) %>"
onChange="dirty = true">
                              </TD>
                      </TR>

                      <TR>
                              <% REM  label: %>
                              <TD VALIGN="TOP">
                                 Sale End:
```

code continued on next page

code continued from previous page

```
                        </TD>

                        <% REM  value: %>
                        <TD VALIGN="TOP">
                            <INPUTTYPE="text"  SIZE=32
NAME="sale_end" VALUE = "<%=
mscsPage.HTMLEncode(rsProduct("sale_end").value) %>"
onChange="dirty = true">
                        </TD>
                    </TR>

                    <TR>
                        <% REM  label: %>
                        <TH ALIGN="LEFT" VALIGN="TOP">
                            Publisher:
                        </TH>

                        <% REM  value: %>
                        <TD VALIGN="TOP">
                            <INPUTTYPE="text"  SIZE=32
NAME="publisher" VALUE = "<%=
mscsPage.HTMLEncode(rsProduct("publisher").value) %>"
onChange="dirty = true">
                        </TD>
                    </TR>

                    <TR>
                        <% REM  label: %>
                        <TH ALIGN="LEFT" VALIGN="TOP">
                            Edition:
                        </TH>

                        <% REM  value: %>
                        <TD VALIGN="TOP">
                            <INPUTTYPE="text"  SIZE=32
NAME="edition" VALUE = "<%=
mscsPage.HTMLEncode(rsProduct("edition").value) %>"
onChange="dirty = true">
                        </TD>
                    </TR>

                    <TR>
                        <% REM  label: %>
                        <TH ALIGN="LEFT" VALIGN="TOP">
                            Author:
```

code continued on next page

code continued from previous page

```
                        </TH>

                        <% REM  value: %>
                        <TD VALIGN="TOP">
                            <INPUTTYPE="text"  SIZE=32
NAME="author" VALUE = "<%=
mscsPage.HTMLEncode(rsProduct("author").value) %>"
onChange="dirty = true">
                        </TD>
                    </TR>

                    <TR>
                        <% REM  label: %>
                        <TH ALIGN="LEFT" VALIGN="TOP">
                            Category:
                        </TH>

                        <% REM  value: %>
                        <TD VALIGN="TOP">
                            <INPUTTYPE="text"  SIZE=32
NAME="category" VALUE = "<%=
mscsPage.HTMLEncode(rsProduct("category").value) %>"
onChange="dirty = true">
                        </TD>
                    </TR>

                </TABLE>
            </TD>
            <TD VALIGN="TOP">
                <TABLE BORDER=0 CELLPADDING=0 CELLSPACING=0>
                    <TR>
                        <TD VALIGN="TOP">
                            <% if Request("image_file").count > 0
then %>
                            <IMG SRC="<%= "/" &
mscsPage.SiteRoot %>/assets/product_images/<%=
mscsPage.HTMLEncode(Request("image_file")) %>"
                                WIDTH="<% =
Request("image_width") %>"
                                HEIGHT="<% =
Request("image_height") %>">
                            <% elseif not
IsNull(rsProduct("image_file").value) and _
```

code continued on next page

code continued from previous page

```
MSCSDataFunctions.CleanString(rsProduct("image_file").value)
<> "" then %>
                              <IMG SRC="<%= "/" &
mscsPage.SiteRoot %>/assets/product_images/<%=
mscsPage.HTMLEncode(rsProduct("image_file").value) %>"
                              WIDTH="<% =
rsProduct("image_width").value %>"
                              HEIGHT="<% =
rsProduct("image_height").value %>">
                      <% else %>
                          <FONT FACE="Arial, sans-serif">No
image entered</FONT>
                      <% end if %>
                      <P>
                      <%
                      cmdTemp.CommandText = "SELECT dept_id,
dept_name FROM fivelakes_dept ORDER BY dept_name"
                      Set rsDept =
Server.CreateObject("ADODB.Recordset")
                          rsDept.Open cmdTemp, , adOpenStatic,
adLockReadOnly

                      if Not rsDept.EOF then
                      %>
                      Department:<BR>
                      <FONT FACE="Arial, sans-serif"
SIZE="-1">(control-click to<BR>
                      select multiple)</FONT><BR>
                      <SELECT NAME="dept_id" SIZE="10"
onChange="dirty = true" MULTIPLE>
                      <%
                      cmdTemp.CommandText = Replace("SELECT
dept_id FROM fivelakes_dept_prod WHERE sku = ?", "?", "'" &
Replace(rsProduct("sku").value,"'","''") & "'")
                      Set rsPDept =
Server.CreateObject("ADODB.Recordset")
                          rsPDept.Open cmdTemp, , adOpenStatic,
adLockReadOnly

                      Do While Not rsDept.EOF
                          selected = ""
                          if Not rsPDept.BOF then
rsPDept.MoveFirst

                          Do While Not rsPDept.EOF
```

code continued on next page

code continued from previous page

```
                                        if CInt(rsPDept("dept_id").value) =
CInt(rsDept("dept_id").value) then selected = " SELECTED"
                                    rsPDept.MoveNext
                        Loop %>
                        <OPTION VALUE="<%=
rsDept("dept_id").value %>"<%= selected %>> <% =
rsDept("dept_name").value %> 
<%                              rsDept.MoveNext
                        Loop
                        %>
                        </SELECT>
                        <BR>
                        <FONT FACE="Arial, sans-serif"
STYLE="{font-family: Arial, sans-serif; font-size: 10pt}">
NOTE: You must add the product to at least one department in order
to make it visible for purchasing.</FONT>
                        <% else %>
                        <FONT FACE="Arial, sans-serif"
COLOR="#FF0000" STYLE="{font-family: Arial, sans-serif;
font-color: red; font-weight: bold; font-size: 10pt}">*** IMPORTANT
*** You must add Departments and select at least one department for
each product to display them in the store.</FONT>
                        <% end if %>
                    </TD>
                </TR>
            </TABLE>
        </TD>
    </TR>
</TABLE>

<TABLE BORDER="0" CELLPADDING="0" CELLSPACING="0">
<TR>
    <TD WIDTH="8"> </TD>
    <TD><INPUT TYPE="SUBMIT" VALUE="Update Product"></TD>
</FORM>
    <TD WIDTH="8"> </TD>
    <FORM METHOD="POST" ACTION="product_delete.asp">
        <INPUT TYPE="HIDDEN" NAME="name" VALUE="<% =
mscsPage.HTMLEncode(rsProduct("name").value) %>">
        <INPUT TYPE="HIDDEN" NAME="sku" VALUE="<% =
mscsPage.HTMLEncode(rsProduct("sku").value) %>">
    <TD>
        <INPUT TYPE="SUBMIT" VALUE="Delete Product...">
    </TD>
    </FORM>
```

code continued on next page

code continued from previous page

```
</TR>
</TABLE>
<H6>
     FIELD LABELS IN BOLD INDICATE REQUIRED FIELDS
</H6>


<% else %>
<P>
<FONT FACE="Arial, sans-serif" COLOR="#FF0000" STYLE="{font-family:
Arial, sans-serif; font-color: red; font-weight: bold; font-size:
10pt}">
<B>Product not found.</B>
</FONT>
<P>
<% end if %>
<BR>

<% REM    footer: %>
<!--#INCLUDE FILE="include/mgmt_footer.asp" -->
```

receipt.asp

```
<%@ LANGUAGE=vbscript enablesessionstate=false LCID=1033 %>

<!--#INCLUDE FILE="i_shop.asp" -->
<!--#INCLUDE FILE="i_ePartner.asp" -->
<!--#INCLUDE FILE="i_util.asp" -->


<%
REM -- Create a storage object for the receipts
Set mscsReceiptStorage = UtilGetReceiptStorage()

REM -- retrieve receipt from storage using the shopper id and
order id:
dim key(1), value(1)
key(0) = "order_id"
key(1) = "shopper_id"
value(0) = Request("order_id")
value(1) = mscsShopperID
on error resume next
set receipt = mscsReceiptStorage.LookupData(null, key, value)
```

code continued on next page

code continued from previous page

```
on error goto 0
if IsEmpty(receipt) then
    items = null
    nitems = 0
else
    set items = receipt.items
    nitems = items.Count
end if
%>

<HTML>
<HEAD>
    <TITLE><%= displayName %>: Receipt: <% =
Request("order_id") %></TITLE>
    <META HTTP-EQUIV="Content-Type" CONTENT="text/html;
charset=ISO-8859-1">
</HEAD>
<BODY
    BGCOLOR="#FFFFFF"
    TEXT=    "#000000"
    LINK=    "#FF0000"
    VLINK=   "#FF0000"
    ALINK=   "#FF0000"
>



<!--#INCLUDE FILE="i_header.asp" -->

<% if nitems <> 0 then %>
<TABLE BORDER="0" CELLPADDING="2" CELLSPACING="1">
    <TR>
        <TH BGCOLOR="#000000" VALIGN="TOP" COLSPAN="9">
            <FONT SIZE="4" COLOR="#FFFFFF"><B> Receipt # <% =
Request("order_id") %>  </B></FONT>
        </TH>
    </TR>
    <% REM ship to & bill to:  %>
    <TR>
        <TH BGCOLOR="#000000" VALIGN="TOP">
            <FONT SIZE="2" COLOR="#FFFFFF"><B> Ship To: </B></FONT>
        </TH>
        <TD VALIGN="TOP">
            <% = mscsPage.HTMLEncode(receipt.ship_to_name) %> <BR>
```

code continued on next page

code continued from previous page

```
                <% = mscsPage.HTMLEncode(receipt.ship_to_street) %> <BR>
                <% = mscsPage.HTMLEncode(receipt.ship_to_city) %>,
                <% = mscsPage.HTMLEncode(receipt.ship_to_state) %> 
                <% = mscsPage.HTMLEncode(receipt.ship_to_zip) %>

        </TD>
        <TH BGCOLOR="#000000" VALIGN="TOP">
            <FONT SIZE="2" COLOR="#FFFFFF"><B> Bill To: </B></FONT>
        </TH>
        <TD VALIGN="TOP" COLSPAN="2">
            <% = mscsPage.HTMLEncode(receipt.bill_to_name) %> <BR>

            <% = mscsPage.HTMLEncode(receipt.bill_to_street) %> <BR>
            <% = mscsPage.HTMLEncode(receipt.bill_to_city) %>,
            <% = mscsPage.HTMLEncode(receipt.bill_to_state) %> 
            <% = mscsPage.HTMLEncode(receipt.bill_to_zip) %>

        </TD>
        <TH BGCOLOR="#000000" VALIGN="TOP">
            <FONT SIZE="2" COLOR="#FFFFFF"><B> Date: </B></FONT>
        </TH>
        <TD VALIGN="TOP">
            <% = MSCSDataFunctions.Date(receipt.date_entered) %>
        </TD>
    </TR>
    <% REM item column labels:  %>
    <TR>
        <TH BGCOLOR="#000000" ALIGN="LEFT">
            <FONT COLOR="#FFFFFF">Label</FONT>
        </TH>
        <TH BGCOLOR="#000000" ALIGN="LEFT">
            <FONT COLOR="#FFFFFF">Name</FONT>
        </TH>

        <TH BGCOLOR="#000000" ALIGN="CENTER">
            <FONT COLOR="#FFFFFF">Unit Price</FONT>
        </TH>
        <TH BGCOLOR="#000000" ALIGN="CENTER">
            <FONT COLOR="#FFFFFF">Today's Price</FONT>
        </TH>
        <TH BGCOLOR="#000000" ALIGN="LEFT">
            <FONT COLOR="#FFFFFF">Qty</FONT>
        </TH>

        <TH BGCOLOR="#000000" ALIGN="CENTER">
```

code continued on next page

code continued from previous page

```
            <FONT COLOR="#FFFFFF">Extra Disc.</FONT>
        </TH>

        <TH BGCOLOR="#000000" ALIGN="CENTER">
            <FONT COLOR="#FFFFFF">Total Price</FONT>
        </TH>
    </TR>
    <% REM row values:  %>
    <% for each row_item in items %>
    <TR>
        <TD WIDTH="75" VALIGN="TOP">
            <% = mscsPage.HTMLEncode(row_item.[_product_sku]) %>
        </TD>
        <TD WIDTH="210" VALIGN="TOP">
            <% = mscsPage.HTMLEncode(row_item.[_product_name]) %>
        </TD>

        <TD WIDTH="60" VALIGN="TOP" ALIGN="RIGHT">
            <% =
MSCSDataFunctions.Money(row_item.[_product_list_price]) %>
        </TD>
        <TD WIDTH="60" VALIGN="TOP" ALIGN="RIGHT">
            <% =
MSCSDataFunctions.Money(row_item.[_iadjust_currentprice]) %>
        </TD>
        <TD WIDTH="30" VALIGN="TOP" ALIGN="CENTER">
            <% = row_item.quantity %>
        </TD>

        <TD WIDTH="60" VALIGN="TOP" ALIGN="RIGHT">
            <% =
MSCSDataFunctions.Money(row_item.[_oadjust_discount]) %>
        </TD>

        <TD WIDTH="60" VALIGN="TOP" ALIGN="RIGHT">
            <% =
MSCSDataFunctions.Money(row_item.[_oadjust_adjustedprice]) %>
        </TD>
    </TR>
    <% next %>

    <% REM divider:  %>

  <TR>
```

code continued on next page

code continued from previous page

```
<%
ship_status = Request("ship_status")
if trim(ship_status) = "Yes" then
   shipping_message = "The order has been shipped"
else
   Shipping_message = "The order has not yet been shipped"
end if
%>
<TH BGCOLOR="#000000">
   <FONT COLOR="#FFFFFF">Shipping Status:</FONT>
</TH>
      <TD>
<B><%=Shipping_Message%></B>
      </TD>
   </TR>
   <TR>
      <TH BGCOLOR="#000000" COLSPAN=8></TH>
   </TR>

   <TR>
      <TH BGCOLOR="#000000" COLSPAN=8 HEIGHT=2></TH>
   </TR>
   <% REM show subtotal:  %>
   <TR>
      <TD COLSPAN="5"></TD>
      <TH BGCOLOR="#000000" VALIGN="TOP" ALIGN="RIGHT">
         <FONT COLOR="#FFFFFF"><B>Subtotal:</B></FONT>
      </TH>
      <TD VALIGN="TOP" ALIGN="RIGHT">
         <B><% =
MSCSDataFunctions.Money(receipt.[_oadjust_subtotal]) %></B>
      </TD>
   </TR>
   <% REM show shipping:  %>
   <TR>
      <TD COLSPAN="5"></TD>
      <TH BGCOLOR="#000000" VALIGN="TOP" ALIGN="RIGHT">
         <FONT COLOR="#FFFFFF"><B>Shipping:</B></FONT>
      </TH>
      <TD VALIGN="TOP" ALIGN="RIGHT">
         <B><% =
MSCSDataFunctions.Money(receipt.[_shipping_total]) %></B>
      </TD>
   </TR>
```

code continued on next page

251

code continued from previous page

```
<% REM show handling:  %>
<TR>
    <TD COLSPAN="5"></TD>
    <TH BGCOLOR="#000000" VALIGN="TOP" ALIGN="RIGHT">
        <FONT COLOR="#FFFFFF"><B>Handling:</B></FONT>
    </TD>
    <TD VALIGN="TOP" ALIGN="RIGHT">
        <%=
MSCSDataFunctions.Money(receipt.[_handling_total]) %>
    </TD>
</TR>

<% REM show tax:  %>
<TR>
    <TD COLSPAN="5"></TD>
    <TH BGCOLOR="#000000" VALIGN="TOP" ALIGN="RIGHT">
        <FONT COLOR="#FFFFFF"><B>Tax:</B></FONT>
    </TH>
    <TD VALIGN="TOP" ALIGN="RIGHT">
        <B><% =
MSCSDataFunctions.Money(receipt.[_tax_total]) %></B>
    </TD>
</TR>
<% REM divider:  %>
<TR>
    <TD COLSPAN="5"></TD>
    <TD BGCOLOR="#000000" COLSPAN="3" HEIGHT="4"></TD>
</TR>
<% REM show total:  %>
<TR>
    <TD COLSPAN=5></TD>
    <TH BGCOLOR="#000000" VALIGN="TOP" ALIGN="RIGHT">
        <FONT COLOR="#FFFFFF"><B>Total:</B></FONT>
    </TH>
    <TD VALIGN=TOP ALIGN=RIGHT>
        <B><% =
MSCSDataFunctions.Money(receipt.[_total_total]) %></B>
    </TD>
</TR>
<% REM divider:  %>
<TR>
    <TD COLSPAN="8" HEIGHT="2"></TD>
</TR>
</TABLE>
<% else %>
```

code continued on next page

code continued from previous page

```
        <TABLE WIDTH="100%" BORDER="0" CELLPADDING="8">
            <TR>
                <TD>
                    <STRONG>Receipt # <% = Request("order_id")
%> not found.</STRONG>
                </TD>
            </TR>
        </TABLE>
<% end if %>
<!--#INCLUDE FILE="i_footer.asp" -->
</BODY>
</HTML>
```

receipts.asp

```
<%@ LANGUAGE=vbscript enablesessionstate=false LCID=1033 %>

<% Response.ExpiresAbsolute=DateAdd("yyyy", -10, Date) %>

<!--#INCLUDE FILE="i_shop.asp" -->
<!--#INCLUDE FILE="i_ePartner.asp" -->
<!--#INCLUDE FILE="i_util.asp" -->

<HTML>
<HEAD>
    <TITLE><%= displayName %>: Order History</TITLE>
    <META HTTP-EQUIV="Content-Type" CONTENT="text/html;
charset=ISO-8859-1">
</HEAD>
<BODY
    BGCOLOR="#FFFFFF"
    TEXT=   "#000000"
    LINK=   "#FF0000"
    VLINK=  "#FF0000"
    ALINK=  "#FF0000"
>

<!--#INCLUDE FILE="i_header.asp" -->

<%

sqlText =
Replace(MSCSQueryMap.receipts_for_shopper.SQLCommand,":1","'"
```

code continued on next page

code continued from previous page

```
& mscsShopperID & "'")
Set rsReceipts = MSCS.Execute (sqlText, nReceipts, adCmdText)
%>
<TABLE WIDTH="400"
    BORDER=     "0"
    CELLPADDING="2"
    CELLSPACING="2"
>
    <TR>
        <TD COLSPAN="3" ALIGN="CENTER" BGCOLOR="#000000">
            <FONT COLOR="#FFFFFF" SIZE="5">
                Order History

            </FONT>
        </TD>
    </TR>
    <TR>
        <TH BGCOLOR="#000000"><FONT COLOR="#FFFFFF">Order
#</FONT></TH>
        <TH BGCOLOR="#000000"><FONT COLOR="#FFFFFF">Date</FONT></TH>
        <TH BGCOLOR="#000000"><FONT COLOR="#FFFFFF">Amount</FONT>
</TH>
    </TR>
    <%
    if Not rsReceipts.EOF then
        set order_idField = rsReceipts("order_id")
        set date_enteredField = rsReceipts("date_entered")
        set totalField = rsReceipts("total")
        do while Not rsReceipts.EOF
            %>
            <TR>
                <TD WIDTH="100" VALIGN="TOP" ALIGN="CENTER">
                    <A HREF="<% = baseURL("receipt.asp") &
mscsPage.URLShopperArgs("order_id",
order_idField.value,"epartner_id",epartner_id) %>"> <% =
mscsPage.HTMLEncode(order_idField.value) %> </A>
                </TD>
                <TD WIDTH="100" VALIGN="TOP" ALIGN="CENTER">
                    <% =
MSCSDataFunctions.Date(date_enteredField.value) %>
                </TD>
                <TD WIDTH="100" VALIGN="TOP" ALIGN="RIGHT">
                    <% =
MSCSDataFunctions.Money(totalField.value) %>
                </TD>
```

code continued on next page

code continued from previous page

```
            </TR>
                <% rsReceipts.MoveNext
        loop
        rsReceipts.Close
        %>

    <% else %>
    <TR>
        <TD COLSPAN="3">
        No receipts found.
        </TD>
    </TR>
    <% end if %>
</TABLE>
<!--#INCLUDE FILE="i_footer.asp" -->
</BODY>
</HTML>
```

xt_orderform_additem.asp

```
<%@ LANGUAGE=vbscript enablesessionstate=false LCID=1033 %>

<!--#INCLUDE FILE="i_shop.asp" -->
<!--#INCLUDE FILE="i_ePartner.asp" -->
<!--#INCLUDE FILE="i_util.asp" -->

<%
function OrderFormAddItem(byVal orderFormStorage, byVal shopperID)
    Set mscsOrderForm = UtilGetOrderForm(mscsOrderFormStorage,
created)

    REM -- retrieve quantity:
    product_qty = mscsPage.RequestNumber("qty", "1", 1, 999)
    if IsNull(product_qty) then
        product_qty = 1
    end if

    REM -- retrieve sku and dept_id:
    sku = mscsPage.RequestString("sku")
```

code continued on next page

code continued from previous page

```
quoted_sku = "'" & Replace(sku,"'","''") & "'"
dept_id = mscsPage.RequestNumber("dept_id")


REM -- retrieve product:
sqlText = MSCSQueryMap.product_info.SQLCommand
sqlText = Replace(sqlText, "?", quoted_sku, 1, 1)
sqlText = Replace(sqlText, "?", dept_id, 1, 1)
cmdTemp.CommandText = sqlText

Set rsProduct = Server.CreateObject("ADODB.Recordset")
rsProduct.Open cmdTemp, , adOpenStatic, adLockReadOnly

list_price = rsProduct("list_price").value
name = rsProduct("name").value
rsProduct.Close

REM -- add item to order form:
set item = mscsOrderForm.AddItem(sku, product_qty, list_price)
item.name = name
item.list_price = list_price
item.dept_id = dept_id

MSCS.Close

REM -- commit order form back to storage:
Call UtilPutOrderForm(orderFormStorage, mscsOrderForm, created)

OrderFormAddItem = true
end function

Set mscsOrderFormStorage = UtilGetOrderFormStorage()


success = OrderFormAddItem(mscsOrderFormStorage, mscsShopperID)
call Response.Redirect("basket.asp?" &
mscsPage.URLShopperArgs() & "&epartner_id=" &epartner_id)

%>
```

xt_orderform_clearitems.asp

```
<%@ LANGUAGE=vbscript enablesessionstate=false LCID=1033 %>

<!--#INCLUDE FILE="i_shop.asp" -->
<!--#INCLUDE FILE="i_ePartner.asp" -->
<!--#INCLUDE FILE="i_util.asp" -->

<%
REM - Create the order form storage
set mscsOrderFormStorage = UtilGetOrderFormStorage()

REM Get the order form
set mscsOrderForm = UtilGetOrderForm(mscsOrderFormStorage, created)

if mscsOrderForm.Items.Count > 0 then
    call mscsOrderForm.ClearItems()

    call mscsOrderFormStorage.CommitData(NULL, mscsOrderForm)
end if

call Response.Redirect("basket.asp?" & mscsPage.URLShopperArgs()&
"&epartner_id=" &epartner_id)
%>
```

xt_orderform_delitem.asp

```
<%@ LANGUAGE=vbscript enablesessionstate=false LCID=1033 %>

<!--#INCLUDE FILE="i_shop.asp" -->
<!--#INCLUDE FILE="i_ePartner.asp" -->
<!--#INCLUDE FILE="i_util.asp" -->

<%
REM Create a storage object for the order forms
Set mscsOrderFormStorage = UtilGetOrderFormStorage()

REM Get the order form
set mscsOrderForm = UtilGetOrderForm(mscsOrderFormStorage, created)

REM Get the index of the item to delete
if mscsOrderForm.Items.Count > 0 then
    index = mscsPage.RequestNumber("index", NULL, 0,
mscsOrderForm.Items.Count - 1)
```

code continued on next page

code continued from previous page

```
        if Not IsNull(index) then
            call mscsOrderForm.Items.Delete(index)

            call mscsOrderFormStorage.CommitData(NULL, mscsOrderForm)
        end if
end if

call Response.Redirect("basket.asp?" & mscsPage.URLShopperArgs()
& "&epartner_id=" &epartner_id)
%>
```

xt_orderform_edititem.asp

```
<%@ LANGUAGE=vbscript enablesessionstate=false LCID=1033 %>

<%Response.Buffer=true%>

<!--#INCLUDE FILE="i_shop.asp" -->
<!--#INCLUDE FILE="i_ePartner.asp" -->
<!--#INCLUDE FILE="i_util.asp" -->

<%
function OrderFormAddItem(byVal orderFormStorage, byVal shopperID)
    Set mscsOrderForm = UtilGetOrderForm(mscsOrderFormStorage,
created)

    if mscsOrderForm.Items.Count >0 then

index=Request.QueryString("index")
call mscsOrderForm.Items.Delete(index)
call mscsOrderFormStorage.CommitData(NULL,mscsOrderForm)
    end if
    REM -- retrieve quantity:
    product_qty = mscsPage.RequestNumber("qty", "1", 1, 999)
    if IsNull(product_qty) then
        product_qty = 1
    end if

    REM -- retrieve sku and dept_id:
    sku = mscsPage.RequestString("sku")
    quoted_sku = "'" & Replace(sku,"'","''") & "'"
    dept_id = mscsPage.RequestNumber("dept_id")
```

code continued on next page

code continued from previous page

```
REM -- retrieve product:
sqlText = MSCSQueryMap.product_info.SQLCommand
sqlText = Replace(sqlText, "?", quoted_sku, 1, 1)
sqlText = Replace(sqlText, "?", dept_id, 1, 1)
cmdTemp.CommandText = sqlText
Set rsProduct = Server.CreateObject("ADODB.Recordset")
rsProduct.Open cmdTemp, , adOpenStatic, adLockReadOnly

list_price = rsProduct("list_price").value
name = rsProduct("name").value
rsProduct.Close

REM -- add item to order form:
set item = mscsOrderForm.AddItem(sku, product_qty, list_price)
item.name = name
item.list_price = list_price
item.dept_id = dept_id

MSCS.Close

REM -- commit order form back to storage:
Call UtilPutOrderForm(orderFormStorage, mscsOrderForm, created)

OrderFormAddItem = true
end function

Set mscsOrderFormStorage = UtilGetOrderFormStorage()


success = OrderFormAddItem(mscsOrderFormStorage,
mscsShopperID)
call Response.Redirect("basket.asp?" &
mscsPage.URLShopperArgs()& "&epartner_id=" &epartner_id)

%>
```

xt_orderform_editquantities.asp

```
<%@ LANGUAGE=vbscript enablesessionstate=false LCID=1033 %>

<!--#INCLUDE FILE="i_shop.asp" -->
<!--#INCLUDE FILE="i_ePartner.asp" -->
<!--#INCLUDE FILE="i_util.asp" -->
```

code continued on next page

code continued from previous page

```
<%
REM Create a storage object for the order forms
Set mscsOrderFormStorage = UtilGetOrderFormStorage()

REM Get the order form
set mscsOrderForm = UtilGetOrderForm(mscsOrderFormStorage, created)

strError = ""
if Not IsEmpty(mscsOrderForm) then
    set items = mscsOrderForm.Items
    for index = mscsOrderForm.Items.Count - 1 to 0 step -1
        set item = items(index)
        quantity = mscsPage.RequestNumber("qty_" &
CStr(index), item.quantity, 0, 999)
        if IsNull(quantity) then
            strError = "nonnumber"
        else
            if quantity = 0 then
                call mscsOrderForm.Items.Delete(index)
            else
                item.quantity = quantity
            end if
            call MSCSOrderFormStorage.CommitData(null,
mscsOrderForm)
        end if
    next
end if

if strError = "" then
    pageRedirect = "basket.asp?" & mscsPage.URLShopperArgs()
else
    pageRedirect = "basket.asp?" &
mscsPage.URLShopperArgs("error", strError,"epartner_id="
epartner_id)
end if

Response.Redirect(pageRedirect)
%>
```

xt_orderform_prepare.asp

```
<%@ LANGUAGE=vbscript enablesessionstate=false LCID=1033 %>

<!--#INCLUDE FILE="i_shop.asp" -->
<!--#INCLUDE FILE="i_ePartner.asp" -->
<!--#INCLUDE FILE="i_util.asp" -->

<%
function OrderFormPrepareArgs(byRef orderForm, byRef errorList)

    orderform.epartner_ID=request.QueryString("epartner_id")

    REM -- shipping method:
    orderForm.shipping_method =
mscsPage.RequestString("shipping_method")


    REM -- ship to:
    ship_to_name = mscsPage.RequestString("ship_to_name",
null, 1, 100)
    if IsNull(ship_to_name) then
        errorList.Add("Ship to name must be a string between 1
and 100 characters")
    else
        orderForm.ship_to_name = ship_to_name
        orderForm.bill_to_name = orderForm.ship_to_name
    end if

    ship_to_street = mscsPage.RequestString("ship_to_street",
null, 1, 100)
    if IsNull(ship_to_street) then
        errorList.Add("Ship to street must be a string between
1 and 100 characters")
    else
        orderForm.ship_to_street = ship_to_street
        orderForm.bill_to_street = orderForm.ship_to_street
    end if
    ship_to_city   = mscsPage.RequestString("ship_to_city",
null, 1, 100)
    if IsNull(ship_to_city) then
        errorList.Add("Ship to city must be a string between 1
and 100 characters")
    else
        orderForm.ship_to_city = ship_to_city
```

code continued on next page

code continued from previous page

```
            orderForm.bill_to_city = orderForm.ship_to_city
        end if
        ship_to_state   = mscsPage.RequestString("ship_to_state",
null, 1, 100)
        if IsNull(ship_to_state) then
            errorList.Add("Ship to zip must be a string between
1 and 100 characters")
        else
            orderForm.ship_to_state = ship_to_state
            orderForm.bill_to_state = orderForm.ship_to_state
        end if
        ship_to_zip     = mscsPage.RequestString("ship_to_zip",
null, 1, 100)
        if IsNull(ship_to_zip) then
            errorList.Add("Ship to zip must be a string between 1
and 100 characters")
        else
            orderForm.ship_to_zip = ship_to_zip
            orderForm.bill_to_zip = orderForm.ship_to_zip
        end if

        ship_to_country = mscsPage.RequestString("ship_to_country",
null, 1, 100)
        if IsNull(ship_to_country) then
            errorList.Add("Ship to country must be a string between
1 and 100 characters")
        else
            orderForm.ship_to_country = ship_to_country
            orderForm.bill_to_country = orderForm.ship_to_country
        end if

        ship_to_phone   = mscsPage.RequestString("ship_to_phone",
null, 1, 100)
        if IsNull(ship_to_phone) then
            errorList.Add("Ship to phone must be a string between 1
and 100 characters")
        else
            orderForm.ship_to_phone = ship_to_phone
            orderForm.bill_to_phone = orderForm.ship_to_phone
        end if

    ship_to_email = mscsPage.RequestString("ship_to_email",
null, 1, 100)
    if IsNull(ship_to_email) then
        errorList.Add("Ship to email must be a string between 1 and
```

code continued on next page

code continued from previous page

```
100 characters")
  else
      orderForm.ship_to_email = ship_to_email
      orderForm.bill_to_email = orderForm.ship_to_email
  end if

  REM Retrieve tax_rate and code from FiveLakes_country table

  quoted_country = "'" & Replace(ship_to_country,"'","''") & "'"
REM -- add quotes
  sqlText = MSCSQueryMap.country_tax.SQLCommand
  sqlText = Replace(sqlText,":1",quoted_country)
  sqlText = Replace(sqlText,":2",quoted_country)
  cmdTemp.CommandText = sqlText
  set rscountry_tax = Server.CreateObject("ADODB.Recordset")
  rscountry_tax.Open cmdTemp, , adOpenForwardOnly, adLockReadOnly
  if not rscountry_tax.EOF then
      orderform.ship_to_country = rscountry_tax("country")
      orderform.tax_rate = rscountry_tax("tax_rate")
  end if
end function

REM Create a dictionary to store errors
Set errorList = Server.CreateObject("Commerce.SimpleList")

REM Get the order form storage
Set mscsOrderFormStorage = UtilGetOrderFormStorage()

REM Get the order form
Set mscsOrderForm = UtilGetOrderForm(mscsOrderFormStorage, created)

REM Retreive the args from the form
Call OrderFormPrepareArgs(mscsOrderForm, errorList)

if errorList.Count > 0 then
%>
    <!--#INCLUDE FILE="i_error.asp" -->
<%

else
    call UtilPutOrderForm(mscsOrderFormStorage, mscsOrderForm,
created)

    call Response.Redirect("payment.asp?" & "epartner_id=" &
epartner_id & "&" & mscsPage.URLShopperArgs("use_form",
```

code continued on next page

code continued from previous page

```
mscsPage.RequestString("use_form", 0)))
end if
%>
```

xt_orderform_purchase.asp

```
<%@ LANGUAGE=vbscript enablesessionstate=false LCID=1033 %>

<!--#INCLUDE FILE="i_shop.asp" -->
<!--#INCLUDE FILE="i_ePartner.asp" -->
<!--#INCLUDE FILE="i_util.asp" -->

<%
function OrderFormPurchaseArgs(byRef orderForm, byRef errorList)
    REM -- cc info:
    cc_name = mscsPage.RequestString("cc_name", null, 1, 100)
    if IsNull(cc_name) then
        errorList.Add("Credit card name must be a string
between 1 and 100 characters")
    else
        orderForm.cc_name = cc_name
    end if

    cc_type = mscsPage.RequestString("cc_type", null, 1, 100)
    orderForm.cc_type = cc_type
    if IsNull(cc_type) then
        errorList.Add("Credit card type must be a string
between 1 and 100 characters")
    else
        orderForm.cc_type = cc_type
    end if

    cc_number = mscsPage.RequestString("_cc_number", null, 13, 19)
    if IsNull(cc_number) then
        errorList.Add("Credit card number must be a string
between 13 and 19 characters")
    else
        orderForm.[_cc_number] = cc_number
    end if
    cc_expmonth = mscsPage.RequestNumber("_cc_expmonth", null,
1, 12)
    if IsNull(cc_expmonth) then
        errorList.Add("Expiration month must be a number
```

code continued on next page

code continued from previous page

```
between 1 and 12")
    else
        orderForm.[_cc_expmonth] = cc_expmonth
    end if
    cc_expyear = mscsPage.RequestNumber("_cc_expyear", null,
1997, 2003)
    if IsNull(cc_expyear) then
        errorList.Add("Expiration year must be a number
between 1997 and 2003")
    else
        orderForm.[_cc_expyear]  = cc_expyear
    end if

    REM -- bill to:
    bill_to_name = mscsPage.RequestString("bill_to_name",
null, 1, 100)
    if IsNull(bill_to_name) then
        errorList.Add("Ship to name must be a string between 1
and 100 characters")
    else
        orderForm.bill_to_name = bill_to_name
    end if

    bill_to_street = mscsPage.RequestString("bill_to_street",
null, 1, 100)
    if IsNull(bill_to_street) then
        errorList.Add("Ship to street must be a string between
1 and 100 characters")
    else
        orderForm.bill_to_street = bill_to_street
    end if
    bill_to_city   = mscsPage.RequestString("bill_to_city",
null, 1, 100)
    if IsNull(bill_to_city) then
        errorList.Add("Ship to city must be a string between 1
and 100 characters")
    else
        orderForm.bill_to_city = bill_to_city
    end if
    bill_to_state  = mscsPage.RequestString("bill_to_state",
null, 1, 100)
    if IsNull(bill_to_state) then
        errorList.Add("Ship to zip must be a string between 1
and 100 characters")
    else
```

code continued on next page

code continued from previous page

```
            orderForm.bill_to_state = bill_to_state
        end if
        bill_to_zip     = mscsPage.RequestString("bill_to_zip",
null, 1, 100)
        if IsNull(bill_to_zip) then
            errorList.Add("Ship to zip must be a string between 1
and 100 characters")
        else
            orderForm.bill_to_zip = bill_to_zip
        end if

        bill_to_country = mscsPage.RequestString("bill_to_country",
null, 1, 100)
        if IsNull(bill_to_country) then
            errorList.Add("Ship to country must be a string between
1 and 100 characters")
        else
            orderForm.bill_to_country = bill_to_country
        end if
        bill_to_phone   = mscsPage.RequestString("bill_to_phone",
null, 1, 100)
        if IsNull(bill_to_phone) then
            errorList.Add("Ship to phone must be a string between 1
and 100 characters")
        else
            orderForm.bill_to_phone = bill_to_phone
        end if

    OrderFormPurchaseArgs = true
end function

function OrderFormPurchase(byRef errorList)
    OrderFormPurchase = null

  Set rsOrderID = Server.CreateObject("ADODB.Recordset")
  REM Extract Order ID value from the table
  cmdTemp.CommandText = "select NewOrderID from FiveLakes_orderid"
  set rsOrderID = cmdTemp.Execute
  New_oid = rsOrderID("NewOrderID")

  temp_val = Int(Mid(New_oid,7)) + Int("1")


    if len(month(now()))=2 then
      next_order_id = month(now()) & year(now()) & CStr(temp_val)
```

code continued on next page

code continued from previous page

```
  else
       next_order_id = "0" & month(now()) & year(now()) &
CStr(temp_val)
  end if

  cmdTemp.CommandText = "update FiveLakes_orderid set
NewOrderID = :1"
  next_order_id = "'" & next_order_id & "'"

cmdTemp.CommandText=Replace(cmdTemp.CommandText,":1",next_order_id)
  set rsOrderID=cmdTemp.Execute

    REM  Create a storage object for the order form
    Set mscsOrderFormStorage = UtilGetOrderFormStorage()

  REM Retrieve order from the storage
    Set mscsOrderForm = UtilGetOrderForm(mscsOrderFormStorage,
created)

  REM Storing the newly created ID
  mscsOrderForm.order_id = New_oid

    REM Retrieve args from form:
    Call OrderFormPurchaseArgs(mscsOrderForm, errorList)

    REM If the order form has no items, add an error
    if mscsOrderForm.Items.Count = 0 then
        errorList.Add("No items to order.")
    end if

    if errorList.Count > 0 then

        REM Save changes to the order form so far
        call UtilPutOrderForm(mscsOrderFormStorage, mscsOrderForm,
created)

        exit function
    end if

    REM Set the verify with flags onto the orderform
    call mscsPage.ProcessVerifyWith(mscsOrderForm)

    REM Create the basic pipe context
    set mscsPipeContext = UtilGetPipeContext()
```

code continued on next page

code continued from previous page

```
      REM Run the plan
      errorLevel = UtilRunPipe("plan.pcf", mscsOrderForm,
mscsPipeContext)

      REM -- Finally if no errors, run the actual purchase
      REM -- Create a transacted pipeline for this execution
      if mscsOrderForm.[_Basket_Errors].Count = 0 and
mscsOrderForm.[_Purchase_Errors].Count = 0 and errorLevel = 1 then

          REM Create the receipt storage
          Set mscsReceiptStorage = UtilGetReceiptStorage()

          REM Add the receipt storage into the pipe context...the
Save Receipt component uses it
          Set mscsPipeContext.ReceiptStorage = MSCSReceiptStorage

          REM Run the transacted pipe
          cmdTemp.CommandText =
Replace(MSCSQueryMap.email_Search.SQLCommand,":1",
Replace(mscsOrderForm.ship_to_email, "'", "''"))
        Set rsEmail = Server.CreateObject("ADODB.Recordset")
          rsEmail.Open cmdTemp, , adOpenKeyset, adLockReadOnly
          if not rsEmail.EOF  then
      errorLevel = UtilRunTxPipe("purchaseupdate.pcf",
mscsOrderForm, mscsPipeContext)
          else
      errorLevel = UtilRunTxPipe("purchaseinsert.pcf",
mscsOrderForm, mscsPipeContext)
          end if
        end if

      if mscsOrderForm.[_Basket_Errors].Count > 0 then
          REM - goto basket to show errors
          Response.redirect "basket.asp?" & mscsPage.URLShopperArgs()
          Response.End
      end if

    if mscsOrderForm.[_Purchase_Errors].Count > 0 or errorLevel > 1
then
        if mscsOrderForm.[_Purchase_Errors].Count > 0 then
            for each errorStr in mscsOrderForm.[_Purchase_Errors]
                errorList.Add(errorStr)
            next
        else
            errorList.Add("Unable to complete purchase at this time")
```

code continued on next page

code continued from previous page

```
        end if
        OrderFormPurchase = null

        exit function
    end if

    REM Save the order id before we delete it
    order_id = mscsOrderForm.order_id

    REM Purchase was successful....delete the order form from
the storage
    call MSCSOrderFormStorage.DeleteData(null, mscsOrderForm)

    REM Return the order id
    OrderFormPurchase = order_id
end function

Set errorList = Server.CreateObject("Commerce.SimpleList")

order_id = OrderFormPurchase(errorList)
if errorList.Count > 0 then
%>
    <!--#INCLUDE FILE="i_error.asp" -->
<%
else
    call Response.Redirect("confirmed.asp?" &
mscsPage.URLShopperArgs("order_id", order_id, "epartner_id=",
epartner_id))
end if
%>
```

Appendix B:
Setup Guide

Technical Requirements

Install and configure your computer by using the following information and instructions.

Required Hardware

- ◆ Personal computer with a 300 MHz Pentium II processor
- ◆ 128 megabytes (MB) of RAM
- ◆ 4-gigabyte (GB) hard disk
- ◆ 12X CD-ROM drive
- ◆ Network adapter
- ◆ 4-MB Video adapter
- ◆ Super VGA (SVGA) monitor (17 inch)
- ◆ Microsoft Mouse or compatible pointing device
- ◆ Sound card with amplified speakers
- ◆ Internet access

Required Software

- ◆ Windows NT 4.0 Server
- ◆ Windows NT Server 4.0 Service Pack 3
- ◆ Internet Explorer 4.01 SP1
- ◆ Windows NT 4 Option Pack
- ◆ Visual InterDev 6.0
- ◆ Front Page Server Extensions
- ◆ Windows NT Service Pack 4 and Y2K Update
- ◆ SQL Server 7.0, Standard Edition

◆ Site Server 3.0

◆ Site Server, Commerce Edition

◆ SiteServer Service Pack 2

◆ Microsoft Data Access Components 2.1 (MDAC 2.1)

◆ Active Directory Services Interfaces 2.5 (ADSI 2.5)

◆ Windows NT Server 4.0 Service Pack 5

Software Sources

Except where noted, this setup guide was developed using software from MSDN 1999 subscription CDs.

Reference Materials

It is recommended that you have a copy of the following reference materials available:

◆ SQL Server 7.0 Documentation

◆ HTML Help

◆ ASP Roadmap

Computer Configuration

The following configuration and naming conventions are used throughout this course and are required for the hands-on labs:

◆ Your computer should be configured as a stand-alone server named **ECOMMERCE.**

◆ When possible **use DHCP** to allocate IP addresses.

Setup Instructions

Use the following procedures to prepare your computer.

Before You Begin

You will need to do the following:

◆ Read through all setup procedures.

◆ Make sure that you have the *Building E-commerce Solutions: Business to Consumer* compact disc that is provided with the book.

Estimated time to set up the computer: 8 hours

Windows NT 4.0 Server

▶ **Installation options**

◆ Set server type as **stand-alone server**.

◆ Format the partition(s) with Windows NT File System (**NTFS**).

◆ Install NT 4.0 to **drive C:**.

◆ **Do not install Internet Information Server 2.0 (IIS)**.

▶ **To install Windows NT 4 Server**

1. From the **MS-DOS Prompt,** change directories to the CD drive's **i386** directory on the installation CD.

2. Type **Winnt /b**.

3. **Windows NT Setup** window appears.

4. A prompt appears asking for a confirmation of the source directory for set-up files, e.g. **E:\i386**. Press **Enter**. A progress bar displays as files are copied.

5. **MS DOS-based portion of setup is complete** dialog box displays. Follow onscreen directions. The computer restarts.

6. **Welcome to Setup** dialog box displays, press **Enter**.

7. **Mass storage detection** dialog box displays, press **Enter**.

8. The **End User License Agreement** appears. Page down to the bottom and press F8.

9. **Hardware and software component list** dialog box displays; press **Enter**.

10. The **Partition choice** dialog box appears. Select the C: drive if it has not been pre-selected. Press **Enter**.

11. In the **Format options** dialog box, use the down arrow to select the **Convert the partition to NTFS** for the C:\ drive. Press **Enter**.

12. A dialog box warning about converting to NTFS displays. Press **C**.

13. Install directory choice dialog box opens. Press **Enter**.

14. NT will examine disks for corruption. This is optional.

15. **Windows NT Server Setup** dialog box displays. Press **Enter**. The files are copied to your C: partition.

16. Remove the CD and press **Enter**. The computer reboots.

17. Windows NT Setup Welcome dialog box displays. Click **Next**.

18. Enter a name and organization name into these fields. Click **Next**.

19. Enter a valid CD Key into the CD Key field. Click **Next**.

Note Depending on the installation CDs you use, MSDN or retail version, a Licensing modes dialog box may displays at this point. If it does, enter 10 concurrent connections.

20. In the **Computer Name** dialog box, name the server **ECOMMERCE**. Click **Next**.

21. In the **Server Type** dialog box, select **Stand-Alone Server**. Click **Next**.

22. In the **Administrator Account** dialog box, type **password** in the password fields. Click **Next**.

23. At the **Emergency Repair Disk** dialog box, you will be prompted to create an emergency repair disk. This is optional. Click **Next**.

24. In the **Select Components** dialog box, accept the defaults and click **Next**.

25. **Windows NT Setup** is now ready to install Windows NT Networking. Click **Next**.

26. At the next dialog box ensure that the **This computer will participate on a network** and **Wired to the network** options are checked. Click **Next**.

Warning Do not install IIS 2.0. IIS will be installed during the installation of Windows NT 4 Option Pack. If for some reason IIS 2.0 is installed in the next step, then use upgrade plus option during option pack installation as noted below, in the installation procedure for Windows NT 4 Option Pack.

27. In the **Install Microsoft Internet Information Server** dialog box, clear the check box. Click **Next**.

28. At the **Network Adapter** search dialog box, set up the network adapter according to the manufacturer's instructions.

29. In **Network Protocols** dialog box, make sure that **TCP/IP Protocol** is selected and clear the NWLink/IPX SPX Compatible Transport selection. Click **Next**.

30. In the **Network Services** dialog box, click **Next**.

31. In the summary screen, click **Next** to install the selected components.

32. A **TCP/IP Setup** dialog box may appear. Click **Yes** if you wish to use DHCP.

33. In the **Network Bindings** dialog box, click **Next**.

34. The **Start the network** message box appears. Click **Next** to start the network.

35. Accept the default settings for **Workgroup and Domain**. Click **Next**.

36. In the final summary dialog box, Click **Finish**.

37. **Date/Time Properties** dialog box displays. Set the current date and time and your time zone. Click **Close**.

38. **Display Properties** dialog box displays. Click **OK**.

39. Click the **Restart** button when it displays.

Configure Drivers

▶ **Install hardware drivers**

Add appropriate drivers for display, sound, and NIC according to the manufacturer's instructions. Some hardware requires that Windows NT Service Pack 3 be installed for the drivers to work correctly.

▶ **Set the Video Display**

It is important to set the install the video driver and set the display properties at some point before installing Site Server Commerce Edition.

1. On the **Start** menu, point to **Settings** and click **Control Panel**. Double-click the **Display** icon. The **Display Properties** dialog box appears.

2. Click the **Settings** tab. In the **Colors** drop-down list box, click **256 Colors**, and set the **Screen area** slider control to **600 by 800 pixels**, and then Click **OK**.

Windows NT Server 4.0 Service Pack 3

1. Run the Windows NT Service Pack 3 Setup application.

2. **Welcome** dialog box appears. Click **Next** or press **Enter**.

3. **Software License Agreement** displays. Click **Yes** to accept.

4. In the **Service Pack Setup** dialog box, Install the Service Pack is selected by default. Click **Next**.

5. **Service Pack Setup** dialog box asks if you want an **Uninstall** directory. This is optional. Click **Next** after choosing one of the options.

6. **Service Pack Setup** dialog box appears. Click **Finish**. **Copying files** dialog box appears.

7. **Windows NT Service Pack Setup** dialog box tells you files have been updated then prompts you to remove any disks and restart your computer. Click **OK**. Computer restarts.

Internet Explorer 4.01 Service Pack 1

▶ **Installation options**

   ◆ Standard installation.

▶ **Install Internet Explorer 4.01**

1. Run the Internet Explorer setup executable.

2. If a **Confirm File Open** dialog box displays. Click **Open**.

3. **Internet Explorer 4.01 SP1 Active Setup** dialog displays. Click **Next**.

4. **License agreement** dialog displays; select **I accept the agreement**, and then click **Next**.

5. **Installation Option** dialog displays; select **Standard Installation**, and then click **Next**.

6. **Windows Desktop Update** dialog displays. The default is Yes to install the update. This is optional.

7. **Active Channel Selection** dialog asks you to select a country: United States is pre-selected. Click **Next**.

8. **Destination Folder** dialog box displays. Leave it at default path and click **Next**.

9. **Preparing setup** displays then begins copying files to the destination path.

10. At the **Setup has finished installing components** dialog, click **OK** to restart your computer.

▶ **Configure Internet Explorer 4.01**

1. Run Internet Explorer to launch the Internet Connection Wizard.

2. **Get Connected!** dialog box appears. Click **Next**.

3. In the **Setup Options** dialog box, choose the **third option** ("I already have an Internet connection setup on this computer and I do not want to change it.") Click **Next**.

4. **Use an Existing Connection** dialog box appears; click **Finish**.

5. An error dialog box may appear informing you that Internet Explorer could not open the Internet site. Click **OK**.

▶ **Set up the proxy in Internet Explorer**

Proceed with this only if you have a firewall and have a proxy installed.

1. Click the **View** pull down menu; click **Internet Options**.

2. Select the **Connection** tab and specify **Access the Internet using a proxy server**. Enter the information for your proxy server in the address and port fields.

3. Make sure that the checkbox for **Bypass proxy server for local (Intranet) addresses** is selected. Click **OK** to apply the settings and close the dialog box.

Windows NT 4.0 Option Pack

Note If during the installation of NT Server 4.0 you installed IIS 2.0, the steps will be different than the ones noted below. If IIS 2.0 is installed then use the Upgrade Plus installation option and choose Custom installation. Within the Custom installation options you will need to check the option to install Index Server.

▶ **Installation options**

◆ Custom installation

◆ Do not install Front Page Server extensions.

▶ **Install Windows NT 4.0 Option Pack**

1. Run the Option Pack setup executable.

2. The **Microsoft Windows NT 4.0 Option Pack Setup** dialog box displays. Click **Next**.

3. **End User License Agreement** displays. Click **Accept**.

4. At the **Installation type** dialog box. Click on the **Custom** installation button.

5. On the **Select Component** dialog box, clear the **FrontPage 98 Server Extensions** check box. Make sure that **Index Server** is checked. Click **Next**.

6. On **Internet Information Server** dialog box, accept the default paths and click **Next**.

7. **Microsoft Transaction Server 2.0** install dialog box appears. Accept the default path and click **Next**.

8. **Configure Administration Account** for Transaction Server 2.0 displays. Accept the default **Local** administration setting and click **Next**.

9. **Index Server Catalog Directory** choice displays. Click **Next**.

10. On the **Microsoft SMTP Service** dialog box accept the default path for the **Mailroot Directory** and click **Next**.

11. The **Completing Installation** dialog box displays while files are copied to your computer.

12. **Windows NT 4.0 Option Pack** dialog box displays, click **Finish.**

13. **Systems Settings Change** dialog box displays. Click **Yes** to restart your computer.

Visual InterDev 6.0

▶ **Installation options for Visual InterDev 6.0**

◆ Typical installation.

▶ **Begin installing Visual InterDev 6.0**

1. Run the Visual InterDev Setup application.

2. In the **Visual InterDev 6.0** welcome dialog box, click **Next**.

3. In the **End User License Agreement** dialog box click **I accept the agreement**, and then click **Next**.

4. In the **Product Number and User ID** dialog box enter a valid CD key into the product ID number field. Click **Next**.

5. In the **Install Microsoft Virtual Machine for Java** dialog box, click **Next**. A progress bar displays as files are copied. **Restart the computer** when prompted.

6. In the **Visual InterDev 6.0 Custom - Server Setup Options** dialog, accept the default setting - **Install Visual InterDev 6.0** and click **Next**.

7. Choose **Common Install Folder** when the dialog box displays; click **Next**.

8. Visual InterDev 6.0 Setup **Welcome** dialog box displays; click **Continue**.

9. **Product ID** message box displays; click **OK**.

10. Visual InterDev 6.0 **Setup installation options** dialog box displays; click **Typical** installation option. A file copy progress bar displays.

11. Visual InterDev 6.0 – **Restart Windows** dialog box displays. Click the **Restart Windows** button.

12. Upon restart, the **Install MSDN** dialog box displays. This is optional.

13. **Server Setups** dialog box displays. Do not launch the BackOffice Installation Wizard. Click **Next**.

14. At the **Register Over the Web Now!** dialog box, clear the **Register Now** checkbox and click **Finish**.

Note If you are installing from a network, and the machine restarts when you finish installing Virtual Machine for Java, you may see an Installation Wizard error message saying that it "encountered a critical error during installation"…"error accessing INI file..."

Just click OK. Then run the Setup program again. The installer will pick up where it left off.

Install Latest Front Page Server Extensions

This file may be downloaded from the Web at: http://officeupdate.microsoft.com/ frontpage/wpp/license.htm.

▶ **Installation steps**

1. Run the **Front Page Server Extensions** setup executable.

2. In the **Welcome** dialog box, click **Next**.

3. In the **License** dialog box, click **Yes**.

4. In the **Administrator Setup for Microsoft Internet Information Server** dialog box, click **OK**.

5. In the **Setup Complete** dialog box, click **Finish**.

6. If prompted to do so, restart the computer.

Windows NT Server 4.0 Service Pack 4

▶ **Installation steps**

1. Run the Windows NT Server 4.0 Service Pack 4 installation executable.

2. In the **Welcome** dialog box, click the **Accept the License Agreement** option, uncheck the **Backup files** option, and then click the **Install** button. Files are copied.

3. When installation is complete the **Windows NT Service Pack 4 Setup** dialog box displays again. Click the **Restart** button. The computer restarts.

4. After the computer restarts, when prompted, do not install the Year 2000 updates. The Y2K updates are installed in one of the later steps.

Internet Explorer 5.0

▶ **Installation options**

♦ Standard installation.

▶ **To install Internet Explorer 5.0**

1. Run the Internet Explorer setup executable.

2. **Welcome to Setup for Internet Explorer and Internet Tools** dialog boxes display. Accept the license agreement and click **Next**.

3. At the Windows update dialog box, click the **Install Minimal,** or **Customize your browser** option. Click **Next.**

4. In **Component Options** dialog box scroll down through the components. Click the **Wallet** check box in the Additional Components section. Click **Next.**

5. **Restart computer** dialog box displays; click **Finish.**

SQL Server 7.0 Standard Edition

▶ **Key installation points**

◆ Standard Edition

◆ Local installation

◆ Services Accounts dialog: set password to **password**

▶ **Installation procedure**

1. Run the SQL Server 7.0 setup executable.

2. At the opening dialog box, select **Install SQL Server 7.0 Components.**

3. In the **Install SQL Server 7.0 Components** dialog, select the **Database Server - Standard Edition** install option.

4. In the **Select Install Method** dialog box, accept the default **Local Install** option and click **Next.**

5. In the **Welcome** dialog box, click **Next.**

6. In the **Software License Agreement** dialog box, click **Yes.**

7. In the User Information dialog box, verify that the information is correct and click **Next.**

8. In the **Setup** dialog box **enter a valid CD key** and click **OK.** Click **OK** again in the **Setup product ID confirmation** message box.

9. In the **Setup Type** dialog box, click **Typical.** Accept the default installation locations, and then click **Next.**

10. In the **Services Accounts** dialog box, accept the default settings and set the password to **password.** Then click **Next.**

11. In the **Start Copying Files** dialog box, click **Next.**

12. In the **Licensing** dialog box click the **I agree that:** option, and then click **Continue.** Some installations may ask you enter the number of users; if this occurs add 25 users to your server.

Note Depending on which CD you use to install (MSDN or the retail version of SQL 7) you may see a **Choose licensing mode** dialog box at this point. If this dialog box comes up, click **Add licenses** and change the quantity to **25.**

13. After setup is done installing files, click **Finish.**

14. Exit the **SQL Server 7.0** setup application.

▶ **Set MSDTC Service to start automatically**

1. On the **Start** menu, point to **Settings, Control Panel** and open the **Services** applet.

2. In the **Services** control panel, scroll down the list of services and select **MSDTC.**

3. Click the **Startup** button.

4. Set Startup Type to **Automatic.**

5. Click **OK.**

6. Click **Start.** The service attempts to start. Once it is successful close the **Services** control panel.

MDAC 2.1

▶ **Installation steps**

1. Run the Microsoft Data Access 2.1 setup program.

2. In the **License Agreement** dialog box, click **Yes.**

3. In the **Microsoft Data Access 2.1 Setup** dialog box, click **Continue.**

4. Click the **Complete** button to install the Data Access components.

5. Restart Windows when prompted.

Tip MDAC 2.1.1.3711.11 (GA) is available for download from: http://www.microsoft.com/data/download2.htm

Create and Configure SQL Databases

▶ Create the FiveLakes SQL database

1. Copy the **FiveLakes** file from the root of the *Building E-commerce Solutions: Business to Consumer* CD into the C:\MSSQL7\Backup directory.

2. On the **Start** menu, point to **Programs, Microsoft SQL Server 7.0,** and then click **Enterprise Manager.**

3. Double-click the **Microsoft SQL Servers** icon in the left pane.

4. Double-click the **SQL Server Group.**

5. Open the group within the SQL server group corresponding to your machine name.

6. Expand the tree for the **Databases** folder and select **Databases.**

7. Right-click in the right pane. A list of options appears. Click the **New Database...** option.

8. Name the database **FiveLakes.**

9. Select the option for **File growth in megabytes.** Enter **10** into the **File growth** box.

10. Click **OK.**

▶ Create the DemoStore SQL database

1. Make sure the **Databases** folder is selected.

2. Right-click in the right pane. A list of options appears. Click the **New Database** option.

3. Name the database **DemoStore.**

4. Select the option for **File growth in megabytes.** Enter **10** into the **File growth** box.

5. Click **OK.**

▶ Restore the FiveLakes SQL database

1. Right-click the FiveLakes database. Click the **All Tasks** option, and then click **Restore Database...**

2. In the **Restore database** dialog box, click the **Options** tab.

3. Select the **Force restore over existing database** option.

4. Click the **General** tab.

5. Select the **From device** option.

6. Click the **Select Devices...** button.

7. Click the **Add...** button.

8. Click the path button (...). Within the C:\MSSQL7\Backup folder, select the FiveLakes database. Click **OK.**

9. Click **OK** to accept the default in the **Choose Restore Destination** dialog box.

10. Click **OK** again at the **Choose Restore Devices** dialog box.

11. Click **OK** to restore the database. A progress bar dialog box appears. Click **OK** when the database has been restored. If you see an error message at this point, you may have missed Step 3 and the **Force a restore** option.

12. Close **SQL Server Enterprise Manager.**

Warning The database name, log location or data location cannot be edited after they are setup. If you mistype one of these and accept changes, you will need to delete the database and recreate it.

▶ Create a System DSN for FiveLakes

1. On the **Start** menu, point to **Settings**, click **Control Panel**, and then double-click the **ODBC Data Sources** icon.

2. On the **ODBC Data Source Administrator** dialog box, click the **System DSN** tab, then click **Add.**

3. On the **Create New Data Source** dialog box, in the **Select a driver...** box, select **SQL Server**, and then click **Finish.**

4. On the **Create a New Data Source to SQL Server** dialog box, type **FiveLakes** in the Name field. In the **Server** drop-down list box, select **(local)**, and then click **Next.**

5. Select the **With SQL Server authentication using a login ID and password entered by the user** option button.

6. Type **sa** into the Login ID field, leave the password blank, and then click **Next.**

7. Select the **Change the default database to** check box, select **FiveLakes,** from the dropdown list. Click **Next.**

8. Click **Finish.**

9. On the **ODBC Microsoft SQL Server Setup** dialog box, click **Test Data Source...** to test connectivity to the database. Click **OK** if the tests complete successfully. If the tests are unsuccessful, review the error information for possible causes.

10. On the **ODBC Microsoft SQL Server Setup** dialog box, click **OK**.

11. On the **ODBC Data Source Administration** dialog box, click **OK** to complete creating a DSN.

▶ **Create a System DSN for DemoStore**

1. On the **Start** menu, point to **Settings**, click **Control Panel**, and then double-click the **ODBC Data Sources** icon.

2. On the **ODBC Data Source Administrator** dialog box, click the **System DSN** tab, and then click **Add**.

3. On the **Create New Data Source** dialog box, in **the Select a driver...** box, select **SQL Server**, and then click **Finish**.

4. On the **Create a New Data Source to SQL Server** dialog box, type **DemoStore** in the Name field. In the **Server** drop-down list box, select **(local)**, and then click **Next**.

5. Select the **With SQL Server authentication using a login ID and password entered by the user** option button.

6. Type **sa** into the Login ID field, leave the password blank, and then click **Next**.

7. Select the **Change the default database to** check box, select **DemoStore**, from the dropdown list. Click **Next**.

8. Click **Finish**.

9. On the **ODBC Microsoft SQL Server Setup** dialog box, click **Test Data Source...** to test connectivity to the database. Click **OK** if the tests complete successfully. If the tests are unsuccessful, review the error information for possible causes.

10. On the **ODBC Microsoft SQL Server Setup** dialog box, click **OK**.

11. On the **ODBC Data Source Administration** dialog box, click **OK** to complete creating a DSN.

Site Server 3.0

▶ Key installation points

- ◆ Need to set user accounts for Publishing and Search options.
- ◆ Choose custom installation: select SQL Server Database support.

▶ Installation steps

1. Run the Site Server 3.0 setup program.
2. In the opening screen, click on **Server Installation**.
3. In **Welcome** dialog box, click **Next**.
4. In the **Read the License Agreement** dialog box, click **Yes**.
5. In the **Specify Product and User Information** dialog box, confirm the Name and Company information, and then type in **a valid CD key** for the software. Click **Next**.
6. Click **OK** in the **Product ID Confirmation** message box.
7. In the **Specify Microsoft Site Server 3.0 Folders** dialog box, click **Next**.
8. In the **Choose Installation Type** dialog box, click the **Custom** icon.
9. The **Select Features** dialog box appears. Click the plus sign (**+**) next to Analysis to display the sub-components. Select the **SQL Server Database Support** option; then click **Next**.

Note If you forget to select SQL Server Database Support then proceed with installation. When Site Server 3.0 installation is complete restart the computer and re-run the installer. Choose to add components and select SQL Server Database Support.

10. In the **Specify a Program Folder** dialog box, click **Next**.
11. In the **Configure User Accounts** dialog box, click **Set User Account**. Type **password** into both password fields, click **OK**, and then click **Next**.
12. In the **Stop Services** dialog box, click **Next** to continue.
13. In the **Start Copying Files** dialog box, click **Confirm**. A progress bar appears.
14. In the **Setup Complete** dialog box uncheck the **Open Readme file** option. Click **Finish**.

15. Restart the computer.

> **Note** When installing Commerce Server 3.0, you may see a dialog box containing a message similar to the following:
>
> ```
> Confirm File Replace
> Source: C:\Microsoft Site Server\_install\_WSH\vbscript
> Target: C:\WINNT\System32\vbscript.dll
> The target file exists and is newer than the source. Overwrite
> existing file?
> ```
>
> Select **No to All** in this dialog box.

Site Server 3.0, Commerce Edition

▶ **Key installation points**

- ◆ Custom installation.
- ◆ Do not install the included sample sites.

▶ **Installation steps**

1. Run the Site Server 3.0, Commerce Edition setup program.

2. On the **Site Server Commerce Edition** opening screen click **Server Installation**.

3. In the **Welcome** dialog box, click **Next**.

4. In the **License Agreement** dialog click **Yes**.

5. In the **Product Information** dialog box, confirm the Name and Company information, then type in a valid CD key for the software. Click **Next**.

6. In the **Product ID Confirmation** message box, click **OK**.

7. In the **Microsoft Site Server 3.0, Commerce Edition** dialog box click **Custom**.

8. Clear the **Ad Manager, Ad Server, Clocktower sample site, Microsoft Market sample site, Microsoft Press sample site** and the **Volcano Coffee sample site** check boxes. Click **Next**.

9. In the **Question** message box, click **Yes**.

10. In the **Microsoft Site Server 3.0, Commerce Edition** dialog box, review the list of features that will be installed. Make sure no sample sites are being installed, and then click **Next**.

11. Clear the **Open ReadMe file** option, then click **Finish**.

12. At the **Site Server Commerce Edition** opening screen, click **Exit**.

Site Server 3.0 Service Pack 2

▶ **Key installation point**

◆ Do not create an uninstall directory.

▶ **Installation steps**

1. Run the Site Server 3.0 Service Pack 2 setup program.

2. In the **Site Server Service Pack 2** dialog box, click **Yes**. A progress bar displays as files are extracted.

3. In the **Welcome** dialog box, click **Next**.

4. In **License Agreement** dialog box, click **Next**.

5. In the **Install the service pack** dialog box, click **Next**.

6. Select the **No, I do not want to create an Uninstall directory** option. Click **Next**.

7. Click **Finish**. Services are finished then files are copied. Services are restarted.

8. At the **Site Server 3.0 Service Pack 2** message box, click **OK**.

9. A final **Site Server 3.0 Service Pack 2** message box displays. Click **OK**.

 Tip Site Server 3.0 Service Pack 2 is available for download from http://www.microsoft.com/siteserver/site/30/downloads/sp2.htm

ADSI 2.5

▶ **Installation steps**

1. Run the setup program.

2. **ADSI Welcome** dialog box displays. Click the **Yes** button.

3. In the **ADSI 2.5 License Agreement** dialog box. Click the **Yes** button.

4. **ADSI installation successful** message box. Click **OK**.

5. After setup is complete, click **Yes** to restart Windows if prompted.

Tip ADSI 2.5 is available for download from http://www.microsoft.com/ntserver/nts/downloads/other/adsi25/

Windows NT Server 4.0 Service Pack 5

▶ **Installation steps**

1. Run the Windows NT Server 4.0 Service Pack 5 installation program.

2. In the **Welcome** dialog box, click the **Accept the License Agreement** option, uncheck the **Backup files** option, and then click the **Install** button. Files are copied.

3. When installation is complete the **Windows NT Service Pack 5 Setup** dialog box displays again. Click the **Restart** button. The computer restarts.

Set Up the Sample Site

▶ **Create a virtual store directory**

1. Start Internet Explorer.

2. Open the URL **http://ECOMMERCE/SiteServer/Admin/Commerce/** to run the Site Foundation Wizard.

3. Click the **Server Administration** link.

4. Click the **Create** button.

5. Select **Default Web Site**, and then click **Next**.

6. Type **SampleSite** in the **Short name** text box. Make sure that there are no spaces between the words. In the **Display name** text box type **SampleSite Publishing**. Click **Next**.

7. On the **Select a Directory Location** screen, accept the default. This is where SiteServer will create a set of Web pages. This is also the destination directory of the sample files you will copy from the CD. Click **Next**.

8. On the **Formulate a Database Connection String** screen, select **FiveLakes DSN** in the list box of **available DSNs**. You may have to scroll down to the bottom of the list to find the **FiveLakes DSN**.

9. In the database login field type **sa**, and leave the password blank. Click **Next**.

10. On the **Specify Manager Account** screen, accept the default **Use an existing Windows NT account.**

11. In the **Select Windows NT Domain** screen, select the domain that corresponds to the machine name, such as **\\ECOMMERCE**. Click **Next.**

12. In the **Select a Windows NT account** screen, leave **Administrator** selected, and then click **Next.**

13. At the **Finish** screen, click the **Finish** button. The **Site Creation Complete** message appears.

14. Copy all the Sample Site files within the SampleSite directory on the *Building E-commerce Solutions* CD to **C:\inetpub\wwwroot\SampleSite.**

15. Start Internet Explorer and type the following URL into the Internet Explorer address field: **http://ECOMMERCE/SampleSite**
    The SampleSite Publishing website should open.

Appendix C:
Microsoft Site Server 3.0, Commerce Edition Performance Kit

Overview

Welcome to the Commerce Server 3.0 Performance Kit. This kit is intended to serve several purposes:

- To help you assess the performance needs of your Commerce Server site
- To show how to measure the performance of your Commerce Server site
- To provide some techniques for optimizing your site depending on your business needs

The performance of your Commerce Server site depends upon many factors. Many of these factors can be controlled by careful analysis and testing.

A good way to balance performance requirements, hardware requirements, and site functionality is to follow these general steps:

- Create a suitable development environment, as discussed below.
- Design and code your Commerce Server site with performance in mind.
- Tune and optimize the server environment.
- Test the performance of your site, at capacity loads, using tools such as WCAT or InetMonitor (described in this document).
- Determine the bottlenecks that impede the performance of your site.
- Make adjustments to the hardware environment, the design of your Commerce Server site, and server settings as needed. Repeat this process until you achieve the desired results.

These steps are described more fully in the following sections.

A companion document, *Commerce Server Capacity and Performance Analysis* is available on the Microsoft Site Server Commerce site (http://www.microsoft.com/siteserver/commerce). That document evaluates the performance and scalability characteristics of a Commerce Server sample site.

Getting Started

Before embarking on the deployment of a Commerce Server site, it's a good idea to assess performance issues. What hardware does a Commerce Server site require? How much bandwidth will the site require for the Internet connection?

Many vendors find the following configuration to be a useful starting point:

◆ A Web/Commerce server consisting of a one-processor computer, with 256 megabytes of memory.

◆ A second computer, identical to the first, to share the Web serving load and to provide redundancy in case of server failure.

◆ A SQL server consisting of a two-processor computer with 512 megabytes of memory.

As a simplified baseline for you to use in determining the hardware requirements for your own site, the following information was recorded by running Commerce Server sample sites on a baseline configuration consisting of :

◆ One computer with a 300 megahertz Pentium II processor, hosting Internet Information Server (IIS) and Commerce Server.

◆ One computer with a 200 megahertz Pentium Pro processor, hosting SQL Server 6.5.

◆ ODBC set to TCP/IP sockets.

◆ ProcessorThreadMax set to 10.

◆ ADO threading model set to BOTH.

The sample site described in this document (VC Turbo) was tested using the above configuration and the shopper profile and methodology that is defined in the Microsoft Site Server 3.0 Commerce Edition Performance and Capacity document (available from http://www.microsoft.com/siteserver/commerce). In this configuration, each server can support 800 simultaneous shoppers. Thus, the estimated total load for the production configuration listed above is 1600 simultaneous shoppers.

The shopper profile used by the scripts in this document assumes that shoppers spend much less time reading and more time navigating and making purchases than the scripts used in the Performance and Capacity document. If you change the shopper profile to match the profile used by the scripts in this document, then the number of simultaneous shoppers is closer to 100 per Commerce Server.

Capacity Planning

The question of what hardware is required and how much functionality can be implemented in a Commerce Server site given the available time, human resources, and site resources depends upon many factors, such as the number of customers that will be attempting to shop and the complexity of the site. Analyzing all the factors involved is as much an art as it is a science. The choices you make depend largely on your own business model, and thus are unique to each business.

In the world of physical retail stores, there is no such thing as the "perfect" model. Successful markets range from elegantly-furnished, well-staffed department stores all the way down to warehouse-style self-serve markets. Each store suits different market needs and customer expectations. In the same way, there is no "correct" hardware configuration for an electronic commerce site. Choices regarding the design and architecture of a commerce site belong with the merchant. The number of shoppers to support, the quality of the shopping experience, and dozens of other factors must be taken into account. Commerce Server provides the flexibility to support a wide range of customizable electronic commerce applications.

As a start, you might begin by asking yourself the following questions.

◆ What is the projected average load (number of simultaneous users connected to a site, which can be estimated by determining how many shoppers you expect to visit the site over a given time)? What is the projected peak load? How often will the site experience peaks? (The number of people visiting any site at a given time is a small percentage of the number of people who regularly visit that site.)

◆ What is the browse-to-buy ratio? On average, how many pages will a shopper visit for each product purchased? How many products will be purchased at one time? In general, browsing a site does not consume as much processing resources as the purchasing process does. The ratio between these types of users will drive many much of your requirements.

◆ How complex is the product database? How large is the product database? How many attributes are supported? How often is the database updated?

- How many external transactions must be supported? A business-to-consumer site typically communicates not only with the shopper but with the payment processor or gateway. A business-to-business site such as Microsoft Market might use both an order processing pipeline (OPP) to process the purchase order, as well as a Commerce Interchange Pipeline to communicate with the supplier.

- How design-intensive is the site? Large, high-resolution graphics and multimedia clips consume more bandwidth, increase response time for the user, and place a greater load on the server.

- To what extent must the site be database-driven? Pages that are hard-coded as HTML can be served more quickly than pages that must be processed by Active Server Pages (ASP).

- Will your site support search? Although a power feature for your shoppers, this functionality places a greater load on the server.

- Does your site use promotions heavily? Marketing tools such as cross-promotions, upsell promotions, and prediction-based promotions can boost sales, but because they involve additional queries and computations, they come at a cost in performance.

- Does the site involve other community-building applications such as events, bulletin boards, or chats? Each of these services adds to the total processing load. Does the site use other features of Site Server? These components may make a difference. For more information, see the Site Server documentation.

- How much analysis will your site require? Logging events consumes processor and I/O resources, although administering a site without some of these tools is not recommended.

- Which pipeline components are required by your business model? Not all components are created equally. Simpler components run faster than more complex components. In addition, components such as Payment, which must send and receive data from another site, are sensitive to Internet latency, the location of the servers involved, and the number of jumps between the Commerce Server and the payment gateway or processor.

- Does the site require international tax computations? These tend to require more computation and therefore place a greater load on the server.

- How much security does your site require? Running secure HTTP consumes more processing resources than non-secure HTTP.

- Will your site enable the Membership feature of Site Server? For more information on the impact of Membership on performance, see "Capacity and Performance Analysis for Membership," which is available on the Microsoft Site Server site (http://www.microsoft.com/siteserver).

◆ What legacy systems must your Commerce Server site connect with? Tying into external inventory and accounting systems can create a bottleneck for the Web server, depending on how they are implemented.

◆ If you are hosting your own Commerce Server site, be sure to invest in sufficient infrastructure to connect your server to the Internet. Depending on where your server is located, it may take a considerable length of time to have new lines installed. To avoid delays beyond your control, make sure that your telephony requirements are designed and managed for future expansion. Often, it is easier and quicker to add more servers than it is to upgrade connection capacity.

◆ What is your strategy for performing backups? This can be a hardware consideration, and can affect your site's availability.

◆ What is your strategy for replicating content?

If you are dealing with an Internet Service Provider (ISP), check the contract to make sure you are not billed excessively for exceeding a prescribed traffic limit.

If you are an ISP, add up the performance requirements of each of the Commerce Server sites that you will be hosting.

Designing for Performance

Performance can be regarded as one of many desirable features of your Commerce Site. Like all features, optimizing for performance comes at a cost: additional development effort, lost opportunity to develop other features, and possibly additional hardware expense. Designing a site for performance, then, requires a delicate balancing act of trading off performance, development complexity, and other site features.

The Turbo Volcano Coffee sample site has been developed to illustrate these tradeoffs.

Turbo Volcano Coffee Sample Site

Commerce Server includes a sample site called Volcano Coffee, a fictitious online retailer of coffee products. For this performance kit, we have modified Volcano

Coffee to demonstrate a number of steps you can take to improve the performance of your Commerce Server site.

The revised version, which we call *VC Turbo*, demonstrates an average performance of 210% that of the original sample site.

Sample site	Average pages/second:
VC30	6.76
VC Turbo	14.2

The following chart illustrates the gains on a per-page basis.

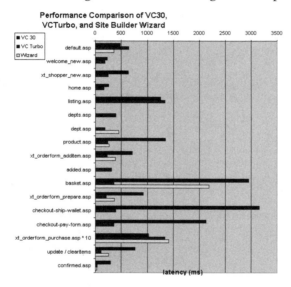

When compared against the original site (VC30), VC Turbo serves as an excellent illustration of how specific tradeoffs enable you to increase speed. The original sample site favors ease of programmability and maintainability, along with a rich user experience. VC Turbo foregoes certain features to provide a faster site that can handle more simultaneous shoppers while retaining essentially equivalent functionality.

The revisions illustrate that performance is a feature which, like any other feature, can be implemented in your site to varying degrees. Like any other feature, performance is achieved at some cost. In many cases, this cost is reflected in increased development time.

Installing VC Turbo

The VC Turbo site is packaged as a self-extracting executable file. To install the site, double-click the VCTurbo.exe file to launch Setup, which installs the site into the appropriate directories. VC Turbo is installed in \inetpub\wwwroot\ or whatever directory you specified as the Web root during the installation of Microsoft Internet Information Server (IIS).

You must have already created a database for the sample site's files. During setup, you must select the name of the DSN to use for connecting to the database, and you must supply the database login name and password. It is recommended that you install VC Turbo in the same database as the one used for the rest of the sample sites during the Commerce Server 3.0 installation.

How VC Turbo Has Been Optimized

The following sections describe the modifications that were made to the site.

Most of these changes are reflected in both the regular Commerce Server site and in the Buy Now site.

Split the Plan Pipeline

In VC30, the Basket page runs the 14-stage Plan pipeline, which performs a number of order calculations, as shown in the figure on the following page.

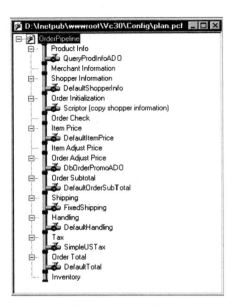

However, the VC30 Basket page simply displays a subtotal for the order. The results of the Shipping, Handling, Tax, and Order Total stages are not used in this page.

In the VC Turbo site, rather than call the Shipping, Handling, Tax, and Order Total stages every time the basket is run, the Plan pipeline is split into two smaller pipelines. The first pipeline (Basket.pcf) consists of five stages: Item Price, Item Price Adjust, Order Price Adjust, Order Subtotal, and Inventory, as shown in the following figure. (The concept of splitting a pipeline into multiple pipelines with fewer functions is handled similarly in sites generated by the Site Builder Wizard, where the Product.asp pipeline configuration includes only the product and shopper information stages, the item price stages, and the inventory stage.)

The second VC Turbo pipeline (Total.pcf) consists of the Shipping, Handling, Tax, and Order Total stages. When the basket is displayed, only the Basket.pcf pipeline is run. When the checkout process occurs (ship, pay), both the Basket.pcf and

Total.pcf pipelines are run. For a purchase, Basket.pcf, Total.pcf, and Purchase.pcf are run. Splitting the larger Plan pipeline into two smaller pipelines eliminates the overhead of running stages that are not used for the purpose at hand.

So what happened to the other five stages of the original Plan pipeline?

◆ The Product Information stage was removed for database performance reasons (see Eliminate the Product Information Stage, in the next section.)

◆ The Merchant Information stage was removed simply because it was not used, even in the original Volcano Coffee site.

◆ The Shopper Information stage was removed in favor of executing the query for shopper information directly on the ASP page.

◆ The Order Initialization stage was removed because the new architecture allocates an order ID by using an **identify** column in the database (see "Improve Generation of Order IDs," on page 313.)

◆ The Order Check stage was eliminated because it was not used.

These stages were deleted from the pipeline configuration using the Win32-based Pipeline Editor in Expert Mode. (For information on expert mode, open the Commerce Server 3.0 documentation and type *expert mode* on the Index tab.)

Eliminate the Product Information Stage

In VC30, the Plan pipeline is run in the Basket.asp, Checkout-pay.asp and Checkout-ship.asp files. The Plan pipeline includes the **QueryProdInfoADO** component (in the **Product Info** stage). The **QueryProdInfoADO** component executes a database query for each line item in the shopping basket.

This query is defined in VC30's Global.asa as follows:

```
MSCSQueryMap.product_purchase.SQLCommand =  "select sku, dept_id,
manufacturer_id, name, list_price, vc_product_family.pfid from
vc_product_variant , vc_product_family  where sku = ? and
vc_product_variant.pfid = vc_product_family.pfid"
```

In VC Turbo, rather than perform these extra queries, an SQL join operation is done against the product table to return the product data. (The **DBStorage** object is not used, as described later.) Instead of being performed in the pipeline, this query is executed in script on the page that is called when the shopper adds an item to the basket (xt_orderform_additem.asp). Then the product information is inserted as a record in the basket item information table, rather than being added to the order form object. See "Changes to the Pages," on page 302.

Running the product query once, and saving the results in the basket table, reduces the database interaction of the line items on the order form and pipeline to just one query.

Eliminate Use of the DBStorage Object

The **DBStorage** object's functionality is powerful and useful, primarily because it enables a flexible database schema. However, this flexibility comes at a cost. The **DBStorage** object must be created on every page on which it is used, due to Microsoft Transaction Server (MTS) considerations. MTS transactional objects are destroyed after the transaction is committed.

Additionally, the creation of this object requires that a query be executed to determine what columns exist in the database. Finally, because it works on the order form as a whole, the order form must be read in from the database, modified, and then written back to the database whenever changes are made.

Instead of using the **DBStorage** object, VC Turbo employs a more traditional database schema for orders and items. This change yields much faster interaction with the database. In the VC Turbo schema, adding an item to a shopping cart simply performs an insert.

MTS transactions can still be supported even though the **DBStorage** object is not used.

The disadvantage is that this architecture requires more programming effort. More ASP script is needed to manipulate the information in the product and basket tables. Also, modifying the order form (for example, adding a gift message) would require a change to the database schema and corresponding changes to the scripts that work against the database.

The following topics explain this change in detail.

Changes to the Database Schema's Basket Table

In VC30, the basket table (which contains the order forms for all shopping sessions currently in progress) consists of a single table (vc30_basket), containing the following columns:

shopper_ID
date_changed
marshalled_order

The marshalled_order column contains the order form for each shopper in a binary stream format. Values added to the order form by the order processing pipeline (OPP) or ASP script are saved automatically (by the **DBStorage** object) into the marshalled_order column, without requiring a change to the database schema.

In VC Turbo however, basket information is stored in two database tables. The order table (vcturbo_basket) and item table (vcturbo_basket_item) mirror the dictionaries for orders and items respectively.

The vcturbo_basket table contains information about the order as a whole:

shopper_id	ship_to_email
order_id	bill_to_name
created	bill_to_street
modified	bill_to_city
ship_to_name	bill_to_state
ship_to_street	bill_to_zip
ship_to_city	bill_to_country
ship_to_state	bill_to_phone
ship_to_zip	bill_to_email
ship_to_country	cc_name
ship_to_phone	

The vcturbo_basket_item table contains information about the individual items in each order:

shopper_id	quantity
created	placed_price
modified	monogram
item_id	attr_text
sku	name
pfid	

Changes to the Pages

In VC Turbo, the xt_orderform_additem.asp is called when the shopper adds an item to the basket. In that page, the function OrderGetItemSQL is first called to run a query on the product tables. The resulting information is then inserted into the vcturbo_basket_item table (as described in "Eliminate Use of the DBStorage Object," on page 300.)

```
Dim sql
sql = OrderGetItemSQL(pfid, attrs)

Set cmdTemp = Server.CreateObject("ADODB.Command")
cmdTemp.CommandType = adCmdText
Set cmdTemp.ActiveConnection = conn
cmdTemp.CommandText = sql
Set rsProduct = Server.CreateObject("ADODB.Recordset")
Dim rsProduct
rsProduct.Open cmdTemp, , adOpenKeyset, adLockReadOnly

if rsProduct.EOF then
    errorList.Add("This product is not available at this time.")
end if

if errorList.Count > 0 then
%>
    <!-#INCLUDE FILE="include/error.asp" _
<%
else
    Dim attr_text, pfReplace, Sku, Price, name

    attr_text    = OrderGetAttributeText(rsProduct, attrs)
    pfReplace    = Replace(pfid, "'", "''")
    sku          = rsProduct("sku").Value
    price        = rsProduct("list_price").Value
    name         = rsProduct("name").Value
    call OrderAddItem(mscsShopperID, sku, pfid, quantity, price,
attr_text, monogram, name)
REM Additional code not shown here
end if %>
```

The OrderGetItemSQL function is defined in Order.asp as follows:

```
function OrderGetItemSQL(pfid, attrs)
    Dim qpfid, I, s, f, w, t
```

code continued on next page

code continued from previous page

```
        qpfid = "'" + Replace(pfid, "'", "''") + "'"

        s = "b.name name, a.sku sku, b.list_price list_price"
        f = "vcturbo_product_variant a, vcturbo_product_family b"
        w = "a.pfid = b.pfid and a.pfid = " & qpfid

        I = 0
        while I < 5
            if attrs(I) <> 0 then
                t = "t" + CStr(I)
                s = s + ", " + t + ".attribute_value attr" + CStr(I)
                f = f + ", vcturbo_product_attribute " + t
                w = w + " and a.attribute" + CStr(I) + " = " +
CStr(attrs(I)) + " and " + t + ".attribute_index = " +
CStr(attrs(I)) + " and " + t + ".attribute_id = " + CStr(I) + " and
" + t + ".pfid = " + qpfid
            else
                w = w + " and a.attribute" + CStr(I) + " = 0"
            end if

            I = I + 1
        wend

        OrderGetItemSQL = "select " + s + " from " + f + " where " + w
end function
```

Here is the definition of the function OrderAddItem, which performs an SQL **insert** statement to add the item to the vcturbo_basket_item table:

```
function OrderAddItem(shopper_id, sku, pfid, quantity,
placed_price, attr_text, monogram, name)

        sql = "insert into vcturbo_basket_item "
        sql = sql + "(shopper_id, created, modified, sku, pfid,
quantity, placed_price, attr_text, monogram, name)"
        sql = sql + " values ( '" + shopper_id + "', GetDate(),
GetDate(), " + CStr(sku) + ", '" + pfid + "', " + CStr(quantity) +
", " + CStr(placed_price) + ", '" + Replace(attr_text, "'", "''") +
"', '" + Replace(monogram, "'", "''") + "', '" + Replace(name, "'",
"''") + "')"

        conn.Execute(sql)
end function
```

Similarly, in VC Turbo, deleting an item simply deletes a row.

Changes to Order Form Creation

In VC Turbo, creating an order form that can be passed as an argument to a pipe-line requires the execution of queries against the order and/or item table.

In Basket.asp, the order form is created as follows:

```
Dim nItemCount
Dim mscsOrderForm

Set mscsOrderForm = UtilRunBasket(mscsShopperId)
nItemCount = mscsOrderForm.Items.Count
```

The function UtilRunBasket is defined in the following script. The function creates an **OrderForm** object, then adds to this object the shopper ID, any items already placed in the basket and saved to the order form database table, and shopper data. Then the function runs the order form through the pipeline, using the basket.pcf configuration, and returns the processed order form object.

```
function UtilRunBasket(mscsShopperId)
      REM Create the order form
      Dim mscsOrderForm
      Dim mscsPipeContext
      Dim errorLevel

      set mscsOrderForm = Server.CreateObject("Commerce.OrderForm")

      REM Set shopper ID order field
      mscsOrderForm.shopper_id = mscsShopperId

      REM Get the items
      call UtilGetItems(mscsOrderForm, mscsShopperId)

      REM Get the shopper data
      call UtilGetShopper(mscsOrderForm, mscsShopperId)

      REM Get the pipe context
      Set mscsPipeContext = UtilGetPipeContext()

      REM Create and run the pipe
      errorLevel = UtilRunPipe("basket.pcf", mscsOrderForm,
mscsPipeContext)
```

code continued on next page

code continued from previous page

```
            REM Return the orderform
            Set UtilRunBasket = mscsOrderForm

    end function
```

The preceding function calls another function, UtilGetItems, which copies all the items in the shopper's basket (the vcturbo_basket_item table) into the order form object. The following script defines UtilGetItems:

```
function UtilGetItems(mscsOrderForm, mscsShopperId)
        Dim rsOrderItem
        Dim sql

        REM Get the item data
        sql = "select sku, item.pfid, item.quantity, item.monogram,
item.item_id, item.name, item.placed_price, attr_text "
        sql = sql + "from vcturbo_basket_item item "
        sql = sql + "where shopper_id = '" & mscsShopperId & "' "
        sql = sql + "order by item_id"
        set rsOrderItem = conn.Execute(sql)

        while Not rsOrderItem.EOF
            Dim item
            set item = mscsOrderForm.AddItem(rsOrderItem("sku").Value,
rsOrderItem("quantity").Value, 0)
            item.monogram = rsOrderItem("monogram").Value
            item.attr_text = rsOrderItem("attr_text").Value
            item.item_id = rsOrderItem("item_id").Value
            item.pfid = rsOrderItem("pfid").Value
            item.name = rsOrderItem("name").Value
            item.[_product_list_price] =
rsOrderItem("placed_price").Value

            rsOrderItem.MoveNext
        wend
end function
```

Changes to Promotions

In VC30, the **QueryProdInfoADO** component performs a query for each line item and writes the product information to the order form. This information can then be used by the promotion component, which looks for name/value pairs that begin with _product_ and that correspond to the columns in the product database.

In VC Turbo, the **QueryProdInfoADO** component is not used. The fields dept_id and manufacturer_id, which are added to the order form in VC30, are not included because they are no longer stored or fetched with the line item in the basket. The manager promotion pages have been modified so that the drop-down menus that that list these fields (in the selections for the award and condition of products) include only those fields that are actually on the order form.

Use Queries for Receipts

VC Turbo also eliminates the **DBStorage** object for saving receipts, for the reasons described in "Eliminate Use of the DBStorage Object," on page 300. The **SaveReceipt** pipeline component is replaced with a call to **SQLOrderADO**.

In VC30's vc_receipt table, each record represents one receipt (corresponding to one purchase transaction), and contains the following columns.

order_id
shopper_id
total
status
date_entered
date_changed
marshalled_receipt

In the same site, records in the vc_receipt_item table contains a subset of information about the individual items in each receipt. This table is provided so that queries can be run against items in the receipts table. The complete information about each item, from the order form, is saved in the marshalled_receipt column of the vc_receipt table. The vc_receipt_item table contains only the following columns.

pfidvarchar
sku
order_id
row_id
quantity
adjusted_price

In VC Turbo, these tables are somewhat different. Vcturbo_receipt does not contain a marshalled_receipt, but instead includes a separate column for each value pertaining to the order, including the shipping and billing addresses, credit card name and type, and order subtotals and totals. The vcturbo_receipt_item contains complete information about each item in the receipt, specifically the following columns.

order_id	quantity
shopper_id	product_list_price
created	iadjust_regularprice
modified	iadjust_currentprice
item_id	oadjust_adjustedprice
sku	monogram
pfid	attr_text
name	

The VC Turbo schema eliminates the redundancy of information that is found in VC30 and in some other Commerce Server sample sites. Manager page functions that display reports on purchases can use this new schema, without requiring redundant information. Similarly, Commerce Server sites that use the **Predictor** object can use this modified receipts schema as the seed table.

Use Queries for Shopper Management

As with shopping baskets and receipts, shopper management in VC Turbo is handled through direct database access instead of using the **DBStorage** object. The table that stores shopper information is directly manipulated and queried from the ASP page.

Replace Select * Queries with Specific Columns

Performance improves greatly when a query specifies only those columns that are actually needed by the ASP script instead of using `select *`.

In VC Turbo, `select *` queries have been replaced with queries that request only the needed columns.

Use Local Variables to Eliminate Repeated Function Calls

In pages where the same value from the **Request** object must be used repeatedly, a small performance gain can be achieved by getting the value once, and then storing it in a local variable for multiple uses on the page.

On pages where the **Replace** function must be called multiple times on the same string, a small performance gain can be achieved by calling the function once and saving the result in a local variable. For example, if the phrase `Replace(Request("pf_id", "'", "''"))` is called multiple times on the same page, you can define it as a local variable, as follows, and then simply refer to the local variable:

```
pfid = Replace(Request("pf_id", "'", "''")
```

In VC30, strings that need to be encoded for HTML are encoded when they need to be displayed on the page. In certain cases, a small performance advantage can be gained by encoding the string once on the page, and saving it in a local variable for repeat use.

For example, VC30's Default.asp contains three calls of the **Page.HTMLEncode** function to encode the site's display name for display on the page. The following is one of the three calls:

```
<TITLE><% = mscsPage.HTMLEncode(MSCSSite.DisplayName) %></TITLE>
```

In VC Turbo, the encoding is performed in Shop.asp (which is included in every page in the site):

```
Dim displayName
displayName = mscsPage.HTMLEncode(MSCSSite.DisplayName)
```

Then, in VC Turbo's version of Default.asp, the three references to the site's display name use the variable, as follows:

```
<TITLE><% = displayName %></TITLE>
```

Improve the Query for Getting Attribute Description Text

In VC30, a utility function retrieves descriptive text for attributes, to be displayed on the basket page. This function executes a query for each attribute set, potentially resulting in five queries. In VC Turbo, one query (albeit a complex multi-join) is executed to minimize hits to the database.

Eliminate the Query Map

In Commerce Server sites, the query map is intended to be used by components in the pipeline that must run SQL queries, and not for queries that are run on the page. In VC Turbo, all page-level queries are executed from SQL text directly on the ASP file. This provides a minor performance improvement because the SQL text does not need to be accessed from a global store. In addition, it allows pages to more optimally construct SQL at runtime.

For example, in VC30, the Global.asa file defines the following query map entry:

```
MSCSQueryMap.product.SQLCommand = "select pfid, dept_id,
manufacturer_id, name, short_description, long_description,
image_filename, intro_date, date_changed, list_price, monogrammable
from vc_product_family  where pfid = ':1'"
```

VC30's Product.asp then uses this query, replacing the string *:1* with the actual pfid:

```
cmdTemp.CommandText =
Replace(MSCSQueryMap.product.SQLCommand,":1",
Replace(rsRelateds("related_pfid").Value, "'", "''"))
```

In VC Turbo, this query is not created in the query map, but rather in the Product.asp where it is used. The pfid is concatenated in the query string:

```
set rsProduct = Conn.Execute("select pfid, monogramable,
list_price, name, image_filename, short_description,
long_description from vcturbo_product_family where pfid = '" &
Replace(pfid, "'", "''") & "'")
```

Optimize Generation of URLs

In VC30, URLs are generated using the **Page.URL** and **Page.SURL** methods. For example, in VC30's Confirmed.asp, the following script uses the **URL** method to generate a link back to the main page:

```
<A HREF = "<% = mscsPage.URL("main.asp") %>"><IMG
SRC="assets/images/btn_continue_shopping.gif" BORDER=0
ALT="Continue Shopping" ALIGN=right valign=top></A>
```

In VC Turbo's Confirmed.asp, a similar reference is made, but using a new function called pageURL instead of the **URL** method:

```
<A HREF="<% = pageURL("listing.asp") %>"><IMG
SRC="assets/images/btn_continue_shopping.gif" BORDER=0
ALT="Continue Shopping"></A>
```

The pageURL function runs faster because the base URL string has been calculated and stored ahead of time. The following is the script that appears in Shop.asp:

```
REM - functions for faster page links

function pageURL(pageName)
    pageURL = rootURL & pageName & "?" & emptyArgs
end function

function pageSURL(pageName)
    pageSURL = rootSURL & pageName & "?" & emptyArgs
end function

function baseURL(pageName)
    REM - you must append your own shopperArgs
    baseURL = rootURL & pageName & "?"
end function

function baseSURL(pageName)
    REM - you must put on your own shopperArgs
    baseSURL = rootSURL & pageName & "?"
end function

Dim displayName
Dim siteRoot
Dim rootURL
Dim rootSURL
Dim emptyArgs

displayName = mscsPage.HTMLEncode(MSCSSite.DisplayName)
siteRoot    = mscsPage.SiteRoot()
rootURL     = mscsPage.URLPrefix() & "/" & siteRoot & "/"
rootSURL    = mscsPage.SURLPrefix() & "/" & siteRoot & "/"
emptyArgs   = mscsPage.URLShopperArgs()

Dim displayName
Dim siteRoot
```

code continued on next page

code continued from previous page

```
Dim rootURL
Dim rootSURL
Dim emptyArgs

displayName    = mscsPage.HTMLEncode(MSCSSite.DisplayName)
siteRoot       = mscsPage.SiteRoot()
rootURL        = mscsPage.URLPrefix() & "/" & siteRoot & "/"
rootSURL       = mscsPage.SURLPrefix() & "/" & siteRoot & "/"
emptyArgs      = mscsPage.URLShopperArgs()
```

Execute Queries Off the Connection Object

In the VC Turbo site, certain queries are performed off the Connection object without having to manually create a **Command** or **Recordset** object. This eliminates the creation of several objects on each page request.

For example, in VC Turbo's Product.asp file, the following script executes the query shown, and returns rsProduct as a recordset:

```
Dim rsProduct

set rsProduct = Conn.Execute("select pfid, monogramable,
list_price, name, image_filename, short_description,
long_description from vcturbo_product_family where pfid = '" &
Replace(pfid, "'", "''") & "'")
```

Where a recordset must be created, VC Turbo reuses it whenever possible.

Remove Next and Previous Buttons

The original Volcano Coffee site displays a list of departments. Clicking a department name displays a product page that includes Next and Previous navigation buttons. While this provides a useful navigation mechanism, it adversely affects performance because it requires additional queries on the product database in the product page.

In the VC Turbo site, the Next and Previous buttons are removed.

Modify Presentation of Cross-Sell and Up-Sell Promotions

In VC30, cross-sell promotions are displayed on the product page, which requires an additional query to be run every time a product page is displayed. Up-sell promotions are displayed on the basket page, requiring an extra query to be run for every line item in the basket every time the basket page is displayed. This heavy use of queries reduces performance.

In VC Turbo, the cross-sell and up-sell data are displayed quite differently. Rather than display promotions on the product page and the basket page, the promotions are displayed only after the shopper adds an item to the basket. The "add item" script checks to see if there are any cross-sell or up-sell promotions in effect for the product being added. If there are none, the script redirects to the basket page. If promotions exist, the script redirects the shopper to an intermediate page. This page thanks the shopper for adding the product to their basket, and presents the cross sell and up-sell products.

Instead of running these queries every time a product is displayed on the product page, and every time each item is displayed in the basket page, VC Turbo runs each query once only.

Use the <OBJECT> Tag

In VC30, objects are created in Global.asa using a call to **Server.CreateObject**. Using **Server.CreateObject** causes the object to be created immediately, and if the object is not used, resources are wasted.

In VC Turbo, many objects in Global.asa are instantiated using the <OBJECT> tag instead. On the site pages, the <OBJECT> tag is also used to create the **Page** object and the **SimpleList** object.

Miscellaneous Non-Performance Improvements

In addition to the performance-specific improvements, the following modifications were made to the VC Turbo site to simplify it and improve its usability.

Simplify Page Layout

The original Volcano Coffee site used multiple nested tables to achieve the navigation bar on the left side of the ASP page, which made the layout complex. In the VC Turbo site, the navigation bar has been moved to the top of the page, greatly simplifying the layout and the resulting ASP and HTML.

Simplify the Creation of the Microsoft Wallet Control

In the VC Turbo site, two new functions have been added to the Wallet Include file (ship-wallet.asp). These new functions can be used to insert the HTML text for the creation of the Wallet control on the ASP page. Using a passed-in variable, they handle all configuration and settings on the controls, including the size (small for Buy Now, large for the Payment page). Hard coded strings were also eliminated from this file in favor of strings passed into the functions as appropriate.

Unlike VC30, VC Turbo supports the Wallet for both Netscape Navigator 3.x and 4.x.

Improve Payment and Shipping Pages

The removal of the nested tables and the addition of the new Wallet helper functions simplified the payment and shipping pages. As a result, the multiple conditional includes could also be eliminated, so the payment and shipping pages in the VC Turbo site have their ASP script inline (with the exception of the Wallet Include file).

Add Receipt View

The VC Turbo site has a new page for viewing the list of receipts for the current shopper. (The original Volcano Coffee site provided viewing of an individual receipt, but not a list of receipts.)

Improve Generation of Order IDs

In the original Volcano Coffee site, order IDs are generated in the pipeline. Because these numbers are generated from globally-unique identifiers (GUIDs), they are difficult for shoppers to read. In the VC Turbo site, order IDs are derived from an **identity** column on the order table in the database, which results in more readable IDs.

An entry for a new shopping basket is inserted into the vcturbo_basket table only when the shopper prepares the order for shipping (when the Checkout-ship.asp page posts data to the xt_orderform_prepare.asp file). The xt_orderform_prepare.asp script calls the UtilGetOrderRowset function (defined in Include\Util), which checks whether an order for the shopper exists in the vcturbo_basket table, and if not, creates one.

In the vcturbo_basket table, the order_id column has been defined as an **identity** column.

Wrap Statements in Global.asa Inside Functions

So that the code in Global.asa is organized more neatly, related operations are grouped together and defined as functions.

In VC30, Global.asa, the site dictionary is read from disk with the following statements:

```
Set MSCSSite = Server.CreateObject("Commerce.Dictionary")
REM - Read Store Dictionary
Set FD = Server.CreateObject("Commerce.FileDocument")
Call FD.ReadDictionaryFromFile( Server.MapPath("/"+SiteName) +
"/config/site.csc", "IISProperties", MSCSSite)
```

The site dictionary is then referenced as an application variable, as follows:

```
Set MSCSSite = Server.CreateObject("Commerce.Dictionary")
```

In VC Turbo, the site dictionary is read from disk by defining a function:

```
REM - Read Store Dictionary
Function ReadsiteDict(SiteName)
REM - Read Store Dictionary
     Call FileDocument.ReadDictionaryFromFile(
Server.MapPath("/"+SiteName) + "/config/site.csc", "IISProperties",
MSCSSite)
     Set ReadsiteDict = MSCSSite
End Function
```

VC Turbo's Global.asa then calls the function, as follows:

```
Set Application("MSCSSite") = ReadSiteDict(sitename)
```

Use Option Explicit

VC Turbo adds the **Option Explicit** statement to the Shop.asp page. This statement forces all variables in the script to be explicitly declared. Use of this statement is considered good programming practice, because errors occur if variables are misused or misspelled.

Eliminate Certain Include Files

The toolbar.asp file was removed from the VC Turbo site, and all toolbar functionality was moved into header.asp (renamed from header-table.asp). The prd_editbody.asp file was removed and its functionality was consolidated into prd_body.asp.

Remove Nested Tables

Nested tables can be confusing to develop and maintain. Most of the nested tables in VC30 have been deleted in VC Turbo. Body text has been placed inside tables so that it appears in the correct position, but these tables are only one level deep. In some cases, Netscape Navigator does not display plug-ins such as the Microsoft Wallet correctly when the plug-ins are nested inside tables.

Also, the tabbing and table structures have been improved throughout the site.

Remove Application.Lock/Unlock

It is preferable not to use **Application.Lock/Unlock** statements in the site's Global.asa.

In VC Turbo, the Application.Lock and Application.Unlock statements have been removed:

```
Set Application("MSCSSite")            = ReadSiteDict(sitename)
Set Application("MSCSQueryMap")        = InitQueryMap
Set Application("MSCSShopperManager")  = InitShopperManager
Set Application("MSCSMessageManager")  = InitMessageManager
Set Application("MSCSDataFunctions")   = InitDataFunctions
Application("MSCSSIDURLKey")           = "mscssid"
```

Tuning the Server Environment

The performance of your Commerce Server site depends greatly on the configuration of the hardware, the operating system, and Internet Information Server (IIS). The topics in this section provide a starting point that you can use to determine what areas you can optimize.

The optimizations described in this section should be kept in perspective. You can spend considerable time and money fine-tuning the performance of your site. Before you do, make sure you know exactly what level of performance you need. Set your goals and then keep tuning until you reach them.

The level of performance that you need depends on your business rules. It should almost never be driven by the software.

Perceived performance does not necessarily correspond to actual performance. Sometimes, doing something as easy as letting the user know that progress is happening and giving them a status indicator to watch solves apparent performance problems.

The results shown in the following table were obtained from tests that were run on the following configuration.

- ◆ Client computer
  - processor = 133 megahertz Pentium
  - system memory = 64 megabytes

- ◆ IIS server computer
  - processor = 300 megahertz Pentium II
  - system memory = 128 megabytes
  - ADO = Free (both), (default = apartment)
  - Page file size = 200 MB (default = 64 MB)
  - Site Server services off

- ◆ SQL server
  - processor = dual 200 megahertz Pentium Pro
  - SQL server system memory = 64 MB
  - SQL user connections = 50

Both 10 Mbit/sec and 100 Mbit/sec networks were tested; no significant difference was measured. This finding, along with other tests, suggests that performance of a Commerce Server site is processor-limited, not bandwidth-limited. However, you should conduct these tests on a private network to minimize the impact of network traffic on the test results.

The numbers in the following table represent pages per second, calculated by dividing successful returns by the test duration. Most numbers represent the average rate from three runs. Tests were conducted on a site generated by the Site

Builder Wizard, VC30, and VC Turbo, at both a 20:1 and 1:1 ratio (pages per second) between visits to the site and actual purchases.

Setting	Wizard 20:1	Wizard 1:1	VC30 20:1	VC30 1:1	VC Turbo 20:1	VC Turbo 1:1
Baseline (ProcessorThreadMax = 10; ODBC = Named Pipes)	11.4	8.53	5.66	5.14	9.45	8.56
ProcessorThreadMax = 15	11.14	8.15	5.79	5.32	10.8	9.06
ODBC = TCP/IP	12.5	9.5	6.76	6.58	14.2	11.3
Database on same computer	9.28	7.03	5.15	4.5	9.67	8.19
ProcessorThreadMax = 15 and ODBC = TCP/IP			5.77	4.76	13.1	11.3

Under the conditions tested, the best performance (marked in gray) was achieved for these stores by using the TCP/IP connection for ODBC, with the database hosted on a separate computer.

As these tests indicate, a particular setting that benefits one Commerce Server site may actually decrease performance for a different site. For this reason, it is essential that you conduct these types of tests on your own site to determine the optimum combination of configuration settings.

Hardware Optimization

Run Commerce Server on a Separate Computer from SQL Server

Hosting SQL Server on a separate computer than the one hosting Commerce Server offers advantages both in performance and in security.

With both Commerce Server and SQL Server running on a 300 megahertz Pentium II, one test measured throughput of 6.0 pages per second. With SQL Server moved onto a dedicated 133 megahertz Pentium II single-processor computer with 64MB of RAM, throughput improved to 7.6 pages per second, a 26% increase.

Provide Sufficient Processing Power

Commerce Server sites, like any ASP-based application, tend to be processor-sensitive. For best performance, use the fastest processors possible for all computers hosting Commerce Server.

Provide Sufficient Physical RAM

Too little memory can significantly decrease performance. In one test, adding 64MB of RAM increased performance by 13%.

SQL Server tends to be memory sensitive. If you are hosting SQL Server on a separate computer from the computer(s) hosting Commerce Server (the recommended configuration), then the SQL Server computer is not constrained so much by processing power as by physical memory. The SQL Server computer should have the amount of memory it needs to handle your data.

Consider Web Farming

Depending on demand, you might consider using multiple computers to host Commerce Server. A large number of servers can be connected to a single computer that is hosting SQL Server.

Microsoft Windows NT Optimization

In the three-volume *Microsoft Windows NT Server Resource Kit* (ISBN 1-57231-344-7), with its companion CD-ROM, you'll find valuable technical and performance information and tools. The Resource Kit is available from Microsoft Press (http://mspress.microsoft.com/) and other booksellers.

You can find studies on the performance of Microsoft Windows NT Server at the following links.

◆ Windows NT Server Performance and Scalability at http://www.microsoft.com/ntserver/Comparisons/performscalable.asp

◆ Microsoft Windows NT Server 4.0 Benchmarks at http://www.microsoft.com/ntserver/Comparisons/benchmarks.asp

Microsoft Internet Information Server (IIS) Optimization

For helpful suggestions on improving performance of IIS, see the product documentation. For example, by adjusting the Number of Connections setting according to your expected traffic, you can increase performance (too many open connections waste memory and therefore reduce overall server performance.)

To find the IIS documentation, on the **Start** menu, click **Programs**, click **Windows NT 4.0 Option Pack**, then click **Product Documentation**. On the **Contents** tab, expand the **Microsoft Internet Information Server** topic, then expand the **Server Administration** topic, and read the sections on **Performance Tuning** and **Performance Monitoring**.

Extensive information on the architecture of Microsoft's Web site (www.microsoft.com) can be found at the following site. This document includes the hardware configuration and current registry settings used by the site, and details on how performance of the site is monitored.

◆ Server Performance Optimization on Microsoft's Web Site at http://www.microsoft.com/workshop/server/feature/serveroptms.asp

The following site describes the Microsoft NT Option Pack Developers Resource Kit, which includes a chapter on *Performance Tuning and Optimization*.

◆ IIS 4.0 Resource Kit Preview with Free Web Capacity Analysis Tool Download at http://www.microsoft.com/workshop/server/toolbox/wcat.asp

You can find more general information on server performance at the following site.

◆ Site Builder Network Server at http://www.microsoft.com/workshop/server

For more information on Internet Information Server, visit the IIS site.

◆ Microsoft IIS site at http://www.microsoft.com/iis/

ASP Optimization

Another important performance consideration is the overhead of running ASP-based scripts.

Often, one of the best measures for improving performance is to evaluate whether a page requires ASP-base scripting at all. Pages with static content can be delivered much more efficiently as HTML. While the performance of ASP files is constrained largely by processing power, the delivery of HTML pages is constrained mostly by bandwidth.

For an excellent set of additional suggestions, see *15 ASP Tips to Improve Performance and Style* at http://www.microsoft.com/sitebuilder/archive/features/asptips.htm.

Internet applications can be developed to run faster by creating Internet Server API (ISAPI) extensions in place of ASP scripts. An ISAPI extension is a DLL that processes input from an HTTP request. ISAPI extensions can be loaded in the same process as IIS for best performance, or into an isolated process to guard against corruption of the IIS process.

For more information on ISAPI, refer to the Windows NT Option Pack documentation. (On the **Start** menu, click **Programs**, click **Windows NT 4.0 Option Pack**, and then click **Product Documentation**. On the **Contents** tab, open the node for **Microsoft Internet Information Server**, then open the node for **Programmer's Reference**, then open the node for **ISAPI**. If the topics are not available, make sure that your Windows NT 4.0 Option Pack setup includes the IIS SDK.)

Database Optimization
SQL Server Configuration

The book *Inside Microsoft SQL Server 6.5*, ISBN: 1-57231-331-5, By Microsoft Corp (Ron Soukup) describes ways to properly configure your SQL Server.

For customers using Site Commerce with SQL Server on a Compaq Server, the following white paper on the Compaq Web set offers valuable advice on running SQL Server.

Configuration and Tuning of Microsoft SQL Server 6.5 for Windows NT on Compaq Servers http://www.compaq.com/support/techpubs/whitepapers/415a0696.html

A good general book on SQL Performance is *The Microsoft SQL Server Survival Guide* published by John Wiley & Sons, Incorporated.

Other information can be found at http://www.microsoft.com/sql

Connection Protocol Configuration

Configure ODBC to use TCP/IP Sockets instead of the default Named Pipes. In some cases this change can result in a significant performance increase.

Other Optimizations

Disable Unneeded Services

Disable all unused processes, including additional software, screen savers, IIS services and Site Server services not used on your site.

Disable Membership If Not Used

If your site does not use Active User Objects (AUO), disable Membership mapping for the default Web site. This change provides a modest improvement (from 7.67 pages per second to 7.83 pages per second, a 2% improvement in the test system).

To disable Membership mapping, on the **Start** menu, click **Programs,** click **Windows NT 4.0 Option Pack,** click **Microsoft Internet Information Server,** then click **Internet Service Manager (MMC).** On the **Console** menu, click **Add/Remove Snap-in...** and click the **Extensions** tab. Make sure the **Personalization and Membership** extension is selected and click **OK.** Expand the **Internet Information Server** node, and then expand the server node. Right-click the Default Web site, click **Task,** then click **Membership Server mapping.** Set the value of **Mapping to Membership Server** to <no mapping>. Click **OK.**

Testing Performance

Which monitoring tool and method you choose depends on the information you need. If you are trying to measure the overall load on your Web server, you can use Performance Monitor to render a week-long plot, showing information such as the number of computer connections and file transfers. Or, if you noticed a slowdown in your server's performance, you could check for errors in Event Viewer, the tool for viewing logs generated by Windows NT.

You can also monitor your server by examining logs generated by IIS.

Your Windows NT documentation is an important source of information about performance monitoring.

Additional information is contained in the Microsoft Internet Information Server documentation. On the **Start** menu, click **Programs**, click **Windows NT 4.0 Option Pack**, then click **Product Documentation**. On the **Contents** tab, expand **Microsoft Internet Information Server**, then expand **Server Administration**. Relevant topics can be found under the headings **Performance Tuning** and **Performance Monitoring**.

Another useful source of information on troubleshooting and capacity planning is *The Windows NT Resource Kit*.

This document describes a number of tools that are useful for testing and measuring the performance of a Commerce Server site:

◆ Performance Monitor

◆ Event Viewer Logs and IIS Logs

◆ Web Capacity Analysis Tool (WCAT)

◆ InetMonitor

Performance Monitor

Performance Monitor (PerfMon) is a powerful tool that you can use to monitor your server's activity and summarize its performance at selected intervals. With Performance Monitor, you can display performance data in real time charts or reports, collect data in files, and generate alerts that warn you when critical events occur. Performance Monitor contains *counters* that monitor the activity of specific *objects*, that is, specific services or mechanisms controlling server resources. For example, if you view the object called Web Service, you can see counters that monitor bytes received per second or connection attempts per second.

Windows NT includes a number of counters, and Internet Information Server (IIS) installs special counters, including Web service counters and counters for Active Server Pages applications.

To run Performance Monitor, click **Start**, point to **Programs**, point to **Administrative Tools**, and then click **Performance Monitor**.

The most useful counters to monitor include the ASP response time, and the Web Service requests executing. Most databases also support counters that are important when identifying database bottlenecks. The following counters may be particularly useful.

Object	Counter	Description
Active Server Pages	Request/Sec	The number of ASP requests executed per second.
Active Server Pages	Request Execution Time	The number of milliseconds that it took to execute the most recent request.
Active Server Pages	Sessions Total	The total number of sessions since the service was started.
Active Server Pages	Memory Allocated	The total amount of memory, in bytes, currently allocated by Active Server Pages.
Active Server Pages	Request Wait Time	The number of seconds the most recent request was waiting in the queue.
Active Server Pages	Requests Executing	The number of requests currently executing.
Active Server Pages	Requests Queued	The number of requests waiting for service from the queue.
Active Server Pages	% processor time	The percentage of processing time consumed.
SQLServer	User Connections	The number of open user connections.

Event Viewer Logs and IIS Logs

Windows NT includes an event-logging service, which records events such as errors or the successful starting of a service. These event logs are viewed by using Event Viewer. (To start Event Viewer, click **Start**, point to **Programs**, point to **Administrative Tools**, and click **Event Viewer**.) You can use Event Viewer to monitor System, Security, and Application event logs. With this information you can better understand the sequence and types of events that led up to a particular performance problem. For details about how to use Event Viewer, see your Windows NT documentation.

InetMonitor

InetMonitor 3.0 (InetMon) is a bottleneck detection program. It can detect hardware bottlenecks in real time, and then generate and log alerts. Based on pre-defined conditions InetMon will make recommendations when it detects bottlenecks. In timed mode, InetMon can capture system status, periodically average it over the given period and report relevant system information.

Unlike WCAT, InetMonitor enables you to simulate a shopping scenario with multiple customers visiting a variety of pages at your site. With InetMonitor, you can specify the ratio of how often product pages are displayed to how often items are placed in the shopping basket.

InetMonitor is available in the *Microsoft BackOffice Resource Kit*. The *Resource Kit* is available from Microsoft Press (http://mspress.microsoft.com/) and other booksellers.

Strategy for Testing with InetMonitor

The following topics provide an overview of a suggested strategy for using InetMonitor to test the performance of your Commerce Server site.

Run the Supplied Test Scripts Against the Sample Sites

Run the tests included in this kit to test the performance of the Volcano Coffee sample site on your server. When you have obtained these test results, you can compare them with the baseline results described earlier in this document. Testing first with an existing sample site and with the supplied test scripts enables you to isolate configuration problems with your server or database connection.

Verify that you can fill the receipt table with orders while running the supplied scripts.

Remember to clear the shopper table intermittently, because the scripts are using a random number between 1000 and 9999 as an identifier. Collisions will result in an invalid sign-on attempt.

Once you can process orders, check how well your server configuration performs compared to our test setup. Does your event log fill up with connection errors under test conditions? If so, check your ADO and SQL configuration. How does the rate of pages served compare to our test results?

Modify the Scripts to Work with Your Store

To conduct performance testing on your own store, you will need to create scripts that match your store configuration. Your scripts must mimic the actions taken by a shopper to sign-on, navigate the store, add items to the basket, and purchase an order. Make sure you can add orders to the receipt table before modifying the script to fit your shopper profile.

The most difficult part of developing InetMonitor scripts for your store is debugging the scripts. You'll need to inspect the database to verify that shoppers have been logged-on successfully and that items can be added to the basket. If you have trouble with a sequence of steps, you can check some steps for completion by copying a line from the script and pasting it into a browser. At times, you may find it useful to use a packet analyzer, such as the Network Monitor in Microsoft Systems Management Server, to check the server response for certain posts.

Modify the Scripts to Emulate a Shopper Profile

Once the script has been debugged, modify the script to emulate a typical shopping scenario for your site. For example, you can modify the script to browse as many items and purchase as frequently as a typical visitor to your site. Use the LOOP command to mimic a shopper's repetitive steps in browsing for a product, and use the SKIP command to traverse different paths.

You may wish to add SLEEP commands into your script to simulate the time it takes a shopper to read a page or supply information to a form to be posted (see vct_shop_20to1s.txt). With sleep commands in your scripts, you can increase the **Number of Users** setting in InetMonitor. Because InetMonitor threads can service multiple clients by switching context as one client goes to sleep, you should not need more than 20 worker threads.

Test Your Site Under Stress

To test if your site is fast enough, manually shop at your site with a browser at the same time that your InetMonitor tests are stressing the server. What is the quality of the customer experience? Is the response time adequate? Is it consistent? Are timeouts or connection errors occurring?

If performance is fast enough, increase the **Number of Users** setting in InetMonitor. Monitor CPU utilization as you do so. As CPU usage approaches 100%, response time will increase. How many users are required to approach 100% CPU usage? Compare this number to the number of visitors you expect to be shopping the store simultaneously. If you need better performance, you may wish to consider upgrading your hardware and/or tuning your pages for better performance.

Analyzing the Data for Bottlenecks

Poorly performing pages can be isolated by analyzing the InetMonitor log files. The response latency is recorded for every response. Usually, latency increases the more a page accesses the database and creates objects. What trends do you observe? Once you identify which pages are performing poorly, you can begin to test them in isolation as you add performance improvements to the page. WCAT may be useful in this endeavor.

Identify performance bottlenecks before adding faster or better hardware. If the CPU is the bottleneck, then it is unlikely a faster hard drive will make much of a difference.

Measure the different performance of individual pages by removing parts of the page and re-running performance gathering tools. This approach helps to identify the portions of the ASP script that take the most amount of time. Try to cache as many processing results as possible to avoid redundant calculations.

InetMonitor Test Files

This Performance Kit includes files that can be used to run InetMonitor tests. The kit includes tests for both the Volcano Coffee and the VC Turbo sample sites. The following table describes the files used in the Volcano Coffee site. The files for testing VC Turbo have analogous names and functions.

File	Description
readme.txt	Last-minute information on this InetMonitor test
vc_shop1to1.inm	InetMonitor configuration for the Volcano Coffee 1:1 browse/shop ratio test. (This file is created and edited using the InetMonitor interface.)
vc_shop1to1.txt	Script for the Volcano Coffee 1:1 browse/shop ratio test.

table continued on next page

File	Description
vc_shop20to1.inm	InetMonitor configuration for the Volcano Coffee 20:1 browse/shop ratio test.
vc_shop20to1.txt	Script for the Volcano Coffee 20:1 browse/shop ratio test.
vc_addproduct.txt	List of URLs for adding products to the shopping basket. The list includes every product and every combination of attributes in the Volcano Coffee sample site.
vc_product.txt	List of URLs for displaying products on the product page. The list includes every product in the Volcano Coffee sample site.
vc_cookie.txt	This file must reside in the same folder as the .inm file, and must be specified as the Cookies file in InetMonitor.

Before You Run the Tests

Because these scripts are not designed to pass the shopper ID in the URL, you must change the site so that it uses cookies instead of URLs for the shopper ID. To make this change, use a text editor to open the site's Global.asa file. Change the following string:

```
'Call MSCSShopperManager.InitManager(SiteName , "URL")
```

so that it reads as follows:

```
Call MSCSShopperManager.InitManager(SiteName , "Cookie")
```

InetMonitor Test Script Design

All of the InetMonitor test scripts in this kit follow the same general design. The following comments apply to the vc_shop20to1.txt script. This particular script is designed to simulate a scenario in which the visit/buy ratio is 20 to 1. This means that for every 20 visitors who enter the site, only one actually completes a purchase. (The vc_shop1to1.txt script simulates the opposite end of the visit/buy scale, in which every visitor makes a purchase.)

This script's scenario assumes that each shopper browses 10 product pages, and places five items in the shopping basket. Of course, you can modify the script to achieve the ratios that you feel are more realistic for your commerce site.

The script simulates the navigational path used by an actual shopper. It navigates first to the Default.asp page and then to the page where the shopper signs in. The script registers as a new shopper, using a random number generator to create a different shopper e-mail name each time. After the new shopper is successfully registered, the site's xt_shopper.new.asp file redirects the browser to the Home.asp page.

```
REM +++ Shopper Sign-In +++
GET url:/vc30/default.asp
GET url:/vc30/welcome_new.asp
POST
url:/vc30/xt_shopper_new.asp?PROPERTIES:email=RAND(1000,9999)&
pwd1=password&pwd2=password&name=sname&street=sstreet&city
=scity&country=USA&state=ss&zip=12345&phone=123-456-7890
```

Next, the script simulates navigation to the product listing page, which the normal store automatically redirects the browser to once the shopper has registered:

```
REM +++ Navigate to product listing after entering +++
GET url:/vc30/listing.asp
```

The next section of the script simulates a shopper browsing the site by navigating from the store directory (Main.asp) to a specific product, then back to the directory, without adding an item to the basket. The product to be displayed is chosen at random from the list in vc_product.txt. Five product pages are visited:

```
LOOP 5
     GET url:/vc30/main.asp
     REM +++ Find Product +++
     GET RANDLIST(vc_product.txt)
ENDLOOP
```

In the next section, the script simulates a shopper visiting five additional product pages, and this time adding the items to the basket:

```
LOOP 5
      GET  url:/vc30/main.asp
      REM +++ Find Product +++
      GET  RANDLIST(vc_product.txt)
      POST RANDLIST(vc_addproduct.txt)
ENDLOOP
```

The final section of the script is executed only 5% of the time. This section makes the actual purchase.

```
REM SKIP THE NEXT 4 COMMANDS 95% of the time
%95 SKIP 4
      REM +++ Shipping Information +++
      GET  url:/vc30/checkout-ship.asp
      GET  url:/vc30/checkout-ship.asp?PROPERTIES:use_form=1
      POST url:/vc30/
xt_orderform_prepare.asp?PROPERTIES:goto=checkout-
pay.asp&use_form=1&ship_to_country=USA&
ship_to_name=Fred&ship_to_street=1313+way+way&
ship_to_city=Springfield&ship_to_state=WA&
ship_to_zip=98765&ship_to_phone=2066551212

      REM +++ Purchase Basket +++
      POST url:/vc30/xt_orderform_purchase.asp?PROPERTIES:goto=
confirmed.asp&error=error.asp&bill_to_name=Fred
&bill_to_street=1313+way+way&bill_to_city=Springfield
&bill_to_state=WA&bill_to_zip=98765&bill_to_country=USA
&bill_to_phone=2066551212&bill_to_email=fred@here.com
&cc_name=mycard&cc_type=Visa&_cc_number=4111111111111111
&_cc_expmonth=12&_cc_expyear=1999

REM END %95 SKIP 4
```

To Run the InetMonitor Tests

1. Copy the supplied scripts, .inm, and other files into a folder on your test computer.

2. Follow the instructions provided with InetMonitor to launch it.

3. On the **File** menu, click **Open**. Navigate to the new folder and select the desired .inm file.

4. On the **HTTP** tab, set the properties as follows (for more information, see the documentation that accompanies InetMonitor):

In this field	Type or select the following value
Target Server	Type the IP address or computer name of the server that is hosting the commerce site.
Number of Users	Type the number of visitors that you want to simulate. At first you can use a smaller number, then increase this number as described earlier.
Users Start Delay	Because shoppers will enter your site at different times, you can balance the load on the registration pages by increasing the delay between the start of each simulated user. This number is entered in milliseconds (1000 equals 1 second).
Test Duration	Type the number of minutes to run the test.
Logging Active	Select this option to enable the creation of a detailed log file. InetMonitor creates a log directory, and creates a new log file each time a test is run. The log contains error information and response times.
Worker Threads	Type the number of separate threads to be used by InetMonitor.
Command Script	Type the name of the test script (for example, vc_shop_20to1.txt). This file must reside in same folder as the .inm file.
Authentication	The default value, (None), specifies Basic Authentication.
Cookies File	Type the name of the cookies file, supplied with this kit. The name must be preceded by RUNTIME. (For example, type RUNTIME vc_cookie.txt).
Client Timeout (s)	Type the length of time which InetMonitor is to wait for a response from the server before timing out, specified in seconds.
Load Images	The setting of this property is not critical for testing Commerce Server sites.
HTTP Version	The version of Hypertext Transfer Protocol used by your server.

Web Capacity Analysis Tool (WCAT)

The *Microsoft Web Capacity Analysis Tool* (WCAT) runs simulated workloads on client-server configurations. Using WCAT, you can test how your Internet Information Server and network configuration respond to a variety of different client requests for content, data, or Hypertext Markup Language (HTML) pages.

InetMonitor (described earlier) works well for simulating a realistic shopping scenario, whereas WCAT is best used after you have determined where the performance bottlenecks occur in your site. At this point, you can use WCAT to perform stress testing on a single page, as you make changes to improve the performance of that page.

WCAT is available from

◆ http://www.microsoft.com/workshop/server/toolbox/wcat.asp

The documentation that accompanies the tool provides instructions for setup and use of WCAT.

This Performance Kit includes three files that can be used with WCAT to test the performance of the Volcano Coffee sample site (VC30).

Conclusion

By applying these suggestions and tools, you should be able to configure your site to achieve the level of performance that you need to support your business model.

To review some of the basic rules of performance testing: remember to design your site with performance in mind, and measure results regularly. Performance of one site is not necessarily a guarantee of similar performance in another site. Don't assume that you know where the bottlenecks are. Don't automatically assume what effect a certain change will have on performance without testing it.

During development, if you encounter an unexpected change in performance, whether for better or worse, make sure that you track down the cause. If you don't, the issue will almost certainly surprise you later. The reason for the change might actually be an error in the test. Take nothing for granted.

Glossary

access control

Granting or denying authorization for users to view and/or alter a directory containing content, a file, or other object.

access control entry (ACE)

An entry in the access control list (ACL) on an object's Security property page consisting of a security principal and the type of control or permission granted or denied to the principal.

access control list (ACL)

An aspect of Microsoft Windows NT security. An ACL contains the Windows NT Server account permissions settings that enumerate which accounts do and do not have access to shared resources and determine how accounts with access can use those resources. See also *discretionary access control list*.

ACE

See *access control entry*.

ACL

See *access control list*.

ACL target

The resource (application, content, directory object, or attribute) to which access is granted or denied by the ACL.

action

The part of a rule that describes an action or actions that should be taken.

Active Channel Agent

Gathers content items from a specified source and places them into a channel. Active Channel Server provides channel agents that gather content items from file directories, databases, Knowledge Briefs, Commerce databases, Index Server, and Search catalogs.

Active Channel Multicaster (ACM)

A set of services running on Windows NT Server 4.0 that delivers files to Windows 95 and Windows NT clients by means of multicast technology.

Active Channel Server

Builds and manages Channel Definition Format (CDF) files, and delivers information to users through channels. Supports delivery of Content Channels, Software Distribution Channels, and Mobile Channels.

Active Directory Service (ADS)

Standard to help businesses and developers access and manage directory services through a common API, such as access to NetWare 3.x and 4.x directories and any other LDAP-compatible directory.

Active Directory Service Interfaces (ADSI)

A component of Windows Open System Architecture (WOSA) Open Directory Service Interfaces (ODSI). A directory service is a part of a distributed computing environment that provides a way to locate and identify the users and resources available in the system. A single, connected system may consist of different network environments from different network providers, each of which may offer different directory services. ADSI defines a common set of interfaces that abstract the properties and methods of directory service objects common to diverse environments, including LDAP-compliant services such as Membership Directory and NTDS.

Active Server Pages (ASP)

A server-side scripting environment that is used to create and run interactive, high-performance, Web server applications, such as the Commerce Server sample sites. ASP scripts run on a Web server rather than on a client, thereby ensuring that the server does all the work involved in generating the HTML pages sent to browsers.

Active User Object (AUO)

A COM object called *Membership.userobjects* that aggregates user properties from multiple Active Directory Service (ADS) property storage mechanisms into a single unified collection (name space). Applications can access a user's properties via AUO without awareness of the actual storage location of the properties, or the user identification mechanism for that provider. The AUO is used in an ASP file as if it were a simple ADS provider, and it transparently handles the user object retrieval across multiple providers.

ActiveX

Microsoft ActiveX technologies is an open technology platform that extends the Windows architecture to include Internet and corporate intranet aspects and capabilities. ActiveX embraces both Java and COM technologies.

ActiveX control

Embeddable control written to the ActiveX specification. An ActiveX control can be embedded in a Microsoft Visual Basic form, a Microsoft Visual C++ resource, or an HTML page.

ActiveX Data Objects (ADO)

Objects that provide access to data stored in ODBC-compliant databases and that can be used for display and processing on Web pages. More information is available in Visual Basic documentation.

ActiveX server component

Typically a dynamic-link library, which makes its functionality available to Active Server Pages through the methods that it defines and implements. Unlike typical Automation objects, an ActiveX control is registered with the operating system specifically to be used by Active Server Pages. See also *Active Server Pages*.

ad

A file or stream of data belonging to an advertiser and placed on content usually for the purposes of subsidizing content development costs.

ad click

The opportunity for a visitor to a site to be transferred to a location by clicking an advertisement, as recorded by the server.

ad request

An opportunity to deliver an advertising element to a visitor to a site. An ad request is a measure of active technology that requires the site visitor to interact with the site before a new advertisement will appear.

Ad Rotator

A tool used to return the HTML code to a content server for a set of scheduled ads on a weighted basis.

Address Book Sample Pages

P&M sample pages that allow the user to search for another user in the address book.

administrator

1. The individual of the administrative security group who has system management privileges within Microsoft Site Server version 3.0 or its components.

2. The individual who manages a computer on which a number of different Commerce Server stores reside.

ADS

See *Active Directory Service*.

ADS provider

Software that supplies implementations of Active Directory Service Interfaces (ADSI), their methods, and their properties. A provider may also support additional interfaces, methods, and properties so that ADSI client applications can use all the capabilities of a particular directory service.

ADSI

See *Active Directory Service Interfaces*.

advertising calendar

A calendar based on weekly dates beginning on Monday and ending on Sunday. The first Monday of a month is the beginning day for that advertising month. For the purpose of reporting, all dates should be aggregated where necessary by using the advertising calendar.

agent

A Windows NT resource used to manage different services between the host and the client. The agent identifies the computer's location, user information, and statistics. The Active Channel Multicaster uses a Multicast Delivery Agent to receive multicast information for client computers.

aggregate bandwidth

A limit on the total amount of data that an Active Channel Multicaster host can stream to clients at any given time. The Active Channel Multicaster host will calculate its aggregate output, based on the sum of the bandwidth of each stream, and limit the bandwidth to the specified aggregate maximum. See also *bandwidth*.

alternate route

Some resources can be reached by means of alternate routes as well as by means of their main routes. An alternate route is a second occurrence of the resource in the map. It indicates that the resource is the target of more than one hyperlink. There may be many alternate routes to a given resource.

ALT strings

The text string that appears in place of an image when a Web page is loading or when graphics are not being displayed. Users who do not have a graphical browser, or users who have chosen not to download graphics, can use the ALT string to identify the graphic that is not being displayed.

analysis project

A Content Analyzer unit of analysis that includes a site definition, map settings, and exploration limits.

anchor

1. A node in the Site Vocabulary whose children are acceptable values for a selected property within a rule.

2. A node in the Site Vocabulary whose child categories appear in the Knowledge Manager's content browser as terms that can be browsed when the content source is selected. Clicking a term will show all content matching that term.

animation

A process in which usage data across time is displayed by using colors to represent hits and hit ranges. One frame in an animation may represent one day of the week, one hour of the day, or another time period.

annotation property

A property whose value is not inherent to the managed object but rather is *attached* as a tracking note.

announcement

Information for a client about an Active Channel Multicaster Multicast Project. See also *Multicast Information File*.

application

A program or set of Web pages that performs a specific task.

Application Server

A collection of software elements that provides a function to the user, such as supporting a Web site. IIS provides several basic application servers, including Default Web Site and Default SMTP Site. These application servers can be mapped to P&M Membership Servers to take advantage of the P&M functionality. Users can also modify other application servers with the P&M SDK in order to map them to P&M Membership Servers.

area

A section of a Web site that provides functionality by addressing one or more business applications or needs. An area typically consists of several HTML pages.

argument

A name/value pair that is passed to a Web server in association with the URL of a dynamic resource, which can take different actions based on the argument. The Web server makes the arguments available to the resource in the course of generating the content that the user sees or hears. The association of arguments with URLs can happen in several ways. Sometimes the arguments appear as name/value pairs following a question mark in the URL and separated by an ampersand (&). Other times the arguments are not part of the URL itself but are embedded in the HTTP request header.

ASP

See *Active Server Pages*.

assets

Files that enhance the functionality of HTML pages, such as graphics files (GIFs, JPEGs, and so on), ActiveX controls, and Java applets.

attribute (syn.: property)

Specific information (an attribute and its value) associated with a file or object.

AUO

See *Active User Object*.

AUOconfig file

An ASP file associated with a Membership Server that is used together with the registry to provide the configuration of the AUO.

AUO provider

An ADSI container object that is used to house user properties and is accessible to the Active User Object (AUO). An AUO provider can be any ADSI-compliant directory service container.

authentication

The process of verifying a user's logon information.

authentication mode

The arrangement under which site users, services, and applications are authenticated, based on the storage location of security credentials. Site Server sites can use either Membership Authentication (credentials are stored in the Membership Directory) or Windows NT Authentication (credentials are stored in the Windows NT Server directory database).

Authentication Service

A P&M component, installed on an application server, that expedites authentication, content access control, and access to users' personalization data.

authoring site

The Web site that is created when one of the Customizable Starter Sites is installed. Authors and administrators can customize this site, adding content and changing the site configuration, before and after the site has been deployed. See also *deployed site*.

authorization

Process of granting or denying permissions to directories or other objects protected with access control.

Automated Refresh

A function that refreshes Channel Project properties and generates an updated Channel Definition Format (CDF) file.

automatic approval

Registration process that takes place online with no administrator intervention.

Automatic Cookie Authentication

A Membership Authentication method in which a user is identified by a GUID instead of a user name. The GUID is stored in a cookie associated with the user's browser.

automation

Using rules to automate tasks, such as updating announcements on certain days, rather than using rules to personalize content.

availability

The difference between capacity and sold impressions.

background texture

The apparent base surface, with a seemingly tactile quality, against which other on-screen objects are displayed.

balanced distribution of values

One of three methods for determining how values should be associated with colors in the Hyperbolic pane of Content Analyzer. In balanced distribution, all eight color ranges have the same number of resources.

bandwidth

The amount of data transferred per unit of time.

Base URL address

The root Web address for all content of a Customizable Starter Sites application, for example, http://NameLevel1/NameLevel2/vroot/.

best effort

A method of file transfer that sends files to recipients but does not allow the recipients to send back transfer status to the host. Best effort file transfer increases the scope of the network by conserving network bandwidth, but data packets might be lost during transfer.

bind

To identify yourself as a user, or to log on to the LDAP Service.

bind as

To log on as a particular user.

Boolean

A type of variable that can have only two values, typically 1 or 0. Boolean variables are often used to express conditions that are either true or false. Queries with Boolean operators (*and*, *or*, *not*, and *near*) are referred to as Boolean queries.

box-whisker graph

Illustrates the spread of data groups around the medians, using a *box* and *whiskers* to break down each data group by percentile.

branch

A node or subarea in a Web site.

branded icons

Unique icons or logos that appear in client browsers and identify the provider of a channel and its content items.

breadth-first (discovery)

A method for setting routes. Routes in your project are set according to the order in which links are discovered on pages.

brief

Information organized on a specific topic used to keep a person, or anyone in the organization, current on that topic. Briefs are composed of two types of sections: lists of useful links and saved searches.

briefing channel

A channel that is set up when Knowledge Manager is installed. The briefing channel contains all the shared briefs created in Knowledge Manager.

broken link

A reference to a resource that Content Analyzer cannot locate because the URL is not valid, the resource to which the link points does not exist, or the server containing the resource is busy or having technical difficulties.

Broker

See *Authentication Service*.

browser

Any application used to locate and display Web pages. Content Analyzer includes an embedded browser: the Browser pane in the Analysis window.

bubble graph

Charts three variables in two dimensions. It is a special form of the scatter graph showing *bubbles*, which are circular markers of variable size plotted on an x-y grid.

build

To build a new version of something, including gathering the data.

Business Internet Site

One of the Customizable Starter Sites. Business Internet Site enables organizations to set up a corporate presence on the Web and to direct appropriate information with personalized content to each customer. Business Internet Site includes areas for information about the company and its products, announcements, press releases, feedback, and a Member Forum for registered users of the site.

Buy Now control

An ActiveX control that enables a shopper to purchase goods from any Web page on the Internet. When the shopper clicks a product image, a dialog appears prompting for shipping address and credit card information.

cache

Small, fast memory holding recently accessed data, designed to speed up subsequent access to the same data.

caching calculations

An aspect of Report Writer that allows the user to save and reuse frequently used calculations. Caching calculations is intended to reduce the time needed to run a report.

calculation

An element of a report definition that acts as a container for dimensions, measures, and presentations. A calculation typically corresponds to one presentation (a table or a graph) in a report.

calculation header

Part of a report. The calculation header includes the calculation name and description.

calculation inventory

The calculation inventory contains a list of all of the calculations in the standard report definitions. Users can add any combination of the calculations to a new report definition.

campaign item

The individual reservation of impressions, click-through, or target user at a certain rate over a specific period of time for a specific customer.

candlestick graph

Consists of a series of boxes with lines extending up and down from the ends, drawn on an x-y grid.

capacity

Total capability of the content system to show ads to customers. Capacity can be measured in number of impressions, click-throughs, and target users.

catalog

A collective term for an index and a property store that can be searched. Catalogs are stored on the search server of a host.

catalog definition

The user-defined instructions and parameters for building a catalog. Catalog definitions are stored on the catalog build server.

catalog build server

The server that gathers information and builds catalogs.

catalog schema

Specification of the columns or properties and their attributes in a Search catalog.

category

1. A value in the Site Vocabulary. Categories can be used as user attribute values and content attribute values.

2. A classification or grouping by type, trait, attribute, or business segment.

CDF file

See *Channel Definition Format file*.

CGI

See *Common Gateway Interface*.

channel

1. A conduit for which information is structured and delivered.

2. The basic organizational structure for arranging service content.

channel agents

The scripts that are executed to collect items for a channel.

Channel Definition Format (CDF) file

Contains URL addresses to channels and their content items, as well as tags that define scheduling and display options. Active Channel Server generates a CDF file for each Channel Project.

channel manager

The MMC snap-in administrator tool that organizes, manages, and fills channels at the ICP.

channel objects

The set of objects representing the service, channels, and items.

Channel Project

Provides centralized channel management and can contain multiple channels and subchannels. It is the building block of an information delivery service.

channel server

The entire suite of services, objects, and tools that make up the push server.

channel subscription

The method by which users elect to receive a content provider's channels. Users do not receive channels unless they subscribe to them.

Clear Text/Basic Authentication

An authentication method in which the user name and password are transmitted in clear text. Transmissions can be encrypted with SSL.

click-through

The act of the user clicking an advertising tracking object.

client

1. The workstation on which the client pieces for Site Server Analysis are installed.

2. A computer system or process that requests a service of another computer system or process (a *server*). For example, a workstation requesting the contents of a file from a file server is a client of the file server.

client browser

Any browser that supports Channel Definition Format (CDF) files and allows users to receive channels.

Client Certificate Authentication

An authentication method in which the user's identity is validated without the use of a password. Validation is performed with computations involving a public key stored in the user's digital certificate and a private key stored on the user's computer.

client computer

A computer that is connected to a server for the purpose of sending and receiving information.

client schedule

The schedule that determines when client browsers retrieve updated CDF files.

clip art

Copyright-free and royalty-free electronic illustrations that can be inserted into a document or page.

code page

A table that relates the binary character codes used by a program to keys on the keyboard or to the appearance of characters on the display. Typically, there are different code pages for different languages or sets of languages. For example, English and Western European languages are supported by code page 850.

color scheme

An arrangement in which resources are displayed in different colors. Content Analyzer includes three color schemes. In the Standard scheme, resources are shown in color according to type (onsite versus offsite, and so on). In the Results scheme, current search results are shown in yellow. In the Numeric scheme, resources are shown in different colors according to the values of their numeric properties.

command line

The area where a Content Deployment command is entered.

Commerce Host Administrator

An application for administering a site or sites. By using the Commerce Host Administrator, you can open, close, or delete a site, or launch the wizards that copy a sample site or create a site foundation.

Commerce Server components

A set of ActiveX server components that provide the run-time environment for the presentation of online commerce sites. These components provide the basic set of services for access to content in a database, for access to shopper information, and for creation of an order form for processing by the order processing pipeline.

Common Gateway Interface (CGI)

An interface for running external programs or gateways under an information server. Gateways are programs that handle information requests and return the appropriate document or generate a document quickly.

component

A section of code that is a piece of a Microsoft Site Server version 3.0 feature.

component user

A user of Microsoft Site Server version 3.0 components. The individual who operates the component after an administrator setup.

condition

Part of a rule that describes when the rule will be applied. If the condition evaluates to true, and there are no exceptions, then the action is taken.

connection name

The display name of a connection string, provided by the connection string map and stored in a Commerce Server site configuration.

connection string

A text string describing properties of a connection as a series of *argument=value* statements separated by semicolons. Typically includes all the information needed to make a connection, including user name and password.

connection string map

An object created in a Commerce Server application to provide an abstraction for detailed database connection strings by mapping connection names to connection strings. The connection string map is saved in a Commerce Server site configuration.

container

An object within a Directory Information Tree (DIT) whose chief purpose is to contain other objects.

content

1. Any amount of information or specified material contained on a site.
2. A collection of files on the host to be delivered to users, either through Active Channels or Active Channel Multicaster.

Content Channels

Used to deliver Web pages or other documents. Based on Channel Definition Format (CDF) technology.

content data

Data that is imported into the Site Server Analysis database from Content Analyzer and either Content Management or Tag Tool. During import, content data and usage data are integrated.

content deployment

A replication that travels *downstream* from the staging server to an end point server.

content group

Content category such as MSNBC news or MSNBC sports in which ad rotation on that content category is scheduled. This usually equates to more than one place where ads can be shown.

content item

A unit of information or a file within a channel.

content manager

The individual who manages the actual content of the channels.

content report

Collection of report elements in a single stream of HTML, possibly broken into pages.

content selection

Part of a rule that describes which content (from the data source defined in the rule set) will be selected and shown to the user.

content source

An object in the Membership Directory that defines content and its location. It is used by ASP pages, Rule Builder, and Knowledge Manager to locate content in a specific content store. Each content source is an instance of one of the following classes: ODBCSource, TripoliSource, or NetLibrarySource.

content source class

Class object associated with a content source, used for processing the type of content store you have chosen. ODBC databases use ODBCSource, Search catalogs use NetLibrarySource, and Index Server indexes use TripoliSource.

content source object

A schema object in the Directory Information Tree that represents one of the following: ODBC database, Search catalog, or Index Server catalog.

content store

An ODBC database, Search catalog, or Microsoft Index Server index used to store information about site content and, in the case of an ODBC database, the content itself.

content template

An ASP page, either a Web content template or a Mail content template, that includes rule sets and personalizations that will be replaced with content when the page is displayed.

content type

A set of attributes shared by similar types of content. These attribute sets are used by the Tag Tool and other authoring tools.

cookie

1. A persistent identification code assigned to the user, which allows you to track the user across visits.

2. A file stored on client computers that provides a means for storing and retrieving information on the client side of a client/server connection, for use by the server. Used to avoid having the user retype a user (shopper) ID at each reconnection.

3. Information that is stored on an Internet client by an Internet server. Automatically passed back from the client to the server as the client browses the site.

Cookie Identification

An identification method under Microsoft Windows NT Authentication in which a user is identified by a globally unique identifier (GUID) instead of a user name. The GUID is stored in a cookie associated with the user's browser.

copy

A media term referring to content in various forms. For the advertising system, it refers to an ad or the page on which the ad is running.

copy blueprint

A set of Active Server Pages template files used by the Sample Site Copy Wizard when making a copy of a sample site. The blueprint files contain scripting expressions (delimited by <%% and %%>) that capture the new site name and DSN selected by the person who runs the wizard. For each blueprint file (.ast file), the wizard generates a standard .asp file that reflects the selected site parameters.

crawl

1. The process through which Content Analyzer examines the site you specify and creates a map. See also *explore*.

2. The process through which Search gathers content by following links contained in documents or by following directory trees in a file system.

crawl catalog

A catalog built by crawling documents on the Internet, on intranets, and on file systems.

crawler

1. A program that automatically fetches Web pages. Crawlers (also called spiders) are used to feed pages to search engines. Crawlers might request all Web pages at a site during a search; therefore, requests by crawlers are typically excluded from request counts.

2. A program that collects files by following links contained in those files (usually over HTTP) or by following directory trees in a file system.

crawling policy

The settings that determine how Search crawls. Search can follow links, crawl files in a directory, or crawl sites for which there are site rules.

credentials

The user name and password, globally unique identifier (GUID), or client certificate whereby a user's identity is authenticated.

.csc file

A file that contains properties of a Commerce Server site. The file typically is named Site.csc and resides in the \Config folder of the site. The information in the Site.csc file is initially configured by the Site Foundation Wizard and can be accessed by using the AdminSite component, the site Dictionary, and the FileDocument component.

CSSs

See *Customizable Starter Sites*.

Custom Import Manager

A window displaying the hierarchy that represents the structure of the Web-site usage data stored in the Microsoft Site Server Analysis database.

customer

The Microsoft Site Server customer who utilizes the Site Server product features and Customizable Starter Sites to develop a Web presence.

customer order

The signed-off number of impressions over time reserved on behalf of the advertiser.

customizable

Able to be modified and personalized by the customer.

Customizable Starter Sites (CSSs)

Applications that enable customers to create Web sites quickly and easily. Each of the CSSs consists of several components joined together by ASP files and customized by the site administrator's selections.

DACL

See *discretionary access control list*.

data editor

A grid that displays the values for a dimension in the Site Server Analysis database. The data editor also displays associations between a dimension and its parent dimensions.

data source name (DSN)

In ODBC, a name given to a set of properties about a database connection. Typically the DSN contains database configuration and location information but not user name or password. DSNs are not used directly in Commerce Server applications.

database catalog

A catalog that is built by crawling a table in an ODBC database.

DCOM

See *Distributed Component Object Model.*

delayed approval

Manual approval process that involves an unrelated verification, such as a credit card check.

deployed site

The Web site that is created when an administrator deploys one of the Customizable Starter Sites. See also *authoring site.*

Design-time control (DTC)

An ActiveX control used from within an authoring environment like Microsoft Visual InterDev or Microsoft FrontPage 98 that helps a developer construct dynamic Web applications by automatically generating standard HTML and/or scripting code. DTCs are used at design time, not at run time.

destination directory

The directory inside the staging server or the end point server to which the deployed content is directed.

dimension

An element of a report definition that typically acts as the data around which the results are grouped in a table or a graph. A dimension is associated with a range of values.

dimension hierarchy

The organization and relationships of dimensions in the Site Server Analysis database. Dimensions are organized into four main categories, which are hierarchically organized in the order of organization, user, visit, and request. Organization dimensions are at the top of the hierarchy, because every user comes from an organization, every visit from a user, and every request from a visit.

direct mail

E-mail that is targeted to a set of users based on their properties or on automation (sometimes called *targeted mail*).

Direct Mailer

A P&M aspect that provides mailing lists, templates, and scheduling for pushing information to visitors through an SMTP server.

directory index file

The files returned when a Web site visitor requests a directory (when the request ends in /).

Directory Information Tree (DIT)

A tree representation of all the entries in the directory information base. The DIT includes both container and leaf nodes.

disallow

Used in rules to disallow processing a specified set of items.

discretionary access control list (DACL)

An aspect of Microsoft Windows NT security. A DACL represents the granted or denied account permissions that allow some users to connect to a shared resource or perform an action while preventing access or operations by other users. A DACL is specified by the object or component owner, such as the administrator of a site. See also *access control lists*.

display name

A name that substitutes for an Internet Protocol (IP) address.

distinguished name (DN)

A text string, composed of a list of values, that uniquely identifies an object in the Membership Directory.

Distributed Component Object Model (DCOM)

A protocol that enables software components to communicate directly over a network in a reliable, secure, and efficient manner. DCOM is designed for use across multiple network transports, including Internet protocols such as HTTP.

Distributed Password Authentication (DPA)

A challenge/response authentication method derived from Microsoft Windows NT Challenge/Response Authentication.

distribution services

The ASP services and CDF generator object for distributing CDF files. Sometimes called distribution agents, delivery agents, or ASP services.

DIT

See *Directory Information Tree*.

DN

See *distinguished name*.

DNS

See *Domain Name System*.

document

A basic unit of information that is gathered, characterized, selected, cataloged, searched, and delivered to the user over the Web.

domain, Windows NT

A logical grouping of network server and other computers that share common security and user account information.

domain name, DNS

A text representative of a resource's IP address, using the unique name of the server computer plus an extension for the type of institution (such as *.com* for a business or *.edu* for a university). Domain names have several parts separated by periods. For example, www.microsoft.com is the domain name for the Microsoft public corporate site, whereas www.microsoft is the unique name for the Microsoft server on the World Wide Web.

Domain Name System (DNS)

A protocol and system used throughout the Internet to map Internet Protocol (IP) addresses to user-friendly names. Sometimes called the bind service.

DPA

See *Distributed Password Authentication*.

DSA-specific entry (DSE) root

The root node containing information relevant to a directory as a whole.

DSN

See *data source name*.

dynamic data

Temporary data not stored on a disk, about online conferences, users who are currently using certain applications, and users logged on to the system. Used by Dynamic Directory and other such applications.

Dynamic Directory

An Internet locating aspect that enables people to find others who are online and set up real-time communication.

dynamic property

Method of retrieving user attributes or other Membership Directory objects by using a dot notation (such as User.name) rather than by using the IADS methods (such as User.get("name")). If the user attribute is found in a secondary AUO provider (such as legacy), use the provider name as part of the dynamic property syntax (such as User("legacy").name).

element

Project, channel, and content item properties become elements in a CDF file. Each element provides direction to client browsers about displaying and managing the channels and content items.

embedded resource

A resource (usually an image, sound, or video) on a Web page. Although an embedded (or inline) resource may have its own URL, from a site visitor's perspective, it is part of the Web page being displayed.

end user

See *user*.

Glossary

...ver

...rvers used by Content Deployment as the ending point for push replications of

...formation Site

...stomizable Starter Sites. Enterprise Information Site enables organizations to set up ...porate intranet, including a personalized home page, areas for organizational ...roduct and service information, an events calendar, a documents library, a ...acts directory, and information about job opportunities.

...search required by some complex query syntax in which the query is compared to ...the catalog and then again to another section of the catalog.

...uage)

...cognized by an object such as an ActiveX control. You can write code to respond to an event.

event sink

An object that receives events.

event source

The point within processing on a server where extension objects can take control.

events (system)

System occurrences, such as user log ons, that are logged to a tool designed to monitor such occurrences and to display them in a window or log them to a file.

exception

Part of a rule that describes when the rule will not be applied. The content appears or the actions are taken only if all exceptions are false.

explore

Process in which Content Analyzer crawls a Web site and adds the pages it finds to the site map. You control how much of the site is explored.

extranet

A collaborative network that uses Internet technology to facilitate relationships between businesses and their suppliers, customers, or other businesses. An extranet may be part of a company's intranet made accessible to other companies or a collaboration between companies. The shared information might be accessible only to the collaborating parties or, in some cases, it might be public.

family account

Group of related accounts in the Membership Directory. Some are designated as parents and others as children of these parents.

feature

A unit of functionality on a Web site consisting of one or more HTML or ASP-based pages, VBScript or JavaScript code, server-side or client-side objects, and associated data that utilizes Microsoft Site Server functionality to add customizable capabilities to a Customizable Starter Site.

File Transfer Method

Sending files over a network by using an agreed-upon protocol for transmitting data between the client and server. The protocol determines the type of error checking to be used, the data compression method, how the server will indicate that it has finished sending a message, and how the client will indicate that it has received a message.

filter

1. A program used to extract the properties and unformatted text from a type of document, such as HTML or Microsoft Word.

2. A string of Boolean name/value pairs used to define a slice of the overall data set upon which the user wishes to report.

filter agent

A process that manages text extraction filter.

fixed distribution of values

One of three methods for determining how values should be associated with colors in the Hyperbolic pane of Content Analyzer. In fixed distribution, you fix the size of the highest and lowest color ranges.

fixed label

A label for a resource. Fixed labels always appear in all Content Analyzer windows.

Forward Error Correction

A method for controlling data-transfer errors in a unidirectional communication system. Extra information is sent, along with the data, that can be used by the receiver to check and correct the data.

foundation

The underlying structure or framework of a Commerce Server site, consisting of the directory structure, Internet Information Server virtual directories, the DSN connect string, and the Microsoft Windows NT Server account used for managing the store.

frame mode

The replication mode that allows replicated content to travel to remote sites.

free content

Content that is available without restriction to any user (requires no user identification, authentication, or permissions).

free-text query

An unstructured query in which site visitors do not need to use any special syntax to specify what they are looking for.

full catalog build

A catalog build that starts with an empty catalog and uses only the start addresses as the starting points for the crawl.

Gantt chart

A specialized version of the horizontal bar graph in simple or stacked form. Used almost exclusively to show a project schedule, with each bar or bar segment marking the start time, duration, and completion time of a task.

gateway

A program that dynamically generates Web content based on the differing values of arguments passed to it. Gateways are often used to process information entered into forms. A gateway has a URL. The Web server makes the arguments associated with that URL in an HTTP request available to the gateway program so that it can process the arguments accordingly.

gather

The automated collection of data files over the Internet or an intranet.

gleam

A notification marker that appears in Microsoft Internet Explorer version 4.x to notify users of channel updates. The marker can appear in the Channel Bar, in the Software Updates folder of the **Favorites** menu, or on an Active Desktop item. The gleam is a red, triangular icon that appears in the upper corner of a channel or a menu item.

Global.asa

1. A file in which you can specify event scripts and declare components for processing by the Active Server Pages scripting environment. Global.asa is not a content file displayed to the users; instead it stores event information and components used globally by the application. This file is required for Commerce Server sites.

2. A file that enables personalized channels.

globally unique identifier (GUID)

A string, usually a number, that uniquely identifies an item, an operation, or an individual. The shopper ID and the order ID used in Commerce Server are GUIDs.

graph

One of two types of a presentation in a report. Tables are the other type.

graphic

A visual element used on a Web page, such as an illustration, photograph, or background texture. Web-based images are in .gif or .jpg formats.

GUID

See *globally unique identifier*.

helper application

Any application used to edit or browse the resources in a Content Analyzer project. Users select the applications that they want to use and start the applications from within Content Analyzer. A typical helper application includes Microsoft Internet Explorer for browsing and Microsoft Notepad for editing HTML pages.

high-low-close graph (HLC)

With HLC, you can chart a range of values on an x-y grid. This range is shown as a vertical bar, with horizontal crossbars for the high, the low, and a normative value usually called the close.

hit

A single action (for example, a click on an advertisement) on the part of the user at a site that results in one line of data being added to the log file.

HLC

See *high-low-close graph*.

home page

1. The root page of a Web site.

2. The root page of a Web site. Often the first page that a visitor to the site sees but not synonymous with the start page. See also *starting page*.

host

A computer using an Internet Protocol (IP) address.

host name

A mechanism for identifying users. A host name has the format *example.microsoft.com*.

hot phrase

The part of a rule fragment that may be modified by a user. The modifications are limited to selecting attributes from the schema or values from the Site Vocabulary.

HREF attribute

Hyperlinks are created by the HREF attribute of the A (anchor) tag in HTML. For example, in <A HREF= "../docs/text.htm"> **Click Here** </A>, **Click Here** is the hyperlink text.

HTML Forms Authentication

An authentication method in which a user name and password are transmitted in clear text in the initial connection request only; validation for each subsequent request in the session is based on a session cookie containing hashed credentials. Transmissions can be encrypted with SSL.

HTML page

One of several types of resources that make up a Web site. Also called *page*.

HTML source code

The HTML code underlying a page or other resource in a Content Analyzer project.

HTML tag

HyperText Markup Language. HTML is a formatting language used to create pages on the World Wide Web. An HTML tag is a command that specifies how information in the page should be displayed in a browser. HTML files are text files.

HTML title lookup

An aspect of Usage Import that associates a title with every HTML file in the Microsoft Site Server Analysis database. This allows reports to contain meaningful document titles rather than only file names.

HTTP response code

The response code associated with a request.

HTTP status codes

HyperText Transfer Protocol. HTTP is the protocol that tells servers and browsers how to transport messages and respond to different commands over the World Wide Web. The server returns HTTP status codes to indicate success or failure. For example, if a resource in a Web site is missing, the browser displays a 404 error, which is one type of HTTP status code.

Hyperbolic pane

The Site window pane that displays a map of the site.

hyperlink text

The text string associated with a hyperlink. When site visitors view a Web page, they can click the hyperlink text to go to another (onsite or offsite) page.

icons

A small picture that represents an object or program. Channel and content item icons appear in client browsers and help users navigate multiple channels.

IFilter interface

Application programming interface (API) designed to extract unformatted text and properties from documents by scanning for plain text and properties.

IIS

See *Internet Information Server 4.0.*

IIS Web site

IIS set of directories used for providing World Wide Web presence that can be accessed directly through HTTP protocol for executing P&M ASP pages. Formerly known as a virtual server.

illustration

An image that uses line, line-and-tone, tone, or paint-like conventions.

image

A visual element used on a Web page, such as an illustration, photograph, or background texture. Web-based images are in .gif or .jpg formats.

Import History Manager

A tool that contains information regarding the log files that have been imported into the Microsoft Site Server Analysis database.

Import Manager

A tool that can be used to import log files into the Microsoft Site Server Analysis database.

impression

A specific delivery of an ad to a Web page.

incremental catalog build

A catalog build that starts with the catalog from the previous build and updates the catalog with any changes made to the content since the last crawl.

indexable column

A searchable column in the catalog.

inferences

A set of rules that make calculated guesses about visit activity. Usage Import applies inferences during import in order to reconstruct data about visit activity about sites.

information consumer

The end user of a channel and its contents who can subscribe to, personalize, read, and unsubscribe from channels and subchannels.

inline link

A link that results in a resource being embedded in the page.

InLinks (from Pages)

Links pointing from a page to other resources in your site. A resource's InLinks all have that resource as the *to* resource of the link, and the various other pages that link to the resource function as the *from* resource of the link.

interactive application

A program written in C, Perl, or as a Microsoft Windows NT Server batch file.

interactive report

An HTML-based report that is displayed in the browser immediately after the queries complete and that contains active links to resources.

Internet address

The Internet address (IP address or host name) from which a request comes and to which the server sends a response.

Internet Information Server 4.0 (IIS)

An Internet application platform that includes a Web server, application development environment, integrated full-text searching, multimedia streaming, and site-management extensions, and is integrated with Microsoft Windows NT Server.

Internet retrieval

A Content Deployment project that is configured to pull content over the Internet from an HTTP or FTP server.

intranet

A communications network, based on the same technology as the World Wide Web, that is available only to certain people, such as the employees of a company.

IP resolution

A process that associates Internet Protocol (IP) address with domain names in the Site Server Analysis database to allow reports to be more meaningful.

ISAPI filter

1. An aspect of ISAPI that allows preprocessing of requests and postprocessing of responses, permitting site-specific handling of HTTP requests and responses.

2. An abbreviation for Internet Server API. The ISAPI filter is an API (application program interface) for Microsoft Internet Information Server. The ISAPI filter allows an IIS server to generate cookies.

job

A collection of tasks that is scheduled to begin on a certain day at a certain time.

Jscript

Microsoft implementation of JavaScript scripting language.

key column

The column in a custom data file that contains key values, which allow custom data to be associated with usage data already in the Site Server Analysis database.

key value

The value in a custom data file that allows custom data to be associated with usage data already in the Site Server Analysis database.

LAN

See *local area network*.

layout

The organization of the elements on a Web page.

layout design template

A file that controls the arrangement of content on top-level pages of the various CSS applications.

lazy provider instantiation

Situation in which the AUO is not set up at initialization but only when a property is referenced.

LDAP

See *Lightweight Directory Access Protocol*.

LDAP interface

Interface in the IIS framework that allows LDAP clients to manipulate and query databases.

legacy applications and data

Applications and data that existed before P&M was installed.

level

A measurement of depth for a Web site. The start page is always Level 1, links from the start page lead to Level 2, and so on.

Lightweight Directory Access Protocol (LDAP)

Internet-standard access protocol that allows Internet client applications to access directory services. P&M uses LDAP to provide client access to the Membership Directory.

linear distribution of values

One of three methods for determining how values should be associated with colors in the Hyperbolic pane of Content Analyzer. In linear distribution, all eight color ranges are the same size.

link

1. A reference to a document. Typically a URL, UNC, or file path.

2. A connection from one Web resource to another.

Links (to Resources)

Links pointing from a page to other resources in the site. Only pages can contain links to other resources.

link list section

A section of a Knowledge Manager brief that contains a list of useful URLs and descriptions of those URLs.

link type

One of three link types included in Content Analyzer: Links (to Resources), InLinks (from Pages), and Links on Route to Resource.

link URL

The URL associated with the link on a page that points to a particular resource. The link URL is the main route for the resource. The link URL can be relative or absolute. If it is relative, the path name is relative to the Web site's root directory or to the page containing the link. If it is absolute, it consists of the full Internet address.

Links on Route to Resource

All links on the route from the site's start page to a specific resource.

local area network (LAN)

A group of computers and other devices dispersed over a relatively limited area and connected by a communications link that enables any device to interact with any other on the network.

local mode

The replication mode that allows replicated content to travel faster at local sites. This mode can be used only for local sites.

locale

Used to indicate language information. Web browsers can specify locale to indicate the language that the user of that browser understands. Documents and Web pages can also specify a locale to indicate what language the text is in.

locale ID

A number that uniquely identifies a locale for Microsoft Windows NT. This number consists of a language code and a sublanguage code.

log data source

A log data source represents an entity that generates log files in a specific format; the entity is typically a physical server.

log file

The file in which data reflecting the actions that a user takes at a site is recorded.

mail content template

The ASP file that selects content from a content source and incorporates it into a Direct Mail message. Also selects attachments.

Mail Delivery

From the Channel Center in Knowledge Manager, users can choose to receive channel updates through e-mail messages. Active Channel Server and the Direct Mailer work together to deliver mail channels.

main route

There is a main route to every resource in your project. It indicates the first hyperlink to the resource that Content Analyzer encountered while exploring the site.

make goods

Undelivered inventory promised to an advertiser, which has to be met.

Managed Push

Client browsers retrieve updated Channel Definition Format (CDF) files from a Web server according to the specified client schedule.

management information base (MIB)

A set of objects that represent various types of information about a device, used by SNMP to manage devices. Because different network-management services are used for different types of devices or protocols, each service has its own set of objects. The entire set of objects that any service or protocol uses is referred to as its MIB. See also *Simple Network Management Protocol*.

manual approval

Registration process that takes place off-line with administrator intervention.

map

1. The contents of the Hyperbolic pane in the Site window.

2. To collect data about a site's structure and resources and display it in a way that can be analyzed and manipulated.

may-have

An attribute whose value is not required to be filled.

MDA

See *Multicast Delivery Agent*.

measure

An element of a report definition that serves as the value that is quantified in a calculation. A measure is associated with only one value.

Member object

Object in the Membership Directory that stores all of the user attributes.

membership

An aspect in P&M that allows the customer to register users, authenticate users, and authorize access to areas of the service on a controlled basis.

Membership Authentication mode

Security mode that uses the Membership feature of P&M for authentication methods. Credentials are stored in the Membership Directory.

Membership Directory

The central repository of user data for Microsoft Site Server version 3.0, including user profiles and address book information.

Membership Directory Manager (MDM)

Administrative tool (MMC snap-in) that manages all aspects of the Membership Directory, including accounts and groups, access control, and the schema.

Membership Directory schema

See *schema*.

Membership DTC

Design-time control that creates registration pages and other forms from information that the user has entered in the HTML form.

Membership Server

A collection of software elements that manage personalization and membership information. Formerly classified as a virtual server.

Membership System

A Microsoft server application that allows you to register new users, authenticate users, authorize access to areas of the service on a controlled basis, and generate billing events for processing by an external billing engine.

metabase

Real-time configuration parameter storage system managed by Internet Information Server.

metadata

Information about data.

META tags

HTML pages can include a tag, <meta name="*name*" content="*content*">, that is used to provide additional information about the page. This additional information can be used to match pages to the Site Vocabulary and to make it easier for site visitors to find a particular HTML page when they are searching. In addition, Content Analyzer reads META tags and converts them into user-defined properties.

MIB

See *management information base*.

Microsoft Management Console (MMC)

An integrated administration user interface that can be used for several applications at the same time by means of snap-ins (administration modules) and that will replace the IIS Internet Service Manager in IIS 4.0 and various Microsoft Windows NT Server administrative tools.

Microsoft Site Server Analysis Database

A database containing imported log file data in a structure that facilitates the analysis of information about usage at a site.

Microsoft Site Server version 3.0 site

A grouping of Microsoft Site Server version 3.0 servers providing infrastructure for a Web site.

.mif

See *Multicast Information File*.

MIME type

Multipurpose Internet Mail Extensions. The file type of an Internet resource. The MIME type has two parts: the general format of the file (the major type) and the specific format (the minor type). For example, an image could have a MIME type of **image/gif** or **image/jpeg**.

Mobile Channels

Used to deliver channels to Microsoft Windows CE mobile devices.

multicast

The transmission of data across the network from a source to all clients who want to receive it.

Multicast Delivery Agent (MDA)

A control installed on client computers that allows them to receive and store files distributed by an Active Channel Multicaster Host. See also *agent*.

Multicast Information File (.mif)

A specific type of announcement used by the Active Channel Multicaster to tell client computers where to receive the information that will be delivered by Active Channel Multicaster. See also *announcement*.

Multicast Project

The content items that are transferred to clients using the Active Channel Multicaster. See also *content*.

multihomed servers

Multiple servers are organized under one log data source in the Server Manager. Setting up multihomed servers is a configuration option that users have when determining how they want log files to be imported into the Site Server Analysis database.

must-have

An attribute whose value must be filled.

National Language Support (NLS)

Helps applications developed for the Win32 application programming interface (API) adapt to the differing language and locale-specific needs of users around the world.

NLS

See *National Language Support*.

node

1. A point on a graph.

2. A location in the Directory Information Tree (DIT) view of the Membership Directory.

noise words

Words that are ignored during cataloging and searching. Typically noise words are common words such as *the*, *and*, *for*, and single characters and numbers.

non-inline (anchor) links

Links that result in hot spots, which provide a way to jump to a different page.

notification catalog

A catalog that is built by receiving information through a notification source.

NTLM Authentication

See *Windows NT Challenge/Response Authentication.*

object model

A collection of objects having properties and methods that provide a specialization namespace for describing a system and its functionality. In the case of the Channel Server, the namespace is based on a channel metaphor.

ODBC

See *Open Database Connectivity.*

offsite link

A link that points to a resource on a site that is different from the site where the link's source page resides.

online post analysis (OPA)

Advertising summary data and reports needed to support the business and customers.

Online Support Site

One of the Customizable Starter Sites. Online Support Site enables organizations to set up a fully functioning customer-support Web site, with a self-help area where users can find product information, answers to frequently asked questions (FAQs), diagnostic tools, and troubleshooting tips. Users can also submit requests for further assistance and check for responses. This site includes an area for support personnel, where they can track requests submitted by customers, respond to them, and post information back to a central solutions area.

onsite links

Links that point to a resource on the same site as their source page.

OPA

See *online post analysis.*

Open Database Connectivity (ODBC)

A technology that provides a common interface for accessing heterogeneous SQL databases.

OPP

See *order processing pipeline.*

order ID

A string stored in the uniform resource locator (URL) of a Commerce Server HTML page. An order ID is assigned during a shopper's initial order activity and is used to track the order through completion.

order processing pipeline (OPP)

A series of processing actions or stages that can occur after a shopper places an order. For example, processing stages can include order verification, tax calculation, and shipping price calculation.

OrderForm

An object that provides nonstructured storage for order data passed from stage to stage of the order processing pipeline. Pipeline components can read data from or write to the **OrderForm** and transform the data therein.

organization

A commercial, academic, nonprofit, government, or military entity that connects users to the Internet.

organization algorithm

An algorithm that flexibly parses host names based on a specified intranet DNS naming scheme.

orphan

A resource or file that exists on your Web server or in your file system, although nothing in your Web site links to it.

P&M Service Administration

A P&M tool that manages application server mapping and security, as well as the following P&M services: AUO, P&M Authentication Service, and LDAP Service.

packet

A transmission unit of fixed maximum size that consists of binary information representing both data and a header containing an ID number, source and destination address, and error-control data.

page hop

A jump from one document to another document.

page layout

The organization of the elements on a Web page.

page view

The transmission of a Web page to an end user.

palette

The colors used by an image. For example, .gif images use a 256-color palette.

parent

A dimension that has a many-to-one relationship with another dimension in the Site Server Analysis database.

pay membership

Approval process that requires payment.

.pcf file

A file that contains order-processing, pipeline-configuration data. Sometimes called a pipeline-configuration file.

Performance Monitor

A Microsoft Windows NT Server administrative tool.

permanent Channel Project

All channels and content items in the project remain constant. Permanent projects do not use Automated Refresh.

permanent channel

A channel within a Channel Project that remains constant and is not updated.

persistent filter

An aspect of Report Writer that allows the user to save and reuse filters that are used frequently. Persistent filters are intended to reduce the time needed to run a report.

Personal Channel Builder

Enables generation of personalized Channel Definition Format (CDF) files and delivery of personalized channels.

personalization

1. Directing Web or mail-based content to users based on their individual or group properties and their need or request for content.

2. Refers to the integration of P&M and Active Channel Server.

personalization sections

Sections of a content template that will be replaced with content or properties when an AUO is present or a rule set fires.

personalized channels

Users select channels in a Channel Project and receive only the selected channels. If users elect not to personalize a project, they receive all channels in the project.

Personalized Push

From the Channel Center in Knowledge Manager, users can select the channels in a Channel Project that they want to receive. Active Channel Server generates personalized Channel

Definition Format (CDF) files based on users' selections, and users receive only the channels they select.

phrase

A sequence of words that can be searched for.

policies

Conditions set by the system administrator, such as, how quickly account passwords expire and how many unsuccessful log on attempts are allowed before a user is locked out.

POP

See *Post Office Protocol 3*.

pop-up label

A text box that appears only when the cursor is passed over a resource in the Hyperbolic pane.

Post Office Protocol 3 (POP3)

Version 3 a protocol designed to allow single user hosts to read mail from a server.

pre-caching

Content items are downloaded and cached onto users' computers for offline browsing.

presentation

A table or graph that appears in a report.

presentation template tag

A tag in an HTML template file that specifies where presentations from a report definition are to be inserted into the template file.

preset

Containing the default attributes and settings when the CSSs were delivered to the Site Server customer.

preview

To display a visual element as it will appear on a Web page.

.prf file

A file that contains a rule set. Sometimes called a rule set file.

private brief

Information organized on a specific topic used to keep a person current on that topic. Only the person who creates a private brief has access to it.

private content

Content to which only registered users can gain access; protection is by means of user authentication. See also *restricted content, secure content*.

project

The parameters that govern an execution of the application and that usually include a pointer to content.

propagate

The process of copying one or more files and notifying a service that will receive them. The receiving service then stops using any older version of the files and starts using the new file(s).

property

1. Specific information (an attribute and its value) associated with a file or object.

2. A unique attribute associated with each resource in a Web site, such as Label, URL, MIME Type, HTTP Status, Hyperlink Text, and so on.

property value

The value assigned to a property in Content Analyzer in either the Property Definitions option or the Resource pane. For example, the value for the property Content Author for a page could be the page's author's name, Martika.

PROPID

An integer that uniquely identifies a property. This integer can be expressed as decimal (10-based) or hexadecimal (16-based) number.

protected content

Content to which access is limited by one or more techniques. See also *restricted content*, *private content*, *secure content*.

protocol

The method by which computers communicate on the Internet. The most common protocol for the World Wide Web is HTTP. Non-HTTP protocols include FTP, Gopher, and Telnet.

proxy settings

Settings that enable a user to connect to the Internet through a proxy server.

proxy server

A server that mediates interactions between a client application, such as a Web browser, and a Web server. It intercepts all requests to the Web server to see if it can fulfill the requests itself. If not, it forwards the request to the Web server.

public area

Set of Web pages or directory tree containing content that is available without restriction to any user (requires no user identification, authentication, or permissions).

public content

See *free content*.

pull project

A pull replication allows content to be pulled from any HTTP or FTP site to the Content Deployment server.

query

1. The process of searching for specific data in a set of files and returning links to the files containing that data.

2. A method for importing usage data into Content Analyzer. The data specified by the query is retrieved from the Site Server Analysis Database.

query string

The syntax used to request information from a database.

RDN

See *relative distinguished name*.

realm

The authority that holds the identification and credentials for authenticating a user.

receipt

An HTML purchase confirmation generated by Commerce Server upon the successful completion of a purchase transaction. The receipt contains the order-tracking number, which can be used by the purchaser for future follow-up on the order. If the pipeline and the database of the Commerce Server site have been configured to save receipts, the purchase history can be displayed to the user or to the manager of the site.

redirector

A tool used to track clicks on ads that transfer the user to the customer's external site.

referrer

The referring URL of the current request (the page containing the link that the user clicked). Some log files contain referrer data that is imported into the Analysis database. Users can then run reports that provide information on, for example, the continent, organization name, and organization city of the referrer.

refresh schedule

The schedule that determines when Active Channel Server refreshes project properties and generates an updated Channel Definition Format (CDF) file.

registration

Process by which a nonregistered user becomes a registered user of a Web site.

registration pages

Membership sample pages that can be customized, added to a Web site, and used to register users to that site.

registry

A Microsoft Windows NT Server database repository for information about a computer's configuration. It is organized in a hierarchical folder-like structure, comprised of subtrees and keys. Keys contain values that describe current hardware and software settings. See Windows NT Server online documentation for more information.

regular expression

A large set of text-processing functions represented as escape characters. Similar to the many variants of UNIX regular expressions or the Microsoft Windows NT Index Server's regular expressions.

relative date filter

Useful in setting up reusable report definitions, relative date filters specify a relative date rather than a specific data. For this reason, relative date filters are always valid. Examples of relative date filters include *ThisWeek* and *Yesterday*.

relative distinguished name (RDN)

The leaf name of an object in the directory service, that is, its name without the full path.

remap

The process through which Content Analyzer updates a project.

remap now

A command that initiates a remap of the current project by re-exploring the site.

remnants

The unsold leftover inventory.

remote

A computer system that is operating in conjunction with other computers that are physically separated from the location of the system being referenced. For example, Active Channel Multicaster Administrator can run on a computer other than the server (a *remote* computer), so that an administrator (a *remote* administrator) can administer the server. Remote services require a suitable means of communication with the server, such as a network.

replication project

Instructions for replicating content.

replication rollback

Returning content to a state prior to deployment.

replication route

A *road map* of Content Deployment servers that a specific replication follows.

report definition

A report definition displays the structure of a report. Elements of a report definition include sections, calculations, dimensions, measures, filters, and presentations. Users can run reports from report definitions.

report header

Part of a report. The report header includes the report name, description, and analysis information.

report header template tag

A tag in an HTML template file that specifies where report header information (time and date of report creation, sites analyzed in a report, timestamp of the first and last requests analyzed in a report, and the report's Table of Contents) will be inserted into a template file.

Report Writer catalog

A catalog that contains the list of standard report definitions. Users can run a standard report definition from the catalog to answer specific questions about usage at their site. Users can also save to the catalog report definitions that they have created.

request

Any connection to an Internet site (a hit) that successfully retrieves content.

reset

Make a potentially incremental process (such as an incremental crawl) start from its initial state (such as an empty catalog).

resource

An object in a Web site, such as a graphic, an audio file, a gateway, or a page.

restricted content

Content that requires the users to fill out a form or questionnaire that collects some specific information before they can gain access. See also *private content, secure content.*

restrictions

URLs that will not be crawled when Content Analyzer creates or remaps a project.

retrievable column

A catalog column in which the value can be displayed in the search results, the search results can be sorted by this column, and queries using relational operators (=, !=, >, >=, <, <=) or regular expressions can be used.

roaming

Signing on to a Web site from a different computer. When a user roams, cookies stored on the user's computer are not available. Sometimes called site roaming.

robot

A program that collects files by following links contained in those files or by following directory trees in a file system. Also called *spider*.

root AUO provider

Required and fundamental AUO provider, whose user properties are accessed directly by using the IADS interface instead of the IADsContainer interface, which is used to access the properties of the secondary providers. The root AUO provider is always the local Membership Directory.

root section

The first section in a report definition. Filters added in the root section apply to the entire report definition.

round robin

A sequential, cyclical allocation of resources to more than one process or device. Usually refers to the scheduling of tasks or requests.

route

1. A path between designated Content Deployment servers where a specific replication project is sent.

2. A series of hyperlink clicks that a site visitor follows to go from the start page to another resource in your site.

rule

A statement, embedded in a Web template or Direct Mail template, that performs an action based on one or more conditions.

rule fragment

The condition, content selection, action, or exception clause of a rule.

rule set

A prioritized list of rules based on a single data source.

rule set file

ASP source code defined by a single rule set and having the .prf suffix.

rule template

A rule without selected hot phrases, used as a basis for new rules.

SACL

See *system access control list*.

Sample Site Copy Wizard

An application that guides you through making a copy of one of the Commerce Server sample sites. This wizard prompts for a new site name, DSN, virtual directories, and Microsoft Windows NT Server account.

sample sites

Demonstration sites provided to illustrate Site Server capabilities.

saved search section

A section of a Knowledge Manager brief that contains a list of useful URLs and descriptions of those URLs.

Scheduler

A Microsoft Windows NT tool used by Site Server Analysis to automate most of the functions of Usage Import, Report Writer, and Custom Import (includes importing log files, performing IP resolution and HTML title lookups, and generating reports); used by P&M to schedule Direct Mail; used by Search to schedule full and incremental catalog builds.

schema

The data structure that defines the data allowed in the Membership Directory.

scope

1. A query scope specifies the set of documents that must be searched. Typically scopes are specified by a file path, such as file:\\c:\docs, or a virtual directory, such as http://myserver/ siteserver/docs.

2. The breadth of a file multicast. Active Channel Multicaster Administrator controls the scope through the time to live parameter. See also *time to live*.

script

1. Code that can be included in HTML pages.

2. A group of directives to an application or utility program.

search server

The server that stores completed catalogs for searching.

secondary AUO provider

AUO provider other than the root provider, which must be specified by a predefined name. See also *AUO provider*.

section

1. An element of a report definition that acts primarily as a container for calculations and as a means of categorizing calculations.

2. A piece of Knowledge Manager brief. There are two types of sections: link lists of useful URLs and descriptions of those URLs, and saved searches.

section header

Part of a report. The section header includes the section name and description.

secure content

Content to which only a subset of registered users can gain access; restriction is by means of both user authentication and access controls. See also *private content*, *restricted content*.

Secure Sockets Layer (SSL)

A connection-oriented protocol that supports authentication of the server, and optionally of the client, based on Public Key certificates. It also provides for negotiation of encryption and/or data integrity services to be applied to the data transferred during the session.

security

A set of procedures and methods to control system access authentication and privileges for users and services.

security context

The identity, groups, permissions, and rights assigned to an authenticated user.

security principal

The entity to which access is granted or denied by an account control entry (ACE). A security principal can be a group, a user, or a service account. The special security principal *SELF* can be used to grant or deny access for the current user to attributes of that user's account. The special security principal *anonymous* can be used to specify access for all anonymous users.

security services

Services to protect the system's data and user information from inside or outside threats.

SEO

See *server extension objects*.

server

Software that provides specific kinds of network services.

server component

A software component that is part of a server.

server extension objects (SEO)

Custom objects, based on the Shinjuku framework, that allow customers to extend service functionality.

Server Manager

A tool that organizes log data sources, servers, and sites hierarchically in a manner that allows log files to be imported into the Microsoft Site Server Analysis database.

service

A Microsoft Windows NT service, running on a server, that implements part of Microsoft Site Server version 3.0.

service manager

A person involved with business decisions related to channels.

shared brief

Information organized on a specific topic used to keep members of the organization current on that topic. Anyone in the organization has access to a shared brief.

shopper ID

A random, 32-character string generated by commerce server to keep track of a shopper's order. The shopper ID is generated when the shopper first enters the site.

shortcut

A fast way to perform an action, such as selecting text or, more usually, opening a file, document, Web page, and so on. A shortcut is usually represented by an icon on the desktop.

signup

The process through which a user goes to become a registered user of a P&M-supported Web site.

Simple Mail Transfer Protocol (SMTP)

A TCP/IP protocol used to send messages between computers on the same network.

Simple Network Management Protocol (SNMP)

A protocol used by SNMP consoles and agents to communicate. In Microsoft Windows NT Server, the SNMP service is used to get and set status information about a host on a TCP/IP network.

site

1. A grouping of Web pages by one or more URL prefixes.

2. A collection of content (World Wide Web, FTP, Gopher, or real-time stream). Sites can be replicated across several servers.

Site Authoring Desk

A Web-based application that allows Business Internet Site authors to add, edit, and delete category, product, and partner information for their sites. Site Authoring Desk also provides links to other authoring tools, such as a site map, content and usage reports, and Site Server features.

Site Builder Wizard

An application that guides you through building a new site. The Site Builder Wizard uses the builder blueprint file and input from you to create a site.

Site Configuration Desk

A Web-based application that allows the Microsoft Site Server customer to administer site-specific information, such as information stored in the Membership Directory, and that provides links to other applications such as WebAdmin or the individual administration tools for a Site Server feature.

Site Foundation Wizard

An application that generates the foundation for a new site. See also *foundation*.

site hop

A jump from a document on one Web site to a document on a different Web site.

Site Manager application

An application for managing an individual Commerce Server site. The Site Manager application enables you to edit product and department information, configure the order processing pipeline, and so on.

site staging server

1. A server in which you can put your Web site to test it before you publish it on a *live* server available to the public.

2. The name given to a server used by Content Deployment as an intermediate staging point for content.

site visitor

An end user who uses a browser to view a Web site that uses Microsoft Site Server.

Site Vocabulary

A hierarchically arranged set of possible values for user and content attributes. The Site Vocabulary is stored in the Membership Directory, and the values, called categories, can be used in the P&M Rule Builder, Knowledge Manager, and Tag Tool.

SMS

See *Systems Management Server*.

snap-in

A software module that integrates with MMC and is used to create administration tools.

SNMP

See *Simple Network Management Protocol*.

source directory

The directory inside the staging server where content is stored prior to deployment.

Software Distribution Channel

Typically used to deliver new software or software updates. Based on Open Software Distribution (OSD) standards.

source page

The page where InLinks (from Pages) originate.

spider

A program that collects files by following links contained in those files or by following directory trees in a file system. Also called *robot*.

SSL

See *Secure Sockets Layer*.

staging server

Any server used by Content Deployment as the starting point for content deployment, Internet retrieval, and component deployment projects.

stand-alone

Describes an application that can be launched by itself.

standard report

A predefined report that the user can generate in Report Writer.

standard report definition

A predefined report definition that users can run to gather a wide range of information about usage at a site.

start address

1. A location from which to start a crawl.
2. The page from which a user begins to crawl a Web site. Not a synonym for home page. See also *home page.*

start page

The page in a Web site at which you want Content Analyzer to begin to map a site. It is usually the site's home page.

static page

HTML page prepared in advance of the request and sent to the client upon request.

stem

The linguistic root of a word. For example, the following words have the stem *fly:* flying, flew, fly, flies.

stitching

Allows log files for two or more sites to be associated during import into the Site Server Analysis database so that a single visit to the sites can be counted as a single visit. Without stitching, the visit would be counted separately.

style

A collection of settings that you define, name, and save.

surface graph

Represents data topographically in three dimensions.

system access control list (SACL)

An aspect of Microsoft Windows NT security. An SACL is maintained by the security administrator for the system. An SACL represents the data structure that contains the access control elements for account permissions.

Systems Management Server (SMS)

A product that runs on Microsoft Windows NT Server that includes desktop management and software distribution that significantly automates the task of upgrading software on client computers.

table

One of two types of a presentation in a report. Graphs are the other type.

tag

A piece of code that denotes the functionality and/or style of specific elements such as text, graphics, and audio on an HTML page.

tag term

See *Site Vocabulary*.

Tag Tool

The tool that lets you apply tags to HTML documents. You can tag documents to categorize them and to improve search results.

tape graph

A three-dimensional form of the line graph.

target directory

The directory inside the staging server or the end point server to which the deployed content is directed. Also called a destination directory.

target resource

A resource pointed to by Links (to Resources). Each page in a Web site contains one or more links to other resources. The resource to which each link points is a target resource. A target resource can be a page, an image, and so on.

task

1. An action that you need to perform to finish creating one of the Customizable Starter Sites (CSSs). The CSS wizards generate a series of Microsoft FrontPage 98 tasks that you must complete before deploying your site. You also can add your own tasks. Tasks and information about how to perform them are displayed in the Task view of FrontPage Explorer.

2. A specific activity in the Scheduler, such as importing a log or generating a report.

template

1. A file used to create full HTML pages in standard formats. Sample sites in Commerce Server provide templates for department, product, and purchasing pages.

2. A predesigned page that you can use as is or as the starting point in designing your own page.

3. A Web page or direct-mail page containing personalization sections.

4. An HTML file with an .mft extension that is automatically created when users choose to create a template from a report definition. The template file has default tags added; users can add more tags or delete some of the default tags to customize the template.

theme

A group of settings that control the colors and style of such elements as graphics, text, and links on the Customizable Starter Sites (CSSs). Each of the Customizable Starter Sites has a default theme that is applied when the site is created. Customers can change the theme for each of the CSSs in Microsoft FrontPage 98. They can choose from a range of predefined themes.

third-party developer

A development partner outside of Microsoft Corporation, such as a solution provider, that will develop and deploy Customizable Starter Sites for Microsoft Site Server customers.

time stamp

The date and time at which the server responded to a request.

time-series graph

A time-series graph consists of a x-y grid in which points are added one at a time to the right edge. When the graph reaches the limit of points it can show, the oldest data begins to drop off the left edge.

time to live

In multicasting, a value that defines the number of routers through which a multicast may pass before a router stops forwarding the multicast. See also *scope*.

token

An access control object.

top-level channel

Active Channel Server automatically creates one top-level channel for each Channel Project.

transaction support

Support of a mechanism that has a two-stage commit: there is a metastage in which part of the transaction has completed, but the transaction can be rolled back until all its parts have completed; it is automatically rolled back unless all parts complete.

unavailable resource

A page or other resource that Content Analyzer cannot retrieve during exploration because the URL is not valid, the resource does not exist, or the server containing the resource is busy or having other technical difficulties.

UNC

See *uniform naming convention*.

unicast

The sending of a separate copy of data across the network from a source to each client requesting it.

unified schema object

Virtual schema object that describes the schema of a single virtual AUO name space.

uniform naming convention (UNC)

A full Microsoft Windows NT name of a resource on a network, which conforms to the *servername**sharename* syntax.

Uniform Resource Identifier (URI)

The generic term for all types of names and addresses that refer to objects on the Web. A URL is one kind of URI.

Uniform Resource Locator (URL)

An address to an object, document, page, or other destination on the Internet or an intranet. The URL also specifies the appropriate Internet Protocol, such as Gopher, HTTP, and so on.

unverified resource

A resource whose existence or accessibility has not yet been verified. This occurs when Content Analyzer finds a link to the resource but has not yet retrieved the resource, either because the level of the resource is excluded by the current exploration limits or because the resource is offsite and offsite resources are not currently being verified.

URI

See *Uniform Resource Identifier*.

URL

See *Uniform Resource Locator*.

URL hierarchy

A method for setting routes. Routes in your project are set according to your site's file structure on the server's hard drive.

usage data

1. Data detailing the sequence of requests and responses relating to an HTTP server or set of servers.

2. Data imported from log files into the Site Server Analysis database.

usage event

A specification that determines what sequence of events client browsers should record during usage logging.

usage logging

Client browsers record information about a user's review of channels and content items and then send log files to a designated server.

user

1. A person who visits the site via a Web browser. Sometimes called an end user or site visitor.

2. Anyone who visits a site at least once.

3. The person visiting the site implemented by the people who buy and configure it (the customer).

4. The recipient of channels and content items.

user account

A record created during a user's initial access or registration that contains the user's credentials; this account may be stored in either the Microsoft Windows NT Server directory database or the Membership Directory. See also *user profile*.

user agent

1. The product name, product version, operating system, and security scheme of the Web browser used for the request.

2. A string that Search uses when crawling Web sites to identify the type of browser that you have.

user algorithm

An algorithm from which visitor and user information are statistically approximated, based on the data in the log files and the logical structure of a site. The algorithm supports cookies and registration.

user data

Data that is imported from Site Server Personalization & Membership's database into the Site Server Analysis database, after which user data and usage data are integrated.

user-defined property

A property associated with resources that can be defined in either of two ways: by the presence of a META tag in an HTML page or by using the Property Definitions dialog box. User-defined properties provide a flexible method by which a user can track arbitrary information about the resources in a site.

user profile

The personal information (other than credentials) gathered about a specific user, which is stored in the Membership Directory. See *also user account*.

user name

The user name used to log in to a site requiring registration.

value

The contents of an attribute in a specific instance of an object.

vector space queries

Queries in which some terms are weighted more heavily than other terms.

verified approval

Delayed approval process that requires the user to respond to an e-mail message.

viewer

A program for opening image files and files in other special formats, such as audio and video.

virtual directory

1. A directory name, used in a URL address, that corresponds to a physical directory on the server.
2. A content directory that typically resides either in a directory different from the home directory (defined by default as C:\Inetsrv\Wwwroot during Internet Information Server setup) or on a different computer. Virtual directories are configured by using Internet Service Manager, and an alias is assigned to each virtual directory. Use of the alias simplifies the URL for accessing content on the virtual directory. By default, Commerce Server creates an alias for each sample site that it installs. See Internet Information Server online documentation for more information.

virtual machine

Software that mimics the performance of a hardware device, such as a program that allows applications written for an Intel processor to be run on a Motorola chip.

virtual private network (VPN)

A set of nodes on a public network such as the Internet that communicate among themselves by using encryption technology.

virtual server

A server instance on the same computer as another server instance. Virtual Web servers allow one single Web server to support multiple sites. Sometimes called a composite site.

visit

A series of consecutive requests from a user to a site.

visit timeout

The length of time after which a visit is determined to have ended. An arbitrary time for a visit timeout is established to prevent visits from being infinite.

VPN

See *virtual private network*.

Wallet

ActiveX controls that enable a shopper to enter payment and address information when initiating an online purchase. The Payment Selector and Address Selector controls reside on the shopper's computer and provide drop-down menus containing credit cards and addresses that are currently stored. Shoppers can enter new information or select an existing entry.

Web content template

The ASP file that selects content from a content source and incorporates it into a Web page.

Web page

1. A page of data (HTML) that can be viewed with an Internet browser.
2. A WWW document.

Web server

Server software that responds to Web client requests, such as requests from a Web browser. A Web server uses the Internet HTTP, FTP, and Gopher protocols to communicate with clients on the TCP/IP networks.

Web site

A specific place on the World Wide Web that provides content to users. See also *content*.

Whois query

A process that associates domain names in the Site Server Analysis database with organization information in order to allow reports to be more meaningful.

Windows default browser

The browser that you have established as the default browser in Microsoft Windows or Microsoft Windows NT.

Windows NT Authentication mode

Security mode that uses Microsoft Windows NT Server for authentication methods. Credentials are stored in the Windows NT Server directory database.

Windows NT Challenge/Response Authentication

An authentication method that uses a challenge/response protocol in which the user's identity is validated by a password. Credentials are not transmitted in clear text. This is the standard method used by Microsoft Windows NT LAN Manager (NTLM) networking; it is also known as NTLM Authentication.

Windows Scripting Host (WSH)

Microsoft Windows NT Server 5.0 language-independent scripting host for 32-bit Windows platforms. Includes VBScript and JavaScript engines.

word breaker

A Search utility that is responsible for identifying words in a document. While the document contents are emitted by the content filter, the work breaker identifies individual words. There is one word-breaking module for each of the languages supported by Search.

word stemmer

A Search component that takes a word and generates grammatically correct variations of that word. Different languages require their own stemmers. For example, the English stemmer, if given the word *swam*, would generate *swim, swum, swimming, swims*, and so on.

WSH

See *Windows Scripting Host*.

zero instance service

A concept in which the service is started with no configured server running but accepts administrator's RPC calls.

Index

Page references occurring in italics refer to graphics and tables.

pipeline configuration files, 82–83
Pipeline Editor, 12, 83
pipelines. *See also specific pipelines*
 business-to-business, 81
 business-to-consumer, 81
 Commerce Interchange, 80, 156
 Order Processing, 11, 79–87
 Plan, *81,* 88–90, *90–92,* 96–97, 99–103, 108–9
 Purchase, *81,* 115–17, 140–43, 148–52
 transacted, 115–16
Plan pipeline, *81*
 adding Scriptor component to, 108–9
 checkout and, 95–96
 components in, 90–92
 editing, 108–9
 executing, 97
 Handling stage, 101
 modifying, 99
 Order Total stage, 103
 Shipping stage, 100
 stages in, 88–90
 Tax stage, 102
price promotions, 62
 adding, 63, 65–67
 enabling, 64–66
 types of, *63*
 viewing on shopping cart page, 67
product_alt.asp file, 234–38
product.asp file, 229–33
product catalogs. *See* catalogs
product_edit.asp file, 238–47
Product Information page, custom attributes on, 46–48
Product Info stage, *89*
 Plan pipeline components and, *91*
Product page, Cross-sell promotions and, 43–44, 48
product pipeline, *81*
products
 adding to shopping cart, 54–59
 computing tax on, 101–3
 information on, *36–38*
 removing from shopping cart, 60–61
 searching for, 8, 41–42

products (continued)
 shopping for, 21–22, 28–29
 updating in shopping cart, 59–60
Product tables, *37*
Promotions Wizard, *44–45,* 48
 price promotions and, 62–67
properties, calling object, 32
Purchase Check stage, 116
purchase confirmation, 119
Purchase pipeline, *81,* 115–16
 editing, 148–49
 modifying, 140–43
 modifying to store shopper information, 148–52
 stages of, 116–17
purchase process, 113–15
PurchaseUpdate.pcf file, editing, *142*
PutShopperID method, *34,* 52–53

Q

queries
 defining descriptions, *37, 40*
 executing appropriate, 41–42
QueryMap Dictionary objects, *36*
QueryMap objects, *32, 35–36*
 adding query to, 144–45
 modifying, 46–47

R

receipt.asp file, 129, 247–53
receipts.asp file, 253–55
RequestNumber method, *34*
RequestString method, *34*

S

Scriptor components, 104
 adding, 104–5
 adding to compute tax, 105–6, 107–10
 configuring, 105, 109–10
 entry points, 105–6
searches
 adding capabilities for, 38–40

W

X

Microsoft Mastering Series

Your *Complete* Training Solution

Print Edition: Study at your own pace.

The Mastering Series Print Editions allow you to get up to speed on new technology whenever and wherever you need it. Print Editions provides in-depth, hands-on training in an affordable package. They are designed for the power user who wants to move to the next level.

▶ *More information:* **http://msdn.microsoft.com/mastering/books**

MSDN Training Online: Get in-depth coverage of the latest technology now.

Mastering Series online courses are offered by training centers around the world. They allow you to combine the best of self-study with the advantages of classroom training — without the hassles of travel and being away from work.

▶ *More information:* **http://msdn.microsoft.com/mastering/online**

Classroom Training: Learn from experienced developer/trainers.

Mastering Series instructor-led training classes are the premium way to get training. You learn in hands-on labs with detailed guidance from veteran developers, at thousands of Microsoft Certified Technical Education Centers around the world. The combination of in-depth training and experienced trainers gives you the clearest possible picture of how to use new technology in the real world.

▶ *More information:* **http://msdn.microsoft.com/mastering**

What's right for you?

If you need help sifting through the many training opportunities available for developers, the professionals at any Microsoft Certified Technical Education Center can recommend the most appropriate training program, tailored specifically for you and your needs! They'll help you decide which critical products and technologies are most important to you. And they will assist you in determining what training formats best suit your preferred learning style and resources. To find the Microsoft CTEC near you, visit the Microsoft Find Training web page at:

http://www.microsoft.com/isapi/referral/product_select.asp?train=84

Microsoft
Mastering Series
Developer Training

Make the *Career You Deserve* with *Microsoft Training Programs*

Why get trained?

As a trained IT professional, you can:

▶ Take advantage of extensive opportunities in a growing industry

▶ Stay on top of changes in the industry

▶ Polish old technical skills and acquire new ones

As an IT manager, hiring trained IT professionals provides you with:

▶ Greater assurance of a job well done

▶ Improved service, increased productivity and greater technical self-sufficiency

▶ More satisfied employees and clients

What's right for you?

The professionals at any Microsoft Certified Technical Education Center can recommend the most appropriate training program, tailored specifically for you and your needs! They'll help you decide which critical products and technologies are most important to you. And they will assist you in determining what training formats best suit your preferred learning style and resources.

How do you get the best training?

With instructor-led, online, and self-paced training and instruction available at locations throughout the world and on the Web, you are sure to find what you need among our industry-renowned comprehensive solutions to give you the right method of training to produce the best results. And a combination of training formats sometimes called hybrid training may be more effective than a single methodology.

Where do you get the best training?

Choose from Microsoft Certified Technical Education Centers, Microsoft Authorized Academic Training Program institutions, Microsoft Press, and, Microsoft Seminar Online to get the job done right.

Microsoft® Authorized Academic Training Program

Microsoft Press

Microsoft Authorized Academic Training Program (AATP) helps full-time and part-time students in participating high schools, colleges and universities prepare for jobs that demand proficiency with Microsoft products and technologies.

For more information, go to: http://www.microsoft.com/astp/

Microsoft Certified Technical Education Centers (Microsoft CTECs) are full-service training organizations that can deliver system support and developer instruction in a variety of flexible formats.

For more information, go to: http://www.microsoft.com/train_cert/

Microsoft Seminar Online delivers a virtual seminar experience right to your desktop, anytime, day or night.

For more information, go to: http://www.microsoft.com/seminar/

Microsoft Certified Professional Approved Study Guides (MCP Approved Study Guides), an excellent way to stay up to date on Microsoft products & technologies, are rigorously developed & reviewed to ensure adherence to certification objectives.

For more information, go to: http://www.microsoft.com/train_cert/train/mcpasg.htm/

Microsoft Press delivers "anytime, anywhere learning" via a full line of Microsoft Official Curriculum (MOC) self-paced training kits enhanced with print & multimedia that prepare you for the MCP exams.

For more information, go to: http://mspress.microsoft.com/

MICROSOFT LICENSE AGREEMENT
Book Companion CD

IMPORTANT—READ CAREFULLY: This Microsoft End-User License Agreement ("EULA") is a legal agreement between you (either an individual or an entity) and Microsoft Corporation for the Microsoft product identified above, which includes computer software and may include associated media, printed materials, and "online" or electronic documentation ("SOFTWARE PRODUCT"). Any component included within the SOFTWARE PRODUCT that is accompanied by a separate End-User License Agreement shall be governed by such agreement and not the terms set forth below. By installing, copying, or otherwise using the SOFTWARE PRODUCT, you agree to be bound by the terms of this EULA. If you do not agree to the terms of this EULA, you are not authorized to install, copy, or otherwise use the SOFTWARE PRODUCT; you may, however, return the SOFTWARE PRODUCT, along with all printed materials and other items that form a part of the Microsoft product that includes the SOFTWARE PRODUCT, to the place you obtained them for a full refund.

SOFTWARE PRODUCT LICENSE

The SOFTWARE PRODUCT is protected by United States copyright laws and international copyright treaties, as well as other intellectual property laws and treaties. The SOFTWARE PRODUCT is licensed, not sold.

1. **GRANT OF LICENSE.** This EULA grants you the following rights:

   a. **Software Product.** You may install and use one copy of the SOFTWARE PRODUCT on a single computer. The primary user of the computer on which the SOFTWARE PRODUCT is installed may make a second copy for his or her exclusive use on a portable computer.

   b. **Storage/Network Use.** You may also store or install a copy of the SOFTWARE PRODUCT on a storage device, such as a network server, used only to install or run the SOFTWARE PRODUCT on your other computers over an internal network; however, you must acquire and dedicate a license for each separate computer on which the SOFTWARE PRODUCT is installed or run from the storage device. A license for the SOFTWARE PRODUCT may not be shared or used concurrently on different computers.

   c. **License Pak.** If you have acquired this EULA in a Microsoft License Pak, you may make the number of additional copies of the computer software portion of the SOFTWARE PRODUCT authorized on the printed copy of this EULA, and you may use each copy in the manner specified above. You are also entitled to make a corresponding number of secondary copies for portable computer use as specified above.

   d. **Sample Code.** Solely with respect to portions, if any, of the SOFTWARE PRODUCT that are identified within the SOFTWARE PRODUCT as sample code (the "SAMPLE CODE"):

      i. **Use and Modification.** Microsoft grants you the right to use and modify the source code version of the SAMPLE CODE, *provided* you comply with subsection (d)(iii) below. You may not distribute the SAMPLE CODE, or any modified version of the SAMPLE CODE, in source code form.

      ii. **Redistributable Files.** Provided you comply with subsection (d)(iii) below, Microsoft grants you a nonexclusive, royalty-free right to reproduce and distribute the object code version of the SAMPLE CODE and of any modified SAMPLE CODE, other than SAMPLE CODE, or any modified version thereof, designated as not redistributable in the Readme file that forms a part of the SOFTWARE PRODUCT (the "Non-Redistributable Sample Code"). All SAMPLE CODE other than the Non-Redistributable Sample Code is collectively referred to as the "REDISTRIBUTABLES."

      iii. **Redistribution Requirements.** If you redistribute the REDISTRIBUTABLES, you agree to: (i) distribute the REDISTRIBUTABLES in object code form only in conjunction with and as a part of your software application product; (ii) not use Microsoft's name, logo, or trademarks to market your software application product; (iii) include a valid copyright notice on your software application product; (iv) indemnify, hold harmless, and defend Microsoft from and against any claims or lawsuits, including attorney's fees, that arise or result from the use or distribution of your software application product; and (v) not permit further distribution of the REDISTRIBUTABLES by your end user. Contact Microsoft for the applicable royalties due and other licensing terms for all other uses and/or distribution of the REDISTRIBUTABLES.

2. **DESCRIPTION OF OTHER RIGHTS AND LIMITATIONS.**

   - **Limitations on Reverse Engineering, Decompilation, and Disassembly.** You may not reverse engineer, decompile, or disassemble the SOFTWARE PRODUCT, except and only to the extent that such activity is expressly permitted by applicable law notwithstanding this limitation.

   - **Separation of Components.** The SOFTWARE PRODUCT is licensed as a single product. Its component parts may not be separated for use on more than one computer.

   - **Rental.** You may not rent, lease, or lend the SOFTWARE PRODUCT.

   - **Support Services.** Microsoft may, but is not obligated to, provide you with support services related to the SOFTWARE PRODUCT ("Support Services"). Use of Support Services is governed by the Microsoft policies and programs described in the user manual, in "online" documentation, and/or in other Microsoft-provided materials. Any supplemental software code provided to you as part of the Support Services shall be considered part of the SOFTWARE PRODUCT and subject to the terms and conditions of this EULA. With respect to technical information you provide to Microsoft as part of the Support Services, Microsoft may use such information for its business purposes, including for product support and development. Microsoft will not utilize such technical information in a form that personally identifies you.

- **Software Transfer.** You may permanently transfer all of your rights under this EULA, provided you retain no copies, you transfer all of the SOFTWARE PRODUCT (including all component parts, the media and printed materials, any upgrades, this EULA, and, if applicable, the Certificate of Authenticity), **and** the recipient agrees to the terms of this EULA.

- **Termination.** Without prejudice to any other rights, Microsoft may terminate this EULA if you fail to comply with the terms and conditions of this EULA. In such event, you must destroy all copies of the SOFTWARE PRODUCT and all of its component parts.

3. **COPYRIGHT.** All title and copyrights in and to the SOFTWARE PRODUCT (including but not limited to any images, photographs, animations, video, audio, music, text, SAMPLE CODE, REDISTRIBUTABLES, and "applets" incorporated into the SOFTWARE PRODUCT) and any copies of the SOFTWARE PRODUCT are owned by Microsoft or its suppliers. The SOFTWARE PRODUCT is protected by copyright laws and international treaty provisions. Therefore, you must treat the SOFTWARE PRODUCT like any other copyrighted material **except** that you may install the SOFTWARE PRODUCT on a single computer provided you keep the original solely for backup or archival purposes. You may not copy the printed materials accompanying the SOFTWARE PRODUCT.

4. **U.S. GOVERNMENT RESTRICTED RIGHTS.** The SOFTWARE PRODUCT and documentation are provided with RESTRICTED RIGHTS. Use, duplication, or disclosure by the Government is subject to restrictions as set forth in subpara-graph (c)(1)(ii) of the Rights in Technical Data and Computer Software clause at DFARS 252.227-7013 or subparagraphs (c)(1) and (2) of the Commercial Computer Software—Restricted Rights at 48 CFR 52.227-19, as applicable. Manufacturer is Microsoft Corporation/One Microsoft Way/Redmond, WA 98052-6399.

5. **EXPORT RESTRICTIONS.** You agree that you will not export or re-export the SOFTWARE PRODUCT, any part thereof, or any process or service that is the direct product of the SOFTWARE PRODUCT (the foregoing collectively referred to as the "Restricted Components"), to any country, person, entity, or end user subject to U.S. export restrictions. You specifically agree not to export or re-export any of the Restricted Components (i) to any country to which the U.S. has embargoed or restricted the export of goods or services, which currently include, but are not necessarily limited to, Cuba, Iran, Iraq, Libya, North Korea, Sudan, and Syria, or to any national of any such country, wherever located, who intends to transmit or transport the Restricted Components back to such country; (ii) to any end user who you know or have reason to know will utilize the Restricted Components in the design, development, or production of nuclear, chemical, or biological weapons; or (iii) to any end user who has been prohibited from participating in U.S. export transactions by any federal agency of the U.S. government. You warrant and represent that neither the BXA nor any other U.S. federal agency has suspended, revoked, or denied your export privileges.

DISCLAIMER OF WARRANTY

MISCELLANEOUS

This EULA is governed by the laws of the State of Washington USA, except and only to the extent that applicable law mandates governing law of a different jurisdiction.

Should you have any questions concerning this EULA, or if you desire to contact Microsoft for any reason, please contact the Microsoft subsidiary serving your country, or write: Microsoft Sales Information Center/One Microsoft Way/Redmond, WA 98052-6399.

Gear Up for *Success*

Register Today!

Return this
Microsoft® Mastering:
eCommerce Development
registration card today to receive advance notice about
the latest developer training titles and courseware!

For information about Mastering series products and training, visit our Web site at
http://msdn.microsoft.com/mastering

OWNER REGISTRATION CARD   0-7356-0891-1

Microsoft® Mastering:
eCommerce Development

FIRST NAME   MIDDLE INITIAL   LAST NAME

INSTITUTION OR COMPANY NAME

ADDRESS

CITY   STATE   ZIP
                                                            (   )
E-MAIL ADDRESS   PHONE NUMBER

U.S. and Canada addresses only. Fill in information above and mail postage-free.
Please mail only the bottom half of this page.

For information about Microsoft Press® products, visit our Web site at **mspress.microsoft.com**

Microsoft Press